The Last Decade

THE WORKS OF LIONEL TRILLING

UNIFORM EDITION

LIONEL TRILLING

THE LAST DECADE

Essays and Reviews, 1965–75

Edited by Diana Trilling

A HARVEST / HBJ BOOK

HARCOURT BRACE JOVANOVICH

NEW YORK AND LONDON

Printed in the United States of America

Library of Congress Cataloging in Publication Data

Trilling, Lionel, 1905–1975.
The last decade.

(A Harvest/HBJ book)
(The Works of Lionel Trilling)
I. Trilling, Diana. II. Title. III. Series:
Trilling, Lionel, 1905–1975. Works. 1977.
PS3539.R56L3   814'.5'2   79–1849
ISBN 0–15–648892–2

First Harvest/HBJ edition 1981

A B C D E F G H I J

Editor's Note

All the pieces in this volume date from the last ten years of Lionel Trilling's life and all but two were published in that period. "Art, Will, and Necessity" has not previously been printed. In various versions it was delivered as a lecture in both England and the United States. The version used in this volume is the last that I can find. "Why We Read Jane Austen" was not yet completed at Lionel Trilling's death and was published posthumously in the form in which it was left.

It is to be kept in mind that the Notes for an Autobiographical Lecture are *only* notes. At the time this lecture was given, Lionel Trilling had very likely begun to think about an intellectual memoir and I include these jottings (though I put them in an Appendix) for the light they cast on what might have been a direction of that projected work.

I wish to express my appreciation to the National Endowment for the Humanities for its support in preparing an archive of my husband's papers. I am also deeply and continuingly grateful to Barbara Crehan for her devoted research assistance.

New York, 1978   D.T.

Contents

The Last Decade

A Novel of the Thirties

[Afterword to the republication of *The Unpossessed*
by Tess Slesinger, Avon, 1966]

I

IN THE 1950's it was established beyond question that the 1930's had not simply passed into history but had become history. The decade had never been thought of as a mere undifferentiated segment of the past, but now it was to be canonized as a veritable epoch or period, an entity with a beginning, middle, and end, and a style appropriate to the discernible logic of its events. Like any authentic period, this one had its characteristic pathos and the power of arousing nostalgia. Intellectuals who had grown up in the intervening time discovered in themselves a lively affinity with the famous years which, they suggested, would have sustained their best impulses, as the year in which they wrote manifestly did not. They thought of the admired age as belonging more truly to them than to the people who had lived in it—their received opinion held that such figures of the decade as were still on the scene had not been equal to, or worthy of, the moral opportunities that had been offered by their high-hearted magnanimous moment.

A survivor of the actualities of the Thirties was bound to meet the celebrations of those hypostatized years with some wryness. At scarcely any point was his own recollection of the decade in accord with the moralizing nostalgia of the younger men. He took what comfort he could from the thought that there can be no history

without myth, that fictions about the past are always being contrived by generous youth. And he was relieved to find a degree of
corroboration of his own sense of things in the view of at least one
writer of a generation later than his. In 1955 Murray Kempton published *Part of Our Time,* in which he looked at the events and
personalities of the period in some detail and with the intention of
objective judgment. One might deplore the rather high, ripe ele-
giacism of his prose, an Ossianic tone perhaps generated by the
subtitle of the book, "Some Ruins and Monuments of the Thirties."
But what he had to say about those years went far toward explaining
why they should have left a sour taste in the mouths of many who
had experienced them. Mr. Kempton did not describe them in an
adversary spirit; he spoke more in wondering sorrow than in dismay
and he knew that for American intellectuals of this century, the
Thirties were the indispensable decade. But he also knew something of the dryness and deadness that lay at the heart of their drama
and that they had brought to the fore a peculiarly American desiccation of temperament. He knew the dull unreverberant minds and
the systematically stupid minds that had been especially valued. He
knew the minds that had corrupted themselves on the highest motives—he had no illusions about the *innocence* of the time, and he
could give a pretty good account of its accepted lies.

For me the authority of Mr. Kempton's book was the greater because it put into evidence Tess Slesinger's novel, *The Unpossessed,*
which it spoke of as "almost forgotten." The characterization took
me aback, for the book had never been forgotten by me, and to see
it referred to in this way was a forcible reminder of how rapidly
the years go by and with what ease they carry things to oblivion.
The fact was as Mr. Kempton stated it—after a sizable flurry of
success on its appearance in 1934, *The Unpossessed* did pass from
memory and Mr. Kempton's reference to it was the only one I could
recollect having seen since a few years after its publication. Mr.
Kempton spoke of it as a "document" and used it as such, and

indeed it does have, as an account of a particular time and place, a certain evidential value. But it deserves to be remembered for more reasons than that, for the spiritedness of its address, for what in it is pertinent not only to its own period but to ours.

The book would not have been forgotten if the author had continued her career as a novelist. Had there been a considerable body of work, *The Unpossessed* might well have been kept in memory as its auspicious beginning. But no novel followed the first; the only other book by Tess Slesinger is the collection of her short stories, *Time: The Present*. She published nothing after this and she died ten years later.

She was, I have no doubt, born to be a novelist. Her talent, so far as she had time to develop it, invites comparison with Mary Mc-Carthy's. She had a similar vivacity and wit, although rather more delicate, and similar powers of social and moral observation, which, like Miss McCarthy's, were at the service of the impulse to see through what was observed. In her satiric enterprise Tess Slesinger was gentler than Miss McCarthy; her animus, although it was strong, was checked by compunction. This was partly because the literary practice of the time still imposed certain restraints, but chiefly for reasons of personal disposition.

Still, her animus *was* strong, and the effect upon it of what I have called her compunction perhaps does something to explain why her career as a novelist came to an end. Those who knew Tess Slesinger when she wrote *The Unpossessed* were aware that the book was not only a literary enterprise but also a personal act. It passed judgment upon certain people; in effect it announced the author's separation from them and from the kind of life they made. The act had in it, I have always thought, more aggression than the compunctious young person could support. I have no doubt that it was a perfectly "healthy" aggression, not any greater than was needed to meet the situation. If there was anger in it, there was no hatred and no malice. But probably it disconcerted Tess to break ties, to judge others to be wrong and to say so publicly, the more because, as I believe, she had not lost her affection for those whom she was judging adversely and from whom she was separating herself.

The burden of uneasy—of "guilty"—feeling must have been increased by the success the book achieved. It was not success of an overwhelming kind, but it was real. And in those days success was not, as now it is, thought to be naturally compatible with purity of intention, even the sign and reward of a special virtue. In the ethos of the time, the idea of "integrity" had great coercive power and it was commonly supposed that success indicated an integrity compromised or even wholly lost; the gratification it brought was almost certain to be shot through with shame. This did not, of course, make success any the less interesting and attractive, and those who constituted the circle of Tess's friends wanted it for themselves, chiefly in the form of fame through literary achievement. But it was Tess who first had it. This must surely have made a difficult situation for her. It would have been difficult for a man; it was even harder for a woman. And it wasn't only as a woman that Tess had done what men wanted to do and hadn't done. She had done it as a girl. She quite liked being a girl and handled the *persona* gracefully, with only an infrequent self-consciousness or affectation; her natural charm was of a daughterly or young-sisterly kind, and in some considerable part consisted of her expectation of being loved, indulged, forgiven, of having permission to be spirited and even naughty. And now by her act, by what the book said and by the success it made, she had, she might well have felt, abolished the person she had known herself to be and liked being. One can understand that she might find the new prospect of a novel rather terrifying.

It was also true that she had wanted to stop being a girl, and daughterly and young-sisterly. She wanted to be quite grown, to the point of having children. It was not a wish that at the time could be thought of as a personal instance of a desire which was in the course of nature; it implied cultural considerations of a quite arduous kind. Young people will perhaps not understand this and I find it harder and harder to do so. Yet it is the fact that the intellectuals of the Twenties and Thirties were likely to assume that there was an irreconcilable contradiction between babies and the good life. The fear of pregnancy was omnipresent and it was not uncommon for young married couples to have a first pregnancy aborted not because they were so very poor but because they were not yet "ready" to have the child. One might have a wide circle of married friends of some maturity without knowing any who were parents. Men were generally presumed not to want children, intellectual men thought of them as "biological traps," being quite certain that they must lead to compromise with, or capitulation to, the forces of convention. There was also the belief that it was wrong to bring children into so bad a world. And quite apart from all practical and moral concerns, the imagination of parenthood was not easily available, or it worked only to propose an absurdity, an image that was at essential odds with that of the free and intelligent person: what parent known to anyone had ever been free and intelligent? That Tess, like Margaret Flinders, one of the two heroines of *The Unpossessed,* should want to be a parent and should avow her wish was a cultural choice of no small import, a mutation in faith, with all the stress that attends such occasions and makes them unpropitious for the writer.

She had her wish. In Hollywood she made a happy second marriage with Frank Davis, a producer, and she bore a son and a daughter. She died of cancer when she was thirty-nine.

II

The first time I saw Tess Slesinger was at her wedding to her first husband, Herbert Solow, on a June evening of 1928. Solow and I had been at Columbia College together, although we were not in the same class and had not known each other until after we had both graduated. He was a man of quite remarkable intelligence, very witty in a saturnine way, deeply skeptical, tortured by bouts of extreme depression. His was the first political mind I ever encountered. Knowledge about power and the means by which it is won was the breath of life to him, the more because his passionate curiosity served high, strict political principle. He was meant to be a great political journalist. I do not know the reasons for his never having made a continued effort toward the career he might have had—our friendship was not intimate, although of long duration—but I suppose them to be connected with his periods of depression. The years of his youth were devoted to radical politics, in which his most notable achievement was the organization of the Trotsky Commission in 1937. He was a member of the staff of *Fortune,* where his work as writer and editor was held in especially high regard. He died in 1964.

The wedding took place in the meeting-hall of the Ethical Culture Society, whose well-known school in the same building on Central Park West Tess had attended. Neither Solow nor I would have been indifferent to the implications of the scene. The Society was not wholly Jewish in its membership, but largely so, and it was often thought of as a means by which Jews of a certain class carried forward their acculturation, although that word, if then invented, was not yet current. The tone of the Society was judged to be that of an unassailable gentility; it was respectable, well-mannered, undistressed. The Jews who belonged to it were chiefly German, more easily detached from their Reform faith than were the East European (generally called Russian) Jews from their orthodoxy. The extent of the acculturation of the German Jews was a matter for pride with them, and they were likely to be envied and resented by East European Jews for what would have been called their refinement. To all that its Jewish members were presumed to want from Ethical Culture, Solow and certain of his friends were antagonistic. Our adverse feeling had been raised to the level of principle by our connection with the *Menorah Journal.*

It can scarcely be a digression from Tess Slesinger if I take notice of this remarkable magazine, for Tess lived in its ambience during an important part of her life, and her debt to its managing editor, Elliot Cohen, was considerable, and one that she was happy to acknowledge.

I should explain that the *Menorah Journal* that I knew is not commemorated in the large anthology edited by Leo Schwarz in 1964 and intended as a memorial to Henry Hurwitz, the founder and chief editor of the magazine. Between Hurwitz and Cohen there were extreme differences of temperament and opinion, and Dr. Schwarz's piety has perpetuated the ancient quarrel by excluding from the anthology any contribution that might seem to have been inspired or influenced by Cohen. No one reading the sedate, temperate, measured, rather elderly volume could possibly know that between 1925 and 1929 the magazine had published the stories, essays, and reviews of a group of lively talented young people who thought of it as the natural medium for their work and gave it a tone of irreverent vivacity that its chief editor had not bargained for and did not want.

The *Menorah Journal* would not have come into being, or continued there, had it not been for Hurwitz, who stubbornly insisted that it be maintained by the Jewish community. But Hurwitz was a man with whom it was impossible to converse, at least if you were young and clever. He was shy and stiff, without wit and no more than a formal humor, and he easily became defensive, although I am sure he meant to be genial and even kind. Cohen was his opposite in every way. He was a Socratic personality, drawing young men to him to be teased and taught. He conversed endlessly, his talk being a sort of enormously enlightening gossip— about persons, books, baseball players and football plays, manners, morals, comedians (on these he was especially good), clergymen (with emphasis on rabbis, one of whom he once described as "the Jewish Stephen Wise"), colleges, the social sciences, philanthropy and social work, literary scholarship, restaurants, tailors, psychiatry. He had gained much from having been born and reared in Mobile,

Alabama; he was proud of his knowledge of an American life that wasn't easily available to New York Jewish intellectuals, and he cherished his feeling (it was not the less genuine because he was conscious of it) for the unregenerate commonplaces of ordinary existence. Indeed, the basis of his intellectual life sometimes seemed to be a feeling for "the people"; he had a reasoned tenderness for the culture of the people such as we find nowadays in the writings of Richard Hoggart and Raymond Williams. At that time, among his younger friends, it seemed almost an eccentricity.

Cohen was not very much older than the youngest of us, but with his great beautiful head he had the aspect of an essential seniority which he was entirely willing to support, for he never played the game of being young. He entranced and infuriated us. He had an infrequent smile that was dazzling in its charm; his surliness, if things did not go as he wished, was impenetrable. No one ever had such pleasing manners, or such bad ones. And no one—certainly none of our teachers—ever paid so much attention to what we thought and how we wrote. He has often been called a great editor and so he was. He gave us things to do and when we had done them, he gave them back to us to do over, and better, having first carefully showed us what was wrong. Eventually one had to set up a protection against Cohen's involvement in one's work. Nothing concerned him so much as the written word, and he wanted above all things to be a writer, but he wrote only with the greatest difficulty, and—except in his letters and in the little ironic pieces he wrote for a time under the *nom de guerre* of "An Elder of Zion"— never in a way that gave a true indication of his quality; as a consequence, one stood in danger of becoming the instrument of his intellectual intentions. But at its beginning his interest in one's writing did only good.

I had come to know Cohen through his having accepted a short story of mine in my senior year at college; at some time in the following year I had brought him together with Solow. The acquaintance flourished; not long after it began, Solow became Cohen's assistant editor and between the two men there developed a close relationship of often painful ambivalence that lasted until Cohen's death in 1958. After her marriage to Solow, Tess Slesinger came into the circle of Cohen's tutelage; no doubt she learned the more from him because he held her in great affection, as she did him. Eventually, like others, she felt the need to work without particular reference to his approval, but, as I have said, she was direct and constant in her gratitude for the help he had given.

What bound together the group around the *Menorah Journal,* what made those of us who came to Solow's wedding take a high line about the Ethical Culture Society, was the idea of Jewishness. This had nothing to do with religion; we were not religious.[1] It had nothing to do with Zionism; we were inclined to be skeptical about Zionism and even opposed to it, and during the violence that flared up in 1929 some of us were on principle pro-Arab. Chiefly our concern with Jewishness was about what is now called authenticity.

The word must not be given too much weight, and some might judge that it can have no weight at all, considering what we were not concerned with. If we excluded religion from our purview, if we excluded Zionism, with all that it implied of the social actualities of Europe as well as of an ethnic aspiration that must inevitably be moving, what could a conception of Jewish authenticity possibly refer to? At this distance in time the answer must seem fairly dull— we had in mind something that probably still goes under the name of a "sense of identity," by which is meant, when it is used of Jews, that the individual Jewish person recognizes naturally and

---

[1] With the exception of Henry Rosenthal, my closest friend at college, who was studying for the rabbinate. Rosenthal gave up his religious profession in the Thirties and took a degree in philosophy, which he now teaches. Other members of the group were Clifton Fadiman and Louis Berg; Felix Morrow came into it at a later date; Meyer Levin, when he was in the city, consorted with it, and so did Albert Harper. Anita Brenner, a young Texan, a precocious scholar of Mexican archaeology, should also be mentioned. Lewis Mumford, a non-Jewish contributor to the *Journal,* was a presence in the offing and I recall encounters with him; but he was an established figure at an early age, and although only ten years older than the youngest of us, he seemed very grand and we were not easy with him; in those days seniority was more of a bar to communication than it has since become.

easily that he *is* a Jew and "accepts himself" as such, finding pleasure and taking pride in the identification, discovering in it one or another degree of significance. From which there might follow an impulse to kinship with others who make the same recognition, and perhaps the forming of associations on the basis of this kinship.

The way in which Cohen and his clever young friends thought about the matter was not essentially at odds with the view of the man they judged to be all too literal and limited—Henry Hurwitz had started the Menorah Society at Harvard to deal with the sense of exclusion felt by Jewish students, the method being to make them aware of the interest and dignity of the Jewish past, to assure them of, as it were, the normality of the Jewish present, toward which they would, it was hoped, have the attitude of *noblesse oblige.* Our intention was much the same, perhaps even to the *noblesse oblige,* although the actual use of the phrase would have appalled us; only our means were different. When it came to the Jewish present, we undertook to normalize it by suggesting that it was not only as respectable as the present of any other group but also as foolish, vulgar, complicated, impossible, and promising. We named names, we pointed to particular modes of conduct. To write our endless reviews of Jewish books, directing our satire at the sodden piety so many of them displayed, to tease Jewish life, as Cohen did in his "Notes for a Modern History of the Jews" and his "Marginal Annotations," to write vivacious stories of modern sensibility in which the protagonists were Jewish, as Tess Slesinger did, was to help create a consciousness that could respond to the complexities of the Jewish situation with an energetic unabashed intelligence.

The situation of the American Jew has changed so much in the intervening years that it may be hard for some to understand the need for such efforts. Nowadays one of the most salient facts about American culture is the prominent place in it that is occupied by Jews. This state of affairs has become a staple subject of both journalism and academic study—for some years now the *Times*

Literary Supplement has found it impossible to survey the American literary scene without goggling rather solemnly over the number of Jews that make it what it is; foreign students have withdrawn their attention from the New Criticism to turn it upon The Jew in American Culture. Jewish protagonists are a matter of course in the contemporary novel, Jewish backgrounds taken for granted. Jewish idioms and turns of speech have established themselves in the language.[2] And, so far as I can make out, there are virtually no barriers to Jews in the universities. But in the time of which I write, things were not so. Jewish writers were not yet numerous and such novelists as there were did not yet find it natural and easy to take their subjects from their own lives. In the universities the situation was very tight indeed. Cohen, after a brilliant undergraduate career at Yale, had given up the graduate study of English because he believed that as a Jew he had no hope of a university appointment. When I decided to go into academic life, my friends thought me naive to the point of absurdity, nor were they wholly wrong—my appointment to an instructorship in Columbia College was pretty openly regarded as an experiment, and for some time my career in the College was conditioned by my being Jewish.

As compared to some anti-Semitic situations that have prevailed, this was certainly not an extreme one, but it had a sufficiently bad effect upon the emotional lives of many who experienced it. Jews who wanted to move freely in the world were easily led to think of their Jewishness as nothing but a burden. One doesn't often encounter nowadays the ugly embarrassment, once quite common, with which Jews responded to an implicit accusation directed against them which they accepted as in some way justified. The young people around the *Menorah Journal* were not much concerned with the anti-Semitism itself. Their interest was in its emotional or characterological effects, which they undertook at least to neutralize.

---

[2] And as elements of American speech are having an effect on English English—"Should, Shmould. Shouldn't, Shmouldn't," is the way a *TLS* reviewer recently expressed his indifference to prescriptive statements.

To wish to create an enclave of culture that would have the effect of advancing Jews—chiefly, of course, Jews of the middle class—toward an "acceptance" of themselves, can scarcely seem a momentous purpose, and, indeed, now that the old state of affairs has gone by, it may be hard to see why it should have engaged the energies of young people to whom cleverness or spiritedness is attributed. And indeed the therapeutic intention I have described, although it was important in our sense of our enterprise, was not at all what made for its excitement. This came from the fact that we had found a way of supposing that society was actual and that we were in some relation to it. If the anti-Semitism that we observed did not arouse our indignation, this was in part because we took it to be a kind of advantage: against this social antagonism we could define ourselves *and* our society, we could discover who we were and who we wished to be. It helped to give life the look of reality.

For a young man in the Twenties, the intellectual or cultural situation was an enervating one. The only issue presented to him was that of intelligence as against stupidity, the fine and developed spirit confronting the dull life of materialist America. With that theme, for what it was worth, Mencken had done all that could be done. I read *The Nation, The New Republic, The Freeman* and hoped that some day I would be worthy to respond to their solemn liberalism with something more than dim general assent. I was addicted to Wells and Shaw but it seemed to me that they spun delightful but fanciful tales about young Philosopher Kings who insisted that their divine right be recognized. I recall my college days as an effort to discover some social entity to which I could give the credence of my sense, as it were, and with which I could be in some relation. But this probably makes me out to be more conscious than I really was—put it, rather, that I was bored and vacuous because I had no ground upon which to rear an imagination of society.

The discovery, through the *Menorah Journal,* of the Jewish situation had the effect of making society at last available to my imagination. It made America available to my imagination, as it could not possibly be if I tried to understand it with the categories offered by Mencken or Herbert Croly, or, for that matter, Henry Adams. Suddenly it began to be possible—better than that, indeed: it began to be necessary—to think with categories that were charged with energy and that had the effect of assuring the actuality of the object thought about. One couldn't, for example, think for very long about Jews without perceiving that one was using the category of social class. It was necessary not merely in order to think about Jews in their relation to the general society but in order to think about Jews as Jews, the class differences among them being so considerable and having so complex a relationship to the general concept of Jewishness that had at first claimed one's recognition and interest.

At least among some of us, feelings about class developed a quite considerable intensity. They became the basis for personal judgments, often quite bitter, for some years before they were politicalized. But the politicalization was not long in coming. The stock-market crash of 1929 and the consequent depression brought to an end the *Menorah Journal* as we knew it. Funds were in very short supply, the magazine ceased monthly publication and became an uncertain quarterly. In 1932, Cohen withdrew from the managing editorship and Hurwitz began his long sad struggle to keep the magazine alive, which, in some sort, he did until 1947. The young contributors turned to the Marxist radicalism of the day.

III

In any view of the American cultural situation, the importance of the radical movement of the Thirties cannot be overestimated. It may be said to have created the American intellectual class as we now know it in its great size and influence. It fixed the character of this class as being, through all mutations of opinion, predominantly of the Left. And quite apart from opinion, the political tendency of the Thirties defined the style of the class—from that radicalism came the moral urgency, the sense of crisis, and the concern with personal salvation that mark the existence of American intellectuals.

The Unpossessed was the first novel to deal with this new class in an effort of realism. Not until two years later did John Dos Passos bring his *U.S.A.* trilogy to its conclusion with *The Big Money,* which, among other records of personal disaster, sets forth the careers of intellectuals who chose the life of liberty and enlightenment and were destroyed by the cold actualities of this ideal existence. What Dos Passos had to say in 1936 about the death of the heart and mind that might overtake the radical intellectual had been exceeded in stringency by Flaubert in 1869, but *L'Education Sentimentale* was not widely known at the time and *The Big Money* was real with shock and bewilderment. The idea that the life of radicalism is not of its nature exempt from moral dangers is still difficult to accommodate—the articles on Dos Passos and *The Big Money* in the latest edition of *The Oxford Companion to American Literature* do not take note of its place in Dos Passos's view of American life and are content to speak of "the vitiation and degradation of character in a decaying civilization based on commercialism and exploitation." *The Unpossessed* cannot claim the force of *The Big Money* and it lacks the detailed verisimilitude which was Dos Passos's *forte,* but it too brought word of danger in the very place where salvation was believed to be certain, and its unhappy news came early.

Not the least interesting element of *The Unpossessed* is its title, which, we may suppose, makes reference to Dostoevski's great novel about radicalism, *The Possessed.* A recent English version corrects Constance Garnett's translation of the name of the book to *The Devils,* a literal rendering which does indeed convey, better than Mrs. Garnett's, the direct force of Dostoevski's adverse judgment of his radical characters. In the word "possessed" there is now a laudatory connotation which is stronger than the pejorative one. To be possessed by a devil is a condition that is indeed bad and even repulsive, but one may also be possessed by a *daimon* or a god, which makes quite a different state of affairs. We intend admiration when we say of a person that he fought or rode or worked "like one possessed," implying an accession of vital energy which carries him beyond his usual powers. Similarly, the man who is said to be possessed by an idea or a purpose, unless it is manifestly evil, is usually regarded with admiration. Like the word "passion," the word "possessed" has subordinated its bad to its good meaning. And it is the good meaning that Tess Slesinger had chiefly in mind—those persons in her novel who are *not* possessed are unfortunate or blameworthy.

The word in the sense she intended, that of not being in the service of some great impersonal vital intention, applies differently to the men and the women of the novel. In the latter case, the old sexual meaning of the word is in point. Neither of the two heroines is possessed by the man she loves. Margaret Flinders, besides being denied the gratifications of motherhood, is frustrated by her husband's refusal to lay full claim to her treasure of frank and open feeling. Elizabeth, adoring her cousin Bruno Leonard, is no less adored by him, but he is unable to take advantage of the commitment she is eager to give him and thus condemns her to a life of sexual promiscuity. The failure of the men to possess the women is consonant with their inability to surrender themselves to the ideals they profess. Miles Flinders is fussy and finicky, his intelligence limited by his conscience, the last man in the world to bear the brunt of the actuality of political power. Bruno Leonard is what is often thought to be the "typical intellectual," egotistical, self-doubting, skeptical of all purpose whatever; at the big party in aid of the Hunger Marchers and his own ill-conceived magazine, he makes a cynical and vulgar speech in which he expresses his disgust with himself and the whole class of intellectuals.

As a document of its time, *The Unpossessed* must be used with caution. I have said that it has a certain evidential value, but it must be added that its testimony is not of a direct and unambiguous kind. Mr. Kempton uses it in an insufficiently critical way and he comes to conclusions that are not to be accepted. From the radical-intellectual characters of the novel Mr. Kempton undertakes to make inferences about the actual persons who were their prototypes and to describe the tendency of their time that they exemplified; he says of the group that it "was an elite not of origin so much as of attitude; like [Edmund] Wilson, its members hated the middle class from above. Its motives were disgust and alienation. . . . It represented an aesthetic rather than a social tendency." Some of the errors of this description arise from Mr. Kempton's reading of the novel: most readers would say, I think, that "hated" is too strong and simple a word for the characters' attitude to the middle class; nor could it accurately be used of the attitude of the actual persons to whom the characters may be thought to refer. And Mr. Kempton's word, "aesthetic," needs explication, for none of the characters is especially concerned with art or displays attitudes derived from such a concern. The word can perhaps be made to serve accuracy if it is taken to suggest a preoccupation with the look and feel of society, the look and feel of the moral life. But such a preoccupation would be, precisely, social. I think that what Mr. Kempton meant to say was that the novel portrays a group whose tendency was social or moral rather than *political*.

This the novel does do, its further intention being to suggest that the characters practice a deception upon themselves when they think of themselves as being political, and that this deception is to be viewed with satiric irony. The situation thus proposed is interesting in itself and it might well be thought to throw some light on the way people act or on the way certain people acted at a certain time. But it does not throw light on the actual group of which some members were, as Mr. Kempton infers, the prototypes of the novel's characters. In point of fact, the group was nothing if not political in the particular mode of radical politics at the time. That mode may be understood from Daniel Aaron's study, *Writers on the Left*. A reading of this useful work might lead to the conclusion that no politics was ever drearier. But it will make clear that the group's participation in it was, if anything, more consciously, and, I think, more intelligently, political than was common.[3] If eventually the group came to regard radical politics with despair, no member of it reached this state of feeling by having passed through Miles Flinders' simplemindedness, nor would he have expressed his hopelessness in anything like the ugly self-pity of Bruno Leonard's drunken speech. The radical politics the group despaired of was that of the Communist Party, which was not the rather comical remote abstraction that *The Unpossessed* represents it as being, and any member of the group would have been able to explain his disillusionment by a precise enumeration of the errors and failures of the Party, both at home and abroad. During the considerable time when Stalinism was established as sacrosanct among a large and influential part of the intellectual class, all the members of the group, on reasoned political grounds, opposed this powerful body of opinion, to which, it must be said, the author of *The Unpossessed* found it possible to give her assent during her Hollywood years.

It cannot be imputed to *The Unpossessed* as a fault that it does not accurately present the people and events it is presumed to have had in mind as the basis of its invention. A novel is not in the first instance a document, and its right to make free with the actuality from which most novels take their start cannot be compromised. To actuality the novel owes nothing, although to reality it gives total allegiance: so runs the prescript of criticism. But sometimes actuality and reality are one, or very nearly so, and *The Unpossessed,* good as

[3] See especially Chapter 14, note 3. Since my name is mentioned in this extended reference to the National Committee for the Defense of Political Prisoners, perhaps it is here that I should correct Mr. Kempton when, if I read him aright, he suggests that I am represented in *The Unpossessed*. This is not the case and was not supposed to be the case by any of the author's friends at the time the book appeared and was much talked about, with, of course, frequent reference to such portrayals of actual people as it was understood to contain. I make the correction partly in the interests of accuracy, partly in order to be able to claim a more nearly complete objectivity in speaking about the book than might be thought possible if I were personally portrayed in it. Perhaps I should add that none of the characters of the novel is a literal, or even nearly literal, representation of the person to whom the character may be referred.

it is, would have been a better book still if the author, by a firmer commitment to actuality, had set a more substantial historical scene, if she had encompassed the political particularities of her time. Politics was not her subject, which is the ironic discrepancy, eventually the antagonism, between life and the desire to make life as good as it might be.

The dialectic is a familiar one and it has attracted literary temperaments as diverse as Molière and Hawthorne. It begins with the discovery that the established values of society are wrong, not only corrupt but corrupting, and with the decision to reject them in favor of other values, which, to all appearance, are far superior, of a different and higher spiritual order. It proceeds in the growing awareness that the preferred new values have their own deficiencies and constitute their own danger. They are by no means proof against human depravity. If they are affirmed by a group, the small dissident social unit is seen to have its own principle of corruption, perhaps different in kind from that of the rejected society but no less active. In the conscious commitment to virtue there is seen to lie a fault which in due time becomes fully apparent—an absoluteness or abstractness which has the effect of denying some free instinctual impulse that life must have. It then seems to be true that the rejected society, for all that its values are wrong, does at least permit "the simple and normal life," as Thomas Mann called it in speaking of his famous story *Tonio Kröger,* in which he expounds an analogous dialectic, that between art and established society. In the antagonism between "nature" and "spirit"—the terms are Mann's—the established society, although it may indeed be the enemy of spirit, is the ally of nature. And if it seems to be after all but an ambiguous ally, it may be the more willingly accepted when it is understood that corrupted spirit is rather worse than corrupted nature.

In the radical political culture of the Thirties, the dialectic was to be perceived at work in its fullest ironic force. The doctrine of the politics affirmed freedom; the conduct of the politics was likely to be marked by a dull rigidity. The doctrine was directed toward the richness and fullness that would eventually be given to human life, but a solicitude for mankind in general and in the future had the effect of diminishing the awareness of actual particular persons within the reach of the hand. One has but to read the politically oriented novels of the time to know the dreary limitation that overtook the imagination of what life is or might ever be.

It is scarcely surprising, since the dialectic is between "spirit" and "nature," that a woman should have been the first to take note of the state of things. For some decades before the Thirties, the belief prevailed that woman stood in a special and privileged relation to "nature," or, as it was sometimes called, "life." Many writers, among them Meredith, Henry James, Shaw, Henry Adams, Wells, Lawrence, and Yeats, had contributed to a rather engaging *mystique* of Woman which developed concomitantly with the feeling that the order of the world as it had been contrived by man was a dismal and possibly a doomed enterprise. The masculine mind, dulled by preoccupation, was to be joined and quickened by the Woman-principle, which drew its bright energies from ancient sources and sustained the hope of new things. Implicit in the *mystique* was a handsome promise made to women—they were to be free, brilliant, and, in their own way, powerful, and, like men, they were to have destinies, yet at the same time they would be delightful, and they would be loved because they were women. The *mystique* faded and the promise lapsed. There are no traces of them in our contemporary literature, and when in older books we encounter the female characters born of that late Victorian and Edwardian dream of Woman, all aglow and shining from the peculiarly close connection with nature, or life, that their authors assigned to them, they appear as the nymphs and goddesses of a vanished age. But up through the Twenties, the *mystique* and its promise could still command the belief of some women.

It was a generous credence. Tess Slesinger set out with it and it made part of her singular personal charm. It probably shaped her style, for better or worse. *The Unpossessed,* quite apart from its *parti pris,* is avowedly and unabashedly a woman's novel and that lack of substantiality of which I have complained is in part the result of a woman writer's stylistic intention—gross and weighty facts were to be kept to a minimum so that there would be little impediment to the bright controlled subjectivity of a feminine prose manner inaugurated by Katherine Mansfield, given authority by Virginia Woolf, and used here with a happy acerbity of wit superadded.

At least a little irony must surely have touched such faith as Tess Slesinger gave to the waning cult of Woman. Yet there is a strange moment in *The Unpossessed* which suggests that the author received it with rather less doubleness of mind than might have been expected of her. Among a small party of friends Margaret Flinders' husband, Miles, has shown great emotional distress. His wife moves quickly to comfort him by her touch and succeeds in doing so. This passage follows: "Had Margaret Flinders sprouted wings? Bruno watched her moving in her sudden radiance. She was beside Miles in a second, her arms about his neck. Something had taken hold of Margaret, filled her with triumphant storm; and Miles, allured, bewildered, stood like a moon beside the sun." It is then said that Miles "was frightened of her. . . . But he was smitten with joy and pride in her." And: "He timidly put out his hand and patted her. The gesture was ridiculous; like patting God."

It is possible, of course, to interpret this in an adversary way. The American litigation between the sexes, after having been quite overt and articulate, has gone into a latent phase, but not before it produced a judgment against women that has established itself in our structure of belief. The substance of this judgment is that women are hostile to men and carry their hostility to the point of being "castrating," or, as some say, thinking it to be a subtler and more scientific word, "castrative." And here in this passage, it will occur to some readers to remark, is the archetypical female fantasy: the woman in her specifically feminine role puts on power, becomes more powerful than the man; in the metaphor of her own perverse mythology, she is the sun to the moon of the frightened and bewildered husband; nor does the fantasy of power stop short of her assumption of a masculine godhead.

The passage is certainly curious. And no doubt there is ground for the adversary reading of it I have supposed, just as there is ground for taking the book as a whole to be that so often graceless thing, a novel of feminine protest. But to settle for this view of *The Unpossessed* would be to misunderstand its real intention, which, as I have said, was to set forth the dialectic between life and the desire to make life as good as it might be, between "nature" and "spirit." That this intention should be susceptible of misunderstanding is, no doubt, the fault of the book itself: had the two terms of its dialectic been of equal substantiveness, had the actuality of politics been more fully realized, the possibility of seeing the issue as merely that between men and women would not have existed. And it is the real intention of the book that gives rise to the imagery of the passage I have quoted—the wings, radiance, triumphant storm, dominant sun, and very godhead are not to be understood as the feminine armament in a war between the sexes: the Blakean paraphernalia are meant to suggest the will and the hope of still uncorrupted nature in its resistance to the tyranny of spirit.

"In our time," said Thomas Mann, "the destiny of man presents its meaning in political terms." Instead of political terms Mann might have said social terms or moral terms, any *terms* at all for the meaning of man's destiny, and still W. B. Yeats would have seized the sentence to inscribe at the head of a poem which says to its solemn epigraph that what it remarks is all very well, and maybe true, but has nothing to do with the real motions of man's heart. Yeats, however, knew that there is no escape from *terms*—the pathetic little tantrum of a poem called "Politics" ("How can I, that girl standing there. . . .") is followed in *Last Poems* by "The Man and the Echo" in which the old poet, searching his life for the harm he may have done others by what he had spoken and written, defends himself from his own accusation by saying that it had not been open to him to "shirk/The spiritual intellect's great work," going on to say that there is no "work so great/As that which cleans man's dirty slate."

It is characteristic of the modern age that an ever-increasing number of people suppose that they must be involved in the spiritual intellect's great work. Whoever can recall the Twenties and Thirties might well have a clear notion of how constant has been the augmentation of their number. The modern person who has reached a certain not uncommon point of intellectual development lives in relation to *terms,* that is to say, to ideas, principles, pasts, futures, the awareness of the dirty slate and the duty of cleaning it. Some stand closer to the activity of the spiritual intellect than others, but all are obedient to its imperative, and proud of their obedience. Yet over this necessity there hovers the recollection, or the imagination, of a mode of existence that is not in the control of the spiritual intellect, the mode of existence that, to use Yeats's language, is of "the body and its stupidity," the blessed stupidity of nature and instinct. Tess Slesinger, who might herself have been "that girl standing there" of Yeats's little poem, enrolled herself early among those who undertook to advance the "great work." Like the friends with whom she began her public intellectual life, she believed that there was no better occupation than to scrub the slate clean of the scrawls made on it by family, class, ethnic or cultural group, the society in general. She did not change her judgment of the enterprise, but in one especially vivacious and articulate moment she took notice of the scribble she had not expected to see on the slate—the one made by the spiritual intellect itself.

James Joyce in His Letters

[*Commentary*, February 1968]

IN 1935, near the end of a long affectionate letter to his son George in America, James Joyce wrote: "Here I conclude. My eyes are tired. For over half a century they have gazed into nullity, where they have found a lovely nothing."

It is not a characteristic utterance. Joyce was little given to making large statements about the nature of existence. As Dr. Johnson said of Dryden, he knew how to complain, but his articulate grievances were not usually of a metaphysical kind. They referred to particular circumstances of practical life, chiefly the lets and hindrances to his work; at least in his later years, such resentment as he expressed was less in response to what he suffered as a person than to the impediments that were put in his way as an artist.

And actually we cannot be certain that Joyce did indeed mean to complain when he wrote to George of his long gaze into "*nulla*"— his letters to his children were always in Italian—or that he was yielding to a metaphysical self-pity when he said he had found in it "*un bellissimo niente.*" The adjective may well have been intended not ironically but literally and Joyce can be understood to say that human existence is nullity right enough, yet if it is looked into with a vision such as his, the nothing that can be perceived really *is* lovely, though the maintenance of the vision is fatiguing work.

To read the passage in this way is in accord with our readiness nowadays to see Joyce as pre-eminently a "positive" writer, to be aware of the resistance he offered to nullity through his great acts of creation. From the famous climactic epiphany of *A Portrait of the Artist as a Young Man,* in which life "calls" in all imaginable erotic beauty and is answered in ecstasy, he went on to celebrate human existence even in the pain, defeat, and humiliation that make up so large a part of its substance. He consciously intended Molly Bloom's ultimate "Yes" as a doctrinal statement, a judgment in life's favor made after all the adverse evidence was in. He contrived a rich poetry out of the humble and sordid, the sad repeated round of the commonplace, laying a significant emphasis on the little, nameless, unremembered acts of kindness and of love—it is much to the point that Joyce as a young man could speak of Wordsworth in superlative praise, for much of the power of his own work derives from the Wordsworthian purpose of discovering a transcendence by which life, in confrontation with nullity, is affirmed.

But this does not tell the whole story of the relation in which Joyce stood to nullity. He was not only resistant to it but also partisan with it. He loved it and sought to make it prevail. The transcendent affirmation of hypostatized life went along with a profound indifference, even a hostility, to a great many of the particularities in which the energies of life embody themselves. He could speak in thrilling archaic phrase of "the fair courts of life" yet the elaborations of developed society were for the most part of no account to him, and to much of the redundancy of culture as it proliferates in objects and practices that are meant to be pleasing he was chiefly apathetic. His alienation from so many of the modes and conditions of human existence is sometimes chilling.

Among life's processes, that of entropy makes an especial appeal to Joyce. The "paralysis" which is representel in *Dubliners* as the pathology of a nation at a particular moment of its history was also known to him as a general condition of life itself, and if he found it frightening, he also found it tempting. *Dubliners* does indeed have the import of social criticism that its author often said it was meant to have. This "chapter in the moral history" of his nation levels an accusation to which the conscience of his race, when at last it will have been forged in the smithy of his soul, must be sensitive. But if the devolution of energy to the point of "paralysis" is, in a moral and social view, a condition to be deplored and reversed, it is also for Joyce a sacred and powerful state of existence. The attraction it had for him is nearly overt in the first story of *Dubliners,* "The Sisters," and in the last, "The Dead." "The special odor of corruption which, I hope, floats over my stories" is the true scent by which life is to be tracked to its last authenticity. It is not without reason that Samuel Beckett is often said to have represented Joyce in the Hamm of *Endgame,* the terrible blind storyteller who presides over the quietus of Nature, himself on the verge of extinction but grimly cherishing and ordering what little life remains, setting against the ever-encroaching void, which he himself has helped bring about, an indomitable egoism that is itself an emptiness.

The power of Joyce's work derives, we must see, not only from the impulse to resist nullity but also, and equally, from the impulse to make nullity prevail. Something of the destructive force was remarked by T. S. Eliot when, taking tea with Virginia Woolf and trying to convince his hostess that *Ulysses* was not to be dismissed as the work of one or another kind of "underbred" person, he characterized the author's achievement and the magnitude of his power by saying that his book "destroyed the whole of the nineteenth century." Eliot meant that Joyce by his radical innovations of style had made obsolete the styles of the earlier time, and also that, as a result of or in concomitance with the obsolescence that Joyce had effected, the concerns and sentiments to which the old styles were appropriate had lost their interest and authority. In 1922 the nineteenth century was not in high repute and one might suppose that the report of its having been killed would make an occasion for hope: with the old concerns and sentiments out of the way, those of the new day might be expected to flourish. But Eliot expressed no such expectation. Although he took it to be part of the great achievement of *Ulysses* that it had shown up "the futility of all the English styles," he went on to say that Joyce had destroyed his own future, for now there was nothing left for him to write about. Nor for anyone else: Eliot later said that with *Ulysses* Joyce had brought to an end the genre of the novel.

If there is truth in Eliot's observation, a phrase of Walter Pater's helps us understand what concerns and sentiments of the nineteenth century Joyce may be said to have killed. In a famous paragraph of the Conclusion to *The Renaissance,* Pater spoke of "success in life." It doesn't matter that he was saying that success in life was the ability to burn with a hard gemlike flame, to make all experience into an object of aesthetic contemplation. The point is that, at the high moment of his exposition of a doctrine directed against crass practicality, Pater could use a phrase that to us now can seem only vulgar, a form of words which scarcely even stockbrokers, headmasters, and philistine parents would venture to use. In the nineteenth century a mind as exquisite and detached as Pater's could take it for granted that upon the life of an individual person a judgment of success or failure might be passed. And the nineteenth-century novel was in nothing so much a product of its time as in its assiduity in passing this judgment.

It was of course moral or spiritual success that the novel was concerned with, and this "true" success often—though not always—implied failure as the world knows it. But a characteristic assumption of the novel was that the true success brought as much gratification as conventional opinion attributed to worldly success, that it was just as real and nearly as tangible. The conception of moral or spiritual achievement was, we may say, sustained and controlled by the society from whose conventions the triumph was wrested. The houses, servants, carriages, plate, china, linen, cash, credit, position, honor, power that were the goods of the conventional world served to validate the goods of the moral or spiritual life. At the heart of the novel is the idea that the world, the worldly world, Henry James's "great round world itself," might have to be given up in the interests of integrity or even simple decency. What made this idea momentous was the assumption that the surrender is of something entirely real, and in some way, in the forcible way of common sense, much to be desired. Upon the valuation of what is given up depends much of the valuation of what is gotten in exchange. Poor Julien Sorel! Poor Pip! Poor Phineas Finn! It was a dull-spirited reader indeed who did not feel what a pity it was that the young man could not make a go of Things As They Are and at the same time possess his soul in honor and peace. But since the soul was one of the possible possessions, it was of course to be preferred to all others, the more because the price paid for it was thought real and high. In the degree that the novel gave credence to the world while withholding its assent, it established the reality of the moral or spiritual success that is defined by the rejection of the world's values.

Credence given, assent withheld: for a time this position of the novel *vis-à-vis* the world was of extraordinary interest. At a certain point in the novel's relatively short history, in the first quarter of this century, there burst upon our consciousness a realization of how great had been its accomplishment, how important its function. It was on all sides seen to be what Henry James in effect said it was, what D. H. Lawrence explicitly called it, "the book of life."

Yet no sooner had the novel come to this glory than it was said, not by Eliot alone, to have died. In all likelihood the report is true. The question of the viability of the novel today is probably to be answered in the spirit of the man who, when asked if he believed in baptism, replied that of course he did, he had seen it performed many times. Novels are still ceaselessly written, published, reviewed, and on occasion hailed, but the old sense of their spiritual efficacy is ever harder to come by. One thing is certain: to whatever purposes the novel now addresses itself, it has outgrown the activity which, in the nineteenth century and in the early days of the twentieth, was characteristic of the genre, virtually definitive of it, the setting of the values of the moral and spiritual life over against the values of the world. This is a confrontation that no longer engages our interest. Which is by no means to say that getting and spending are not of great moment, or that moral and spiritual sensibility have declined. As to the latter, indeed, it flourishes in a way that is perhaps unprecedented—it may well be that never before have so many people undertaken to live enlightened lives, to see through the illusions that society imposes, doing this quite easily, without strain or struggle, having been led to the perception of righteousness by what literature has told them of the social life. Whatever we may *do* as persons in the world, however we behave as getters and spenders, in our other capacity, as readers, as persons of moral sensibility, we *know* that the values of the world do not deserve our interest. We know it: we do not discover it, as readers once did, with the pleasing excitement that the novel generated as it led toward understanding. It is a thing taken for granted. That the world is a cheat, its social arrangements a sham, its rewards a sell, was patent to us from our moral infancy, whose first spoken words were, "Take away that bauble."

So entirely, and, as it were, so naturally do we withhold our assent from the world that we give it scarcely any credence. As getters and spenders we take it to be actual and there; as readers our imagination repels it, or at most accepts it as an absurdity. What in the first instance is a moral judgment on the world intensifies and establishes itself as a habit of thought to the point where it transcends its moral origin and becomes a metaphysical judgment.

More and more the contemporary reader requires of literature that it have a metaphysical rather than a moral aspect. Having come to take nullity for granted, he wants to be enlightened and entertained by statements about the nature of nothing, what its size is, how it is furnished, what services the management provides, what sort of conversation and amusements can go on in it. The novel in some of its experimental and theoretical developments can gratify the new taste, but this is more easily accomplished by the theater, which on frequent occasions in its long tradition has shown its natural affinity for ultimate and metaphysical considerations. By means of the irony which it generates merely through turning a conscious eye on its traditional devices of illusion, the theater easily escapes from its servitude to morality into free and radical play with the nature of existence as morality assumes it to be. That life is a dream, that all the world's a stage, that right you are if you think you are—such propositions can be forcibly demonstrated by the theater, which, defined by its function of inducing us to accept appearance as reality, delights in discovering in itself the power of showing that reality is but appearance, in effect nothing.

At least at one point in his life Joyce rated drama above all literary forms and made what he called the "dramatic emotion" the type of the "aesthetic emotion" in general. With the metaphysical potentialities of drama he was not concerned in an immediate way, but his famous account of the "dramatic emotion" has an obvious bearing upon the theater's ability to control, even to extirpate, the credence given to the worldly reality. Dedalus explains to Lynch that this emotion is "static," that it is brought into being by the "arrest" of the mind. "The feelings excited by improper art are kinetic, desire and loathing. Desire urges us to possess, to go to something; loathing urges us to abandon, to go from something. The arts which excite them, pornographical or didactic, are therefore improper arts. The aesthetic emotion (I use the general term) is therefore static. The mind is arrested and raised above desire and loathing."

Nothing, of course, could be further from the aesthetic of the novel in its classic phase. The novel was exactly, in Joyce's sense of the words, both pornographical and didactic, having the intention to generate desire and loathing, to urge the possession of the good, the abandonment of the bad. Assuming the prepotency of the will, the novel sought to educate and direct it by discriminating among the objects to which it might address itself. But Joyce characteristically represents the will in entropy, in its movement through ambiguity and paralysis to extinction. In *Ulysses,* for example, the objects of desire or intention of virtually all the characters are either of no great moment as the world judges, or they exist in unrealizable fantasy, or in the past.

There is one exception. The will of one person is represented as being, although momentarily in abeyance, on the point of becoming prepotent, and its object is represented as both capable of attainment and worth attaining: Stephen Dedalus means to become a great writer and we know, of course, that he does. The will of the artist is accepted in all its legendary power and authority, fully licensed. And the worldly traits of the particular artist Stephen Dedalus are entirely acknowledged—his bitter intention of fame, his pride, his vanity, his claim to unique personal superiority, touched with class feeling, his need to be ascendant in every situation. Yet the world to which these traits refer, that world to which Yeats—the admirer of Balzac!—gave so lively a recognition, in which the artist wins his prizes, has no existence in *Ulysses*. On the evidence that the book provides, there is nothing that can signalize the artist's achievement of success in life. There is no person, let alone a social agency, component and empowered to judge his work and tell him that he has triumphed with it, that he has imposed his will upon the world and is now to be feared and loved. The honor he deserves cannot be accorded him, since the traditional signs of honor are wanting— there is no fine house to inhabit, no comfort or elegance that can gratify his heroic spirit after strenuous days, no acclaim or deference appropriate to his genius. His prepotent will lifts him above the primitive life, the everlasting round of birth, copulation, and death, making him peerless: his only possible peers are a certain few of the pre-eminent dead, among whom God is one, on the whole the most congenial of the small company. It is chiefly in emulation of the work of this particular colleague that Joyce undertakes his own creation, intending that his book shall be read as men formerly "read" the "book of the universe." In his eyes a thousand years are as but a day, or the other way around, and the fall of the sparrow does not go unnoticed. The round of birth, copulation, and death receives his sanction under the aspect of eternity and in the awful silence of the infinite spaces, and his inscrutable but on the whole affectionate irony is directed upon all that men contrive in their cities for their survival, with a somewhat wryer glance toward what they contrive for their delight. Who that responds to the subtle power of his work can ever again, as a reader, give serious thought to the appointments of the house, the ribbon in the buttonhole, the cash in the bank and the stocks in the portfolio, the seemliness of the ordered life, the claims of disinterested action (except as they refer to certain small dealings between one person and another, especially between father and child), the fate of the nation, the hope of the future? And however else we read *Finnegans Wake,* we cannot fail to understand that it is a *contra-Philosophie der Geschichte,* that its transcendent genial silliness is a spoof on those figments of the solemn nineteenth-century imagination—History, and World Historical Figures, and that wonderful Will of theirs which, Hegel tells us, keeps the world in its right course toward the developing epiphany of *Geist.*

But if Joyce did indeed kill the nineteenth century, he was the better able to do so because the concerns and sentiments he destroyed made so considerable a part of the fabric of his being. To read his letters as we now have them is to be confirmed in our sense of his denial of the world, but it is also to become aware that what is denied was once affirmed with an extraordinary intensity. It is to understand how entirely Joyce was a man of the century in which he was born, how thoroughgoing was his commitment to its concerns and sentiments, how deeply rooted he was in its ethos and its mythos, its beliefs and its fantasies, its greedy desires, its dream of entering into the fair courts of life.

In 1957 Stuart Gilbert brought out a volume called *Letters of James Joyce* which gave us most, though not all, of the letters that were available at the time. Taken as a whole, the collection proved disappointing. It included relatively few letters of the early years, always likely to be the most interesting period of a writer's correspondence; by far the greater number date from the years of maturity, beginning at a time when, although not yet famous, Joyce was already a figure, and of these a great many are devoted to business in the unremitting and often trifling detail in which Joyce carried it on. Nothing that bears upon Joyce's life can fail to command attention, but there is not much in Mr. Gilbert's collection that goes beyond the well-known public aspects of the career to make the appeal of intimacy.

It is true that some reviewers remarked on a quality of warmth and gaiety that they found in the letters and on how much more "human" this showed Joyce to be than had hitherto been supposed. By his middle years Joyce had developed a talent, if not for friendship, then at least for friendliness; whatever else his friends may have been to him, they were his aides, adjutants, and ambassadors, and in the letters in which he did business with them and through them there sounds a note of geniality, often of a whimsical kind, which, as the reviewers noted, is at variance with what is often reported of his forbidding reserve. But it is possible to feel that the genial air is rather *voulu*, even contrived,[1] and at least one reviewer put the matter of the "humanness" in a qualified way—Philip Toynbee said no more than that the letters "reveal a far less inhuman man than the myth had led us to believe." They may be thought to reveal a man who, out of his sense of what is seemly, or perhaps for reasons of policy, wished to conceal the full extent of his "inhumanness," of his detachment from the affections. On the evidence of the first published letters only one event of his middle age seems ever actually to have reached Joyce, his daughter's extreme mental illness. Even here the *apatheia* is to some degree in force, in part through the self-deception as to the true state of affairs that Joyce practiced, although we are in no doubt about the bitterness of his grief.[2] For the rest, the personal life seems to have been burned out,

---

[1] The letters to Frank Budgen are exceptional in suggesting Joyce's actual enjoyment of a relationship with another person.

[2] Joyce's long refusal to recognize the seriousness of Lucia's condition was abetted by the doctors, who, whether out of ignorance or compunction, seem never to have offered a firm diagnosis.

calcined. The difficulties of the once obsessing marriage appear to have been settled one way or another and no new erotic interests are to be discerned. The dialectic of temperament has come to an end—there are scarcely any indications of an interplay between the self and the life around it, the existence of which is recognized only as the world rejects or accepts Joyce's art.

Immediately after the appearance of Mr. Gilbert's collection there came to light a great trove of Joyce's letters, preserved through many vicissitudes. They were available to Richard Ellmann in the research for his definitive life of Joyce, and Professor Ellmann has edited them with the erudition and intelligence that make his biography the superlative work it is. The two collections have been conjoined to make a new *Letters of James Joyce* in three volumes, of which Mr. Gilbert's is now Volume I, Professor Ellmann's Volumes II and III. The arrangement is anomalous and of course awkward, since the collections cover the same span of time although in different degrees of completeness. But the practical nuisance should not be exaggerated. The Joyce scholars are inured to worse difficulties than those to which the arrangement subjects them. And the general reader will inevitably conclude that Volumes II and III make the corpus of the *Letters* to which Volume I serves as a supplement. His conclusion will be based not merely on the greater scope of the later volumes but on the extent of their interest, which is beyond comparison with that of their predecessor.

The letters of the mature years that are given in Professor Ellmann's collection do not change in any decisive way the impression made by those of Volume I, although they do modify it in some respects. It turns out not to be true, for example, that there are no moments of crisis in the marriage after the removal to Paris. In 1922 Nora Joyce went off to Ireland with the children, threatening that she would not return. Joyce writes in desperate appeal to "my darling, my love, my queen," telling her that the check for her fur is on the way, that he will live anywhere with her so long as he can be "alone with her dear self without family and without friends.

Either this must occur or we must part for ever, though it will break my heart." He goes on to report in detail his "fainting fit in Miss Beach's shop," and concludes: "O my dearest, if you would only turn to me even now and read that terrible book which has now broken the heart in my breast[3] and take me to yourself alone to do with me what you will!"

The substance of the marital correspondence at forty is not different from that of the twenties: the same belief in the importance of gifts, especially of fur; the extravagant demand for devotion made through the avowal of infantile weakness; the plea to be dealt with ruthlessly in his total and pathic dependence. But as compared with the earlier letters of similar import that we now have, the energy of this one seems but dutiful, almost perfunctory. It appears early in Volume III and is the last expression not only of erotic feeling but of strong personal emotion of any kind.

From here on, the new letters of the later years are at one with those of the 1957 collection in suggesting that, however powerful Joyce's creative will continued to be, his affective will had been outlived. *"Only disconnect!"* had long been an avowed principle of his life, but not until now had it been put fully in force. It is true that the paternal tenderness and solicitude do not abate, that the form of courteous geniality is maintained, that an enterprise of helpfulness is not precluded, such as involved Joyce with the career of the tenor Sullivan, and we must suppose that some other magnetism in addition to that of his genius drew many people to his service. But nothing in the ordinary way of "humanness" contradicts our sense that the letters of the years of fame were written by a being who had departed this life as it is generally known and had become such a ghost as Henry James and Yeats imagined, a sentient soul that has passed from temporal existence into nullity yet still has a burden of energy to discharge, a destiny still to be worked out.

We are tempted to deal with the uncanny condition by bringing it into the comfortable circle of morality. Joyce's disconnection

---

[3] Even two years later Nora had not yet consented to read *Ulysses.*

from the world, we may want to say, is the ground of his indomitable courage, before which we stand in awed admiration. The man who had ventured and won so much with *Ulysses* now pushes on with *Finnegans Wake* under the encroaching shadow of blindness and to the disapproval of his patron and virtually all his supporters: how else save by a disconnection amounting to "inhumanness" can he pursue the enterprise? Or our moralizing takes the adversary tack and notes the occasions when the disconnection issues in an ugly coarseness of behavior in regard to others. Joyce, who concerned himself with every detail of the promotion of his own books and enlisted everyone he could in the enterprise, when asked to support one of the posthumous novels of Italo Svevo, whose work he admired, not only refuses the request but sneers at the very idea of literary publicity. When his daughter-in-law, Giorgio's first wife, suffers an extreme mental collapse, he writes of the disaster in anger and describes the deranged conduct with contemptuous bitterness.

Eventually, however, we come to feel that no moral judgment can really be to the point of Joyce's state of being in his latter years. And psychology seems as limited in its pertinence as morality. It is inevitable that psychological speculation will be attracted to the often strange and extreme emotional phenomena that the new letters record, especially to what the early ones tell us of the extravagant energy of affective will that was to devolve into the disconnection from the world, the existence in nullity. Neither Joyce's representation of himself as Dedalus, nor Professor Ellmann's detailed account of his youthful temperament, nor yet the two taken together quite prepare us for the intimacy and violence of Joyce's early relation to the world, the urgency with which he sought to requisition the world's goods. And certainly the devolution (if that is the word) from this early egotism of the world to the later egotism of nullity is a biographical event that asks for explanation. But however brilliant and even true may be the insights into the disposition of the internal forces that brought it about, they will fail to do justice to its significance, which is finally not personal but cultural. The process recorded by the letters proposes itself as a paradigm of the nineteenth-century will *in extremis*. It leads us to reflect less on what transpired in the life of James Joyce than on what could formerly happen and cannot happen again—never in our time will a young man focus this much power of love and hate into so sustained a rage of effectual intention as Joyce was capable of, so ferocious an ambition, so nearly absolute a commitment of himself to himself.

Joyce was of course not exceptional in being a continuator of the titanism of the nineteenth-century artistic personality. The literary culture of the first quarter of the twentieth century is differentiated from that of our own time by nothing so much as the grandiosity, both in purpose and in achievement, of its pre-eminent figures. In this respect their sense of life is alien from ours and is not uncommonly felt to alienate them from us. In one point of temperament, in the unremitting energy of their inner-direction, they have a closer affinity with their nineteenth-century predecessors than with their successors. But as compared with Joyce, none of the great modern chieftains of art put himself so directly and, as one might say, so *naïvely,* in the line of the powerful personalities of the age before his own. None so cherished the purpose of imposing himself upon the world, of being a king and riding in triumph through Persepolis.

If Joyce did indeed derive the impetus to his achievement from his acceptance of the ethos and mythos of the nineteenth century, a first salient example is his response to an idea that we take to be characteristic of the ideology of the period, the idea of the nation. One of the best-known things about Joyce is his ambivalence toward Ireland, of which the hatred was as relentless as the love was unfailing. With this passionate relationship his lust for pre-eminence and fame is bound up, and the more so because his erotic life is intricately involved with it. He is twenty-seven and on his first visit to Dublin after his exile and he is writing to Nora, telling her of the part she plays in his inspiration. "My darling," he says, "tonight I

was in the Gresham Hotel and was introduced to about twenty
people and to all of them the same story was told: that I was going
to be the great writer of the future in my country. All the noise and
flattery around me hardly moved me. I thought I heard my country
calling to me or her eyes were turned toward me expectantly." He
goes on to tell Nora that she is more important to him than the
world and that everything comes from her. But in his thought of
fame he cannot separate her from the nation, the "race": "O take
me into your soul of souls and then I will indeed become the poet
of my race." And among the things he has loved in her—"the
image of the beauty of the world, the mystery and beauty of life
itself . . . the images of spiritual purity and pity which I believed
in as a boy"—there are "the beauty and doom of the race of whom
I am a child." He calls her "my love, my life, my star, my little
strange-eyed Ireland!"

And yet, of course, "I loathe Ireland and the Irish. They themselves stare at me in the street though I was born among them.
Perhaps they read my hatred in my eyes." The hatred was of the
essence of his ambition quite as much as the love. Three years
later he is again in Dublin and he writes: "The Abbey Theatre will
be open and they will give plays of Yeats and Synge. You have a
right to be there because you are my bride and I am one of the
writers of this generation who are perhaps creating at last a conscience in the soul of this wretched race."

Some considerable part of Joyce's ambition consisted of what the
nineteenth century called aspiration and conceived to be a mode of
feeling peculiarly appropriate to generous minds, artists perhaps especially but also soldiers, statesmen, engineers, industrialists. Aspiration was the desire for fame through notable and arduous achievement. The end in view which defined it was the realization of one's
own powers. That in order to reach this end one might be involved
in competition with others, seeking to surpass and overcome them,
was a frequent but accidental circumstance of aspiration which was
not thought to qualify its noble disinterestedness. That this is a

reasonable way of looking at the matter is suggested by the astonishing letter the nineteen-year-old Joyce addressed to Ibsen. He makes
a full and grandiose communication of his admiration and then
goes on to say to the sick old man, "Your work on earth draws to a
close and you are near the silence. It is growing dark for you." But
there is a comfort that he can offer, the assurance that One—an
unnamed but unmistakable One—comes after to carry on the great
work. It is in all conscience a crueller letter than the young writer
chose to know, yet the competition with the Father, the Old
King, is sanctioned not only by tradition but by the very nature of
life, and Joyce invests it with an absurd but genuine nobility by
which the Master Builder, after a wince or two, might well have
been grimly pleased.

But Joyce's competitiveness, which was extreme, was not always,
not characteristically, in the grand style; as it showed itself in his
relations with his age-mates it was often vindictive and coarse.
Through all the early years in Trieste and Rome, Joyce lived in
bitter jealous hatred of his former friends and companions in
Dublin. He cannot mention them and their little successes without
an expression of disgust: "Their writings and their lives nauseate
[me] to the point of vomiting." The new letters make clear to how
great an extent Joyce in his youth conceived of his art as a weapon
to be used in personal antagonism, especially in vengeance. "Give
me for Christ' sake a pen and an ink-bottle and some peace of mind
and then, by the crucified Jaysus, if I don't sharpen that little pen
and dip it into fermented ink and write tiny little sentences about
the people who betrayed me send me to hell." The chief object
of his bitterness, of course, was Gogarty, from whom, after the
quarrel, he would accept no tender of reconciliation. It was his
belief that the man who had so terribly offended him sought to make
peace out of fear of how he would be delineated—the belief finds
expression in the first chapter of *Ulysses:* "He fears the lancet of
my art as I fear that of his. Cold steelpen."—and as early as 1905
it was assumed by Joyce's Dublin friends that a great revenge was in

train; the form it would take was already known. "[Elwood] says," writes Stanislaus Joyce, "he would not like to be Gogarty when you come to the Tower episode. Thanks be to God he never kicked your arse or anything." Gogarty himself had every expectation that revenge would be duly taken, and Joyce coolly confirmed him in this; he reports that in refusing Gogarty's attempt to renew the friendship, he had said: "I bear you no ill will. I believe you have some points of good nature. You and I of 6 years ago are both dead. But I must write as I have felt!" To which Gogarty replied, "I don't care a damn what you say of me so long as it is literature."[4]

The unremitting bitterness with which Joyce remembered and commemorated his relation with Gogarty serves to remind us of the great authority that the ideal of male friendship formerly had. In this, as in so many other respects, the nineteenth century maintained its connection with the courtly cultures of earlier epochs. Out of the dream of the true friend arose the possibility of the false friend, and it is an element of the *Heldenleben,* as the nineteenth century understood the genre, that the hero is beset by treacherous comrades envious of his powers and eager to subvert them. Had these dwarfish natures been lacking in the actuality of his life, Joyce would have been quick to supply the want. His genius throve upon his paranoia, which was capable of anything—it is quite in his style to say in an early letter to Lady Gregory that the college authorities were determined that he should not study medicine, "wishing I dare say to prevent me from securing any position of ease from which I might speak out my heart." A belief in a hostile environment, in persecution and personal betrayal, was necessary

---

[4] In the event this proved not to be true—Gogarty cared many a damn when *Ulysses* appeared. As well he might, if only because Joyce led all the world to believe forever that he and not Gogarty-Mulligan was the rightful tenant of the tower and that the famous key was his: any statement of the fact of the matter, that the opposite was the case, will always be received with surprise and incredulity and soon forgotten. Such is the power of the literary imagination in the service of self-justification. Partisans of simple justice—alas, there are virtually none of Gogarty— may find some encouragement in the display of the actual lease in the tower; that a signboard calls the tower James Joyce's should not dismay them: the rights of the ultimate possession are now absolute.

to his mission. But in point of fact the false friends and the malice of their envy were real enough; they were fostered by Dublin life before they were cherished by Joyce as a condition of his art and the testimony of his being a dedicated spirit, singled out. Long before Joyce had anything like a career his promise of genius was taken for granted by those who knew him and Stanislaus's diary records the envy with which he was regarded by his contemporaries. In his early days of exile, when his thoughts turned homeward, it was to inquire what these lesser impotent beings said of his courage, his freedom, his unconventional marriage, and, as time passed, his approach to success. Their mischievous impulses in relation to him came fully to light in the strange episode of his friend Cosgrove telling him, falsely and seemingly out of the gratuitous impulse to play Iago to this Othello, that before the elopement Nora had been unfaithful to him, a communication that for a time had all its intended effect of making chaos come again.

The social life of late nineteenth-century Dublin as Joyce's class situation permitted him to know it was obviously in most respects quite elementary, but it was certainly not wanting in concern with social status, in judging who was "better" and stood higher than whom, and to such questions the young Joyce gave the most solemn attention. It was surely an important circumstance of the last interview with Gogarty that it took place in Gogarty's elaborate house and that the former friend, now set up in medical practice, well-to-do and well married, should have invited Joyce to come with him in his motorcar to have lunch in his country home. The social advantages that Gogarty had previously enjoyed, perhaps especially his having gone to Oxford, were of the greatest moment to Joyce, who was at constant pains to enforce the idea that, when it came to social establishment, Stephen Dedalus, if the truth were seen, was the superior of anyone.[5] Joyce was in nothing so much a man of

[5] In the tower scene Mulligan tells Stephen, "You know, Dedalus, you have the real Oxford manner." And he speculates that this is why Haines, the Englishman who is staying with them, can't make Stephen out. Haines is rich and himself an Oxford man and Mulligan twice remarks that he thinks Stephen isn't a gentleman.

the nineteenth century as in the sensitivity of his class feelings. No less than Dickens he was concerned to be a *gentleman* and he was as little shy as Dickens about using the word, the Victorian force of which maintained itself for at least two of the Joyces in the face of the family's rapid downward mobility. In the midst of an expression of disgust with his situation at Rome James remarks to Stanislaus, "I feel somehow that I am what Pappie said I wasn't [,] a gentleman."[6] He was at the time working in a bank as a correspondence clerk; he lived with his wife and infant son in a single small room; often his wages did not meet his weekly expenses and the letters of the period are chiefly to Stanislaus in Trieste, their whole burden being that money must be sent at once. The conversation of his fellow clerks, as he describes it, is simian; he has no ordinarily decent social intercourse with anyone, yet he finds it in his heart to describe his circumstances not as unfit for a human being but as unfit for a gentleman.

His feeling for the social forms could be strict, often in a genteel, lower-middle-class way. Although in 1910 black-edged writing paper was still used by proper people in a period of mourning, the faintly barbaric custom was not universally observed, but Joyce, at the death of his uncle John Murray, thought it necessary to his sense of how things should be done.[7] When he was virtually starving during his first sojourn in Paris, he regretted that he could not attend the Irish Ball because he had no dress suit. He is still working as a Berlitz teacher in Trieste and the family in Dublin

---

[6] The occasion of the judgment was John Joyce's reading *Gas From a Burner*. Stanislaus seems not to have shared the social feelings of his father and elder brother. Perhaps it was his puritanical rationalism that led him to adopt a rather plebeian stance. The youngest surviving Joyce brother, Charles, apparently laid no continuing claim to being a gentleman; when last we hear of him he is a postal clerk in London. The idea of social status was part of the fabric of the Joyce family life—it is well known how preoccupied John Joyce was with the superiority of his own family to his wife's, which of course had some bearing on James's choice of a wife whose pretensions to breeding were notably less than his own.

[7] Joyce took account in *Ulysses* of his response to the claims of funeral pomp. "He can't wear them," Mulligan says when his offer of a pair of gray trousers has been refused by Dedalus because he is in mourning for his mother. "Etiquette is etiquette. He kills his mother but he can't wear gray trousers."

is on the verge of destitution, but he directs his father to arrange to sit for his portrait. The family crest was his treasured possession.

At the present time feelings about class in their old form are in at least literary abeyance and it is hard to remember the force they once had and the extent to which they defined the character and aspirations of the artist.[8] In an age when the middle classes seemed to be imposing their stamp upon the world, a young writer was led to set store by what he imagined to be the aristocratic qualities of grace, freedom, and indifference to public opinion, and the aristocratic mode of life seemed the model for what all men's lives should be. It was the rare writer who did not think himself to be "well born" in some sense of the phrase, and if he had any reason to think that he was actually of distinguished blood, he was pretty sure to find the circumstance of value. George Moore said no more than the simple truth when he remarked that "Yeats's belief in his lineal descent from the great Duke of Ormonde was part of his poetic equipment." Writing in admiration of Tolstoy, Joyce associates his genius with his class position and his ability to remember "the Christian name of his great-great-grandfather." And the young man who felt himself excluded from the patrician literary circle of Dublin and expressed his resentment in rude mockery of its members shared Yeats's dream of the culture—the word is Joyce's own—of the great houses and the ancient families. Writing to Nora, who had been a chambermaid in a Dublin hotel when he had first met her and whose lack of grammar he was not above mocking to his brother, he explains to her the inspiration of *Chamber Music*: "You were not in a sense the girl for whom I had dreamed and written the verses you now find so enchanting. She was perhaps (as I saw her in my imagination) a girl fashioned into a curious grave beauty by the culture of generations before her, the woman for

---

[8] A few years ago I had occasion to remark in an essay that my students, no matter what their social origins, were not prevented by Yeats's snobbery from responding to his poetry. One reviewer took me sternly to task for obscuring the transcendent achievement of the great poet by speaking of him as a snob. What made especially interesting the view of life and letters implied by the rebuke was that the reviewer was Leon Edel, the biographer of Henry James.

whom I wrote poems like 'Gentle Lady' or 'Thou leanest to the shell of night.' " He goes on, surely in entire sincerity: "But then I saw that the beauty of your soul outshone that of my verses. There was something in you higher than anything I had put into them. And so for this reason the book of verses is for you. It holds the desire of my youth, and you, darling, were the fulfillment of that desire." Yet the discrepancy between the robust, barely literate chambermaid who had to be told not to copy her love-letters out of a letter-book and the girl fashioned into a curious grave beauty by her lineage was often a pain to Joyce, and much as he needed Nora's earthy strength, he flinched at the rudeness—so he called it—that went with it. It was certain that he was a gentleman, but whatever else Nora was, she was, alas, no lady.

That Joyce's preoccupation with his social status should go along with an avowed interest in subverting the society in which he held his valued rank does not make a contradiction. It was quite common in the nineteenth century for gifted men to find sanction for their subversive intentions toward society in such aristocracy or gentility as they could claim.[9] But that Joyce should ever have been political at all will for most of his readers make an occasion for surprise. For a few years of his young manhood, between the ages of twenty-two and twenty-five, Joyce called himself a socialist. Again and again in his letters to Stanislaus he insists on the importance to the artist of a radical political position: "I believe that Ibsen and Hauptmann separate from the herd of writers because of their political aptitude—eh?" "It is a mistake for you to imagine that my political opinions are those of a universal lover: but they are those of a socialistic artist." He scolds Stanislaus for not sharing his "detestation of the stupid, dishonest, tyrannical and cowardly burgher class." He explains the opposition of the Church to "the quite unheretical theory of socialism" as being an expression of the belief that a socialist government would expropriate ecclesiastical "landed estates . . . and invested moneys." His

9 This was especially true of the anarchists in Russia, France, and Italy.

cogent objection to the Irish nationalist movement is that it takes no account of economic realities and is not aware that "if the Irish question exists, it exists for the Irish proletariat chiefly." And it is a further black mark against Gogarty that his political views exclude economic considerations. "Gogarty would jump into the Liffey to save a man's life but he seems to have little hesitation in condemning generations to servitude."[10]

Joyce never committed himself to political action or association, and although he had a knowledgeable interest in the Italian radical parties, he seems never to have put himself to the study of socialist theory; the only reference to Karl Marx occurs in the course of an excited and rather confused account of the apocalyptic Jewish imagination derived from Ferrero's *Young Europe*. By 1907 his socialism had evaporated, leaving as its only trace the sweet disposition of Leopold Bloom's mind to imagine the possibility of rational and benevolent social behavior and the brotherhood of man. This, however, is a residue of some importance in the history of literature: it makes *Ulysses* unique among modern classics for its sympathy with progressive social ideas.

In one of his early poems Yeats speaks of the places where men meet "to talk of love and politics." To us at our remove in time the conjunction of the two topics of conversation seems quaint, for of course by love Yeats did not mean the rather touching interfusion of *eros* and *agape* that young people have lately come to use as a ground of social and political dissidence: he meant a love much more personal and egotistic, that ultimate relation between a man and a woman the conception of which had descended from courtly love, the "gay science" of the late Middle Ages, to become one of the powerful myths of the nineteenth century. Its old force has greatly diminished, perhaps to the point of extinction. No matter how gravely and idealistically we may use our contemporary names for the relation between a man and a woman, "sex" and "mar-

---

[10] Joyce's disgust with Gogarty on political grounds was made the more intense by Gogarty's anti-Semitism.

riage," and even the phrase that is a vestige of the old name, "in love with," do not suggest, as "love" did for an age in whose sensibility *Tristan and Isolde* occupied a central position, the idea of life realized and transfigured by the erotic connection, fulfilled by its beauty, sustained by the energy and fidelity that constituted its ethos.[11] In the nineteenth century, politics was a new activity of free spirits and it naturally found affinity with a conception of love that made large promises of perceptivity, liberty, and happiness. Love was understood to be art's true source and best subject, and those who lived for love and art did harm to no one, lived the right life of humanity: so Tosca in a passion that reaches B-flat informs the tyrant Scarpia. The operatic example is much in point, for opera was the genre in which love and political virtue joined hands to make a lyric affirmation of life. The contemptuous indifference in which opera is held by our intellectual culture is not qualified by recognition of its political tendency. For Joyce, as everyone knows, opera was a passion. With a most engaging simplicity he gave the genre the response it asked for; he found it, as people used to say, ravishing. He would have been astonished and dismayed by the contemporary snootiness to Puccini; he held *Madame Butterfly* to be a work of transcendent beauty and power, most especially the aria *"Un bel di"* which at one period seems to have woven itself into the very fabric of his emotional life; when Butterfly sang the "romance of her hope" of what would come to her over the sea, his soul (as he wrote bitterly to Nora, who was not similarly moved) "sway[ed] with languor and longing": in the face of the harshness of circumstance, life is affirmed in erotic ecstasy, as when, in *A Portrait of the Artist,* Stephen has sight of the girl on the strand, gazing out to sea. For Joyce, as still for many men of the time in which he was young, human existence was justified by the rapture—lost archaic word!—of love.

11 For an account of what *Tristan and Isolde* meant to the epoch, see Elliot Zuckermann's admirable *The First Hundred Years of Wagner's Tristan* (New York: Columbia University Press, 1964).

Perhaps nothing in Joyce's life is more poignant and more in-
dicative of the extent to which his imagination was shaped by the
mythos of his time than the episode, on the threshold of his middle
age, in which the famous vision of the lovely girl standing with
high-kilted skirts at the water's edge, the most grandiose of the
epiphanies, seemed to have presented itself as an attainable actuality.
Martha Fleischmann was a young woman, seemingly Jewish,
though not so in fact, beautiful, provocative but apparently not
disposed to go beyond elaborate flirtation, whom Joyce came to
know in Zurich in the autumn of 1918. As Martha recalled their
meeting nearly a quarter of a century later, the scene stands all
ready for the librettist. She was coming home "one evening at
dusk" when a passerby stopped and looked at her "with an expression of such wonder on his face that she hesitated for just a
moment before entering the house." The stranger spoke, explaining
his astonishment by saying that she reminded him of a girl he
had once seen "standing on the beach of his home country."[12]
Martha's erotic temperament was ambiguous to a degree. She had a
devoted "guardian," as she called him, and he expressed jealousy
of her relation with Joyce, but there is some question as to whether
her connection with this man was sexual in any ordinary sense
of the word. On one occasion Joyce addressed her as "Nausikaa,"
signing himself "Odysseus,"[13] and it would seem that the Gerty
MacDowell of the "Nausikaa" episode of *Ulysses* commemorates her
genteel narcissism and sentimentality. Joyce's own erotic disposition at this time was scarcely of a more direct kind. His lust, like

---

[12] The quoted passages are from Professor Straumann's account of his interview
with Martha when, in Zurich in 1941, she called to inquire about selling the four
letters and the postcard that Joyce had written to her. Professor Straumann did not
make the purchase on that occasion, but he did so at a later time, in 1943, when,
Martha being ill, her affairs were in the charge of her sister—at least he bought the
letters; the postcard had vanished. Professor Straumann's account of the relationship
of Martha and Joyce appears as a preface to the letters as given in Volume II, pp.
426–436; it is less full and circumstantial than Professor Ellmann's earlier account
in his biography.

[13] The salutation and the subscription were, Professor Straumann says, the whole
message of the lost postcard.

Mr. Bloom's, was chiefly of the eye and the mind. What seems to have been the climactic assignation of these two fantasts of love took place in Frank Budgen's studio on February 2, which was Joyce's birthday and the feast of Candlemas, and Joyce borrowed from a Jewish friend a *Menorah* so that he might gaze on Martha's beauty by candlelight, perhaps the sole intention of the meeting.[14] With the passage of years the exquisite virgin, *La Princesse loin-taine,* came to be represented in the great "Nausikaa" episode as nothing more than the sad, silly figment of ladies' magazines, and the dream of love-and-beauty as an occasion of masturbation. But at the time his feelings for Martha seemed to Joyce to challenge comparison with Dante's for Beatrice and Shakespeare's for the Dark Lady; at least he meant them to. "And through the night of the bitterness of my soul," he wrote in the last of his letters to Martha, "the kisses of your lips fell on my heart, soft as rosepetals gentle as dew," and concludes, "O rosa mistica [*sic*], ora pro me."

One of the four letters is mutilated—we are told that Martha "tore off the lower right-hand edge of the second sheet . . . be-cause it contained what she considered an indelicate expression." The judgment on the offending word or phrase cannot be set aside out of hand as one of Martha's neurotic gentilities. The chances are that Joyce did actually write an indelicacy, even an obscenity, for his concern that the erotic object and situation be of an extreme re-finement and beauty went together with a no less exigent desire for all that is commonly thought to sully, besmirch, and degrade the erotic activity, and he derived a special pleasure from expressing this desire in writing.

The dialectic between the essential innocence and the essential

---

[14] Candlemas commemorates the purification of the Virgin Mary and the presenta-tion of Christ in the Temple. "The blessing of candles is now the distinctive rite of this day. . . . Beeswax candles, which are blessed, distributed, and lit whilst the Nunc Dimittis is sung, are carried in a procession commemorating the entrance of Christ, the 'True Light' (cf. Jn. I.9) into the Temple."—*The Oxford Dictionary of the Christian Church.* In his second letter to Martha, remarking on his impression that she was a Jewess, Joyce says, "If I am wrong, you must not be offended. Jesus Christ put on his human body: in the womb of a Jewish woman."

shamefulness of the sexual act has in our time lost much of its old force, at least overtly. If nowadays we obey the command of Blake's Los to "Consider Sexual Organization," it does not seem naturally to follow, as the demiurge thought it would, that we "hide . . . in the dust" for shame. Crazy Jane's observation that love has pitched his mansion in the place of excrement is received as an interesting reminder of the actual state of affairs rather than as the expression of a distressing (or exciting) thought in the forefront of consciousness. The words of Yeats's poem echo those of another divine utterance in *Jerusalem:* "For I will make their places of love and joy excrementitious," but the circumstance as Yeats refers to it is not conceived to be a curse: we understand Yeats to be remarking on an anomaly that makes human existence more complex and difficult than his long celebration of the *Rosa Mystica* would suggest, or more "ironic," or more "tragic," but for that reason more substantive and the more interesting. His sense of the shameful arrangements of the erotic life stands midway between the neutralizing view of them that our contemporary educated consciousness seems determined to take and the eager response to them made by Joyce, for whom shame was a chief condition of sexual fulfillment.

In the course of the two visits he made to Ireland in 1909, Joyce in his letters to Nora ran through the whole gamut of his erotic emotions and in full voice. Within a week of his first arrival in Dublin, Cosgrove imparted the news of Nora's double dealing in the betrothal time, and although the false friend spoke only of kisses, Joyce of course imagined more and questioned whether Nora had actually come to him a virgin—"I remember that there was very little blood that night. . . ."—and whether Giorgio is in truth his son. He is shattered by the dreadful revelation—"I shall cry for days"—but a fortnight has not passed before he can report blandly that everything has been cleared up by Byrne's having said that Cosgrove's tale is "all a 'blasted lie' "; and after having called himself a "worthless fellow," he vows to be "Worthy of your love, dearest," and goes on to speak of a shipment of cocoa he has sent, that same cocoa that he later urges Nora to drink a good deal of so that she will increase the size of "certain parts" of her body, pleasing him by becoming more truly womanly. His marital resentments are bitter and explicit: Nora, whose great fault is her rudeness, had called him an imbecile, had disagreed with his expressed opinion that priests are disgusting, had been indifferent to *"Un bel di"*; his apologies, when his recriminations have proved offensive, are abject. He is much given to expressions of tender and poetic regard and is engagingly proud of the courtly ingenuity of a gift of jewelry he has designed and had executed, a necklace of gold links, five cubes of old ivory and an ivory plaque bearing in ancient lettering words from one of his poems, which is to symbolize the lovers' years together and their sadness and suffering when they are divided; his Christmas present is *Chamber Music* copied out of his own hand on parchment, bound with his family crest, on the cover the lovers' interlaced initials. But his lively imagination of the elegances of love goes along with fantasies and solicitation that, as he says, make him the object of his own disgust and, he insists on supposing, of Nora's.

Professor Ellmann has not found it possible to carry out his intention of publishing in its entirety the group of obscene love-letters from Dublin preserved in the Cornell Library. What he is able to publish does indeed, as he says, suggest the tenor of these extraordinary documents (the adjective is Joyce's) but not the force and the strange dignity that they seemed to me to have when I read them at Cornell some years ago. It may be, of course, that my memory plays me false, but I recall the letters read in the completeness of the holograph as making the effect of having been written under a more driving compulsion, a more exigent possession, than appears in the curtailed printed version. Perhaps it was the holograph itself that contributed to the impressiveness, enforcing the situation in something like the awesomeness that Joyce himself felt it to have: the man who may well be the greatest literary genius of his age submits to the necessity of taking in hand

his sacred cold steel pen and with it to sully sheet after virgin
sheet of paper with the filthy words that express all that he feels in
the way of delight at the dirtiness of his exalted nature. The words
themselves have for him a terrifying potency. One of his letters
has induced Nora in her reply to use what he can refer to in no
other way than as "a certain word." The sight of it, he says,
excites him terribly—"There is something obscene and lecherous
in the very look of the letters. The sound of it too is like the act
itself, brief, brutal, irresistible and devilish."

His longed-for perversities and depravities—we had best call them
that without permissive apologies, since he thought of them so
and we ought not deny the ground of his pleasure—were not of
an especially esoteric kind. He expresses the wish to be flogged
and not merely in show but fiercely, to the end of his feeling real
pain; he blames himself for writing "filth" and instructs Nora, if
she is insulted by it, to bring him to his senses "with the lash, as
you have done before." Nora is an "angel" and a "saint" who
guides him to his great destiny, and he longs to "nestle" in her
womb, and he seeks to "degrade" and "deprave" her, he wants her
to be insolent and cruel and obscene. Perhaps the controlling and
to him most puzzling and most significant component of his
polymorphous perversity is his delight in the excrementitiousness
of the places of love and joy, what he called his "wild beast-like
craving . . . for every secret and shameful part" of his wife's body,
"for every odor and act of it." "Are you offended because I said I
loved to look at the brown stain that comes behind on your girlish
white drawers? I suppose you think me a filthy wretch."

No one, I think, will be so armored in objectivity as not to be
taken aback by the letters. But their shocking interest fades as we
become habituated to them, or to the idea of them. In the way of
all drastic personal facts, especially in our time, they cease to be
dismaying or amazing soon after they are brought into the light
of common day and permitted to assume their institutional status

—one might say their prestige—as biographical data. What does not fade, however, is the interest of the literary use to which Joyce put the erotic tendencies that the letters disclose and indulge.

To a reader of *Ulysses* nothing in the substance of the letters comes as a surprise. All the fantasies are familiar to us through our having made acquaintance with them in the mind of Leopold Bloom. But what exists in the mind of Mr. Bloom is of a quite different import from the apparently identical thing as it exists in the mind of James Joyce or might exist in the mind of his surrogate Stephen Dedalus. The reader of the letters will not fail to conclude that it required a considerable courage for Joyce to write them. His doing so went against the grain of a decisive and cherished part of his nature, his austere, almost priestly propriety. "As you know, dearest," he writes in one of the letters, "I never use obscene phrases in speaking. You have never heard me, have you, utter an unfit word before others. When men tell in my presence here filthy or lecherous stories I hardly smile." Yet he put on paper and sent through the mail what was not to be countenanced and, although he urged Nora to be watchful in guarding the secrecy of the letters, since he did not destroy them when he might have done so, he must be thought to have wished that they be preserved. One thing, however, he would not—could not—do: attribute the fantasies of the letters to the mind of Stephen Dedalus.

By assigning them to Mr. Bloom, he of course quite changes their character. As elements of Mr. Bloom's psyche, they become comic, which is to say morally neutral. Our laughter, which is gentle, cognizant, forgiving, affectionate, has the effect of firmly distancing them and at the same time of bringing them within the circle of innocence and acceptability. We understand that nothing very terrible is here, nothing awesome, or devilish, or wild-beast-like—only what we call, with a relishing domesticating chuckle, *human.* And the chuckle comes the more easily because we recognize in Mr. Bloom, as we are intended to, the essential innocence of the child; his polymorphous perversity is appropriate to his infantile state. This innocence, it would appear, is part of Joyce's conception of Jews in general, who, he seems to have felt, through some natural grace were exempt from the complexities of the moral life as it was sustained by Christians. Writing to Stanislaus of his son having been born early, with nothing prepared, he says, "However, our landlady is a Jewess and gave us everything we wanted." The implication is that a Christian might or might not have provided the necessary things; Christian kindness would result from the making of a choice between doing the good deed and not doing it, and would therefore, by the Aristotelian definition, be moral; but a Jewish good deed was a matter of instinct, natural rather than moral. It is in natural goodness rather than in morality that Mr. Bloom has his being, and in the ambience of his mind the perverse fantasies have nothing of the fearsome significance they had for Joyce when he entertained them.

It is possible to say that the translation of the fantasies as they existed in the mind of James Joyce, and might have existed in the mind of Stephen Dedalus, into what they become in the mind of Leopold Bloom is a derogation of Joyce's courage as an artist. A Stephen Dedalus whose rigorous moral being is assailed and torn by sinful desires is readily received as a heroic figure so long as the desires can be supposed sinful in a received way. But a polymorphous-perverse hero would make a difficulty, would be thought a contradiction in terms. For Joyce the Aristotelian categories of tragedy and comedy, the one showing men as "better," i.e., more dignified, than they really are, the other showing men as "worse," i.e., more ignoble, than they really are, had an authority that, at the time of *Ulysses,* was not to be controverted.

It is also possible to say that Joyce's refusal to assign the perverse fantasies to Stephen is a derogation of personal courage. A polymorphous-perverse Leopold Bloom stands as testimony to his author's astonishing powers of imagination, of sympathetic insight into the secret places of nature at the furthest remove from his own. But a polymorphous-perverse Stephen Dedalus must advertise the polymorphous perversity of the author whose fictive surrogate he is inevitably understood to be. To this personal disclosure Joyce could not consent.

His fictional disposition of the polymorphous perversity must make a salient question in any attempt to understand the mind of James Joyce. What I have called—with, I should make plain, no pejorative force—a derogation of courage is an answer that has a kind of provisional cogency. But a comment on the obscene letters made by Professor Ellmann in his Introduction seems to me to initiate an explanation that goes deeper. Professor Ellmann says of the letters that they have an "ulterior purpose," that Joyce, in writing them, had an intention beyond immediate sexual gratification. One thing he intended was "to anatomize and reconstitute and crystallize the emotion of love." And, Professor Ellmann says, "he goes further still; like Richard Rowan in *Exiles,* he wishes to possess his wife's soul, and have her possess his, in nakedness. To know someone else in love and hate, beyond vanity and remorse, *beyond human possibility almost* [my italics], is his extravagant desire."

If this is so, as I think it is, it brings the obscene letters into accord with what I have proposed as the controlling tendency of Joyce's genius—to move through the fullest realization of the human, the all-too-human, to that which transcends and denies the human. It was a progress he was committed to make, yet he made it with some degree of reluctance. Had the obscene fantasies been assigned to Stephen Dedalus, they would have implied the import that Professor Ellmann supposes they had for Joyce himself. But Joyce, we may believe, did not want, not yet, so Hyperborean a hero as he then would have had. The ethos and mythos of the nineteenth century could still command from him some degree of assent. The merely human still engaged him, he was not wholly ready to go beyond it. The fair courts of life still beckoned invitation and seemed to await his entrance. He was to conclude that their walls and gates enclosed nothing. His genius is defined by his having concluded this rather than taking it for granted, as many of the generation that came after him have found it possible to do.

What Is Criticism?

[Introduction to *Literary Criticism: An Introductory Reader,* edited by Lionel Trilling, Holt, Rinehart & Winston, 1970]

I

THE word criticism derives from the Greek word meaning judgment. A critic does more things with literature than judge it, but his judicial function is involved in everything else that he does. That literature should have called into being an attendant art of judgment tells us something about the nature of literature—that it is an enterprise which is inherently competitive.

In the conventional praise that is nowadays likely to be given to the literary art, this characteristic is overlooked or implicitly denied. The pious view of the serious and dedicated author represents him as being superior to such crass considerations as the acknowledged degree of his excellence in relation to his fellows. He is presumed to be motivated by nothing but a disinterested desire to make his own work as good as his native talent and devoted application will permit. The Greeks, of course, thought otherwise. Their poets and dramatists wrote in open institutional contest with each other—we know how many times Pindar took first prize in music and poetry, we wonder how it could have happened that in one or another year Sophocles was awarded only second place in

tragedy.[1] Dante, Shakespeare, and Milton were overt in their desire for pre-eminence and spoke shamelessly of the peculiar fame
that was its due. In our own day a convention of modesty prevails
among writers, making it startling when one of them—Ernest
Hemingway, for example, or Norman Mailer—publicly estimates
his powers and achievements by comparison with what his predecessors or contemporaries can show, but we may be sure that he
is exceptional only in his avowal, not in his competitive concern.

There are several kinds of literary competition that the critic is
called upon to judge. One is in essence the rivalry that goes on
among tradesmen or craftsmen as to who can give, and be known
to give, the best value. A memorable scene in Aristophanes' comedy,
The Frogs, represents Aeschylus and Euripides in Hades contend-
ing over which of the two gives better measure in point of sheer
weight. A great pair of scales is brought onto the stage, the dramatists take turns delivering what each takes to be his most ponderous
lines, and the scales tip this way or that. The division of literary
epochs into those that are "golden" and those that are "silver" is
an old one, and the same metals are used to classify poets of any
one age: the title of Gerald Bullett's anthology, *Silver Poets of the
Sixteenth Century,* suggests that the poets included—Wyatt, Surrey,
Sidney, Ralegh, and Davies—although precious indeed, are not so
valuable as other poets of the period, such as Spenser and Shakespeare.

"There is no competition among poems," Allen Tate has said.

---

[1] Lemprière's *Classical Dictionary,* after telling us that Pindar "conquered Myrtis
in a musical contest," goes on to say, "He was not, however, so successful against
Corinna, who obtained five times, while he was competitor, a poetical prize, which
according to some, was adjudged rather to the charms of her person than to the
brilliancy of her genius, or the superiority of her composition. In the public as-
semblies of Greece, where females were not permitted to contend, Pindar was
awarded the prize in every other competition. . . ." And this is how *The Oxford
Companion to French Literature* describes a moment in the career of Racine: "His
Andromaque (1667) rivalled Corneille's *Le Cid* in its success, and in 1669, after
the appearance of his comedy *Les Plaideurs* in 1668, he challenged the older dramatist
on his own ground with the political play *Britannicus.* The contest was repeated in
1670, and the younger poet was held the victor, when his *Bérénice* and the *Tite et
Bérénice* of Corneille appeared almost simultaneously. . . ."

"A good poem suggests the possibility of other poems equally good." There are occasions in our experience when the first sentence is true. And although the second sentence is always true, it affords the ground for denying the permanent truth of the first. For no sooner have we said "equally good" than we conjure up "not quite so good" and "even better." If the "equally good" poems are peaceable among themselves, it is because the competition has already taken place and been judged. Poems are not competitive as poets are, out of natural depravity. Their competitiveness is imposed on them by us, by our restless need to discriminate among degrees of excellence.

In some sense, a work of art is a commodity. The word "artist," to which we now give a highly honorific significance, was once exactly synonymous with the word "artisan," that is, a skilled workman who offers the products of his skill for sale. The word "poet" derives from the Greek word meaning "maker," and indeed "maker" was the common English word for poet up to the sixteenth century. Like other objects that are made for the use or pleasure of the customer, the literary object is to be judged by the materials out of which it is fashioned and by the skill of the fashioning. The title of Cleanth Brooks's book about poetry, *The Well Wrought Urn,* suggests that a poem, whatever else it may be, is an object of *virtu,* prized for its shapeliness and for the ingenious craft that went into the shaping. We may surmise that Professor Brooks wanted to revive in his readers the sense that was stronger in an older time than it is now, that a poem is a *made* thing, seeking to qualify our modern tendency to think that what we call a work of art is not so much made as *created:* the important place in the moral and spiritual life that we assign to it seems to suggest that it is not really a *thing* at all. In this regard it is useful to reflect that things which in our culture are thought of as the products of "mere" craftsmanship are in other cultures respected in an ultimate degree and considered to have the same transcendent value which we attribute to a work of "high" art. To a Japanese, swords of the thirteenth or fourteenth century, the period of the great sword-smiths of his country, will yield an experience no less profound, transcendent, and valuable than that which might be afforded by a great poem or painting, and he holds the great smiths in as much reverence as great poets or painters.

In one of his functions, then, the critic is the kind of judge that we call a connoisseur, preferably one who has a pretty thorough knowledge—although not necessarily a practical command—of the technical means the artist or craftsman uses, and the ability to perceive and point out the particular merits of the work, how one or another difficulty was overcome or how this or that detail was scamped or crudely handled. His judgment of any one object involves comparison, whether explicit or implied, with other objects of the same genre. In regard to certain objects, such as Greek or Chinese urns, or Japanese swords, or paintings, or furniture, or gems, the results of these comparative judgments are expressed, in auction rooms and dealers' shops, in monetary terms: the presumed or agreed upon artistic value of the object determines the price it will bring from those who desire to possess objects of this kind.[2] The expression of artistic value in monetary terms cannot be made in the case of literary objects, but the process of connoisseurship, of making judgments of comparative values, is not essentially different from that which is applied to other artistic works.[3]

[2] Jakob Rosenberg, the eminent historian of art, begins his book, *On Quality in Art: Criteria of Excellence, Past and Present* (Princeton, N.J.: Princeton University Press, Bollingen, 1967), with the following statement: "In recent years we have witnessed an astonishing rise in the prices paid for works of art, both of old and of modern masters. It has been a rise sensational to a degree hardly ever equalled in the past. Naturally one wonders about the causes and the justification for such a development, and this leads to a feeling of uncertainty about the real value of these works of art. We are not concerned [in this book] with the prices of art objects, with their material value, but with their aesthetic value, their quality. Yet if the market acts on a sound basis, the material value should reflect the true artistic value or quality. Thus the problem with which we are concerned in this volume, namely, how to make a proper quality judgment, is as important for the art historian and the art critic as it is for the collector, the museum man, and the serious art dealer."

[3] Of course a literary work is sold and bought, but the price that the customer pays for it is determined not by its artistic merit but by the cost of printing, binding, and distributing the book in which it appears, and of giving the author some some return on his labor and the publisher a profit; we pay no more for a copy of the

Another kind of literary competition which the critic adjudicates is more grandiose. In it the writer figures not as a craftsman of however exalted a character, pursuing a craftsman's purpose of satisfying the expectations of the customer or patron, but rather as some great feudal lord who asserts his claim to dominion over territories and populations in rivalry with other feudal lords having the same end in view. The critic who exercises his function of judging in this situation is less the connoisseur than a justice of some high court. He judges the work not primarily in regard to its merit or excellence or degree of preciousness, as a thing to be possessed and cherished, but in regard to its power and "greatness," as claiming possession of us.

There are, it will be seen, two issues to be adjudicated in the contention. One is the legitimacy of any single author's claim to assert dominion over his readers. The other is the conflict of claims among rivals for power.

The latter issue, the jealous rivalry among literary earls and dukes, or, as Hemingway put it, candidates for the presidency, engages the modern critic rather less than might be supposed, and much less than it engaged critics of a former time. D. H. Lawrence and James Joyce are thought by many to be the two pre-eminent prose writers in English of the first third of the twentieth century. Each disliked the work of the other (thinking it objectionable for, among other reasons, its obscenity); each thought that praise given to the work of the other diminished his own standing, and that the mind of any reader who admired the rival was insofar corrupted as to be unable to respond properly to him. There are indeed critics who undertake to continue the antagonism—for example, the admiration that F. R. Leavis gives Lawrence is sustained by his condemnation

---

Iliad (perhaps less: Homer does not receive royalties) than for a copy of a detective story. The case is different, to be sure, when what is in question is the original manuscript, the work as it came from the author's hand, or a rare first edition. The artistic value imputed to the work then determines the price it will bring in the open market. The recently discovered manuscript of the first version of T. S. Eliot's *The Waste Land,* a work that can be bought in print for not much more than a dollar, is, as we say, priceless.

of Joyce's methods and sensibility. Most critics, however, do not feel it necessary to make the choice a matter of absolute decision. Perhaps drawn by temperament more to one than to another, they find it possible (even gratifying) to recognize the power of both. To be sure, if one has for a time submitted to the power of Lawrence, it is not easy to submit soon to the power of Joyce, and *vice versa*. Nor, perhaps, should it be. But when one is free from both dominations, it may well seem, as one considers them in recollection, that there is no choice to be made.

This is not to say that the modern critic is wholly indifferent to the hierarchy of literary status. Where the judgment of "great" is made, it is inevitable that judgments of greater and greatest will follow. But the modern critic is less inclined to press toward hierarchical strictness than critics formerly were. Matthew Arnold, in his essay "The Study of Poetry," undertook to designate the canon of the truly great poets of the world and of England. It is not an enterprise that is likely to be repeated in our day.

More than exercising judgment upon the conflicting claims of authors as to how much dominion is their due, the critic, so far as he is a judge, concerns himself with the other issue raised by the *power* of literature—with, that is, the rights of the author as over against those of the reader. What is the legitimacy of the power over us that Shakespeare exercises through *King Lear?* He overcomes our minds, requiring us to behold things from which we want to turn away in horror and disgust. He leads us to the very point of despair, and, as Keats said in the sonnet in which he expressed his fears "on sitting down to read *King Lear* once again," even carries us beyond that point. By what right does he do this? By what right does any author invade our privacy, establish his rule over our emotions, demand of us that we give heed to what he has to say, which may be wholly at odds with what we want to hear said if we are to be comfortable? Joyce said that the ideal reader of his difficult *Finnegans Wake* was someone with an ideal insomnia. By what right does he make this exorbitant demand?

That there is in the abstract such a right is the assumption of any critic. Not infrequently his judicial task is to affirm the right in some particular instance of its having been unjustly denied, the responsibility for the miscarriage of justice lying, of course, at the door not only of the public but also of impercipient critics. Blake's poems, now so much admired and happily submitted to, were scarcely read for decades after their publication, not until a few critics undertook to declare that this was an impermissible state of affairs. *Moby-Dick* fell virtually into oblivion upon its first appearance in 1851 and was not allowed to exercise its power until critics in the 1920's aroused themselves to say that it should and must. It can happen that time and fashion rescind a right that was once in force, as in the case of John Donne, greatly admired in his own day, then scolded and condescended to in the eighteenth century, then for two centuries largely ignored, and restored to admiration by critical opinion at the beginning of this century.[4] And of course there are instances of criticism undertaking to reverse favorable judgments made by earlier courts. Matthew Arnold said that Dryden and Pope were not properly to be called poets at all. In our time Milton and Shelley have suffered from influential adverse opinions, of which the best known are those delivered by T. S. Eliot; in the case of Milton, Eliot subsequently reversed himself. When, after an extended advocacy, the high status of Henry James was accepted as legitimate, Maxwell Geismar undertook to question the correctness of the decision and even the disinterestedness of the

---

[4] It is a view commonly held that criticism is insensitive and resistant to new work of high quality and habitually delays its acceptance by the public. On the whole, this is not so. The large majority of notable works in all ages have quite quickly captured the interest and esteem of a significant body of readers. I have noted some exceptions and of course their number could be extended, but they do not support the view that as a rule genius is not readily recognized. It is no doubt true that new work sometimes meets with hostility from influential quarters. But the contemned artist usually (not always) has his own supporting group and the history of modern culture suggests that dissident opinions prevail over conventional ones and in relatively short time. The fullest statement of the opposite view is that made by Henri Peyre in his *The Failures of Criticism* (Ithaca, N.Y.: Cornell University Press, 1944).

judges who had made it, but he seems not to have succeeded in sending the case back for review.

II

If we survey the exercise of criticism's judicial function through its long history, we discern certain striking changes in the criteria which have controlled judgment. One such change has already been touched on, the diminishing (but by no means defunct) tendency in modern times to think of the writer as a craftsman and of his work as a made thing. At this point it will be useful to be aware of the successive assumptions about literature on which criticism has operated. These have been systematically and lucidly described by M. H. Abrams in his well-known book, *The Mirror and the Lamp,* and what follows is chiefly a paraphrase of Professor Abrams' admirable first chapter.[5]

Professor Abrams begins by observing that in all comprehensive theories of art there are four elements of the artistic situation which are dealt with in one or another degree of emphasis. The first of these is the work of art itself. The second is the maker of the work, the artist. The third is the subject of the work, what the work "is about," and this Professor Abrams denotes by a term that he chooses because it is "neutral and comprehensive": the universe. And finally there is the audience, those who hear or see or read the work. The difference among various theories of art and among the kinds of judgment that follow from these theories lies largely in the varying emphasis that is placed on one or more of the four elements.

The ancient Greeks thought of art primarily in terms of the relation between the work and the universe. Plato takes for granted the common idea that the essence of any work of art is that it repre-

---

[5] New York: Oxford University Press, 1953. I should emphasize *chiefly,* for I have at several points touched upon considerations that were not to Professor Abrams' purpose. And even where I have followed Professor Abrams, the responsibility for the ideas set forth, it goes without saying, is mine.

sents or imitates some part of the universe. The imitative nature of art makes the ground for the low esteem in which Plato held it, at least for his philosophical purposes. (It is plain that, in what we may speak of as his personal opinion, he held art in high regard; he had a considerable reputation as a poet and some of his philosophical dialogues are intensely admired for being in themselves works of art.) Plato distinguishes three degrees of reality. Of these the universe of things as we know them through the senses is in a median position: the things which we know and use in daily practical life are but imitations of eternal Ideas of things—any object, a bed, a table, a jar, is but the imperfect representation or imitation of the abstract and perfect Idea of the bed, table, or jar, just as the circle we draw on the blackboard in a geometry lesson is but the imperfect representation or imitation of the Idea of the circle. For Plato the Idea is the reality, the real reality. And if the objects of sense that we habitually and unreflectively think of as real are in truth not real at all but copies or shadows of reality, then how much further removed from reality are art's imitations of these objects. They are the copies of copies, the shadows of shadows.

No less than Plato, Aristotle conceived of art as imitative. He speaks of all the arts as being "modes of imitation." But he does not intend this to be in the least a pejorative characterization. For one thing, because he rejects Plato's doctrine of Ideas, he does not conceive of art as imitating reality at two removes; if it is indeed a copy, it is not a copy of a copy. What is more, it is apparent that by imitation Aristotle means something more than mere copying; the two English words by which the Greek word *mimesis* may be translated, imitation and representation, are close in meaning but they are not exactly the same, and it is representation rather than imitation that Aristotle has chiefly in mind. Although it is true that art refers to existing things, it is by no means wholly controlled by what is habitually observed of these things. Each art follows the laws of its own being in its mode of imitation. Aristotle says of tragedy and comedy that they show men as, respectively, "better than they really are" and "worse than they really are" and that each of them uses a selection of language appropriate to its intention. This gives a very considerable latitude to representation. Nowhere does Aristotle speak of a literary genre that represents men just as they really are.

Yet, for all the license that Aristotle grants to representation, his *Poetics* served to establish the mimetic doctrine, the critical mode that concentrates on the relation of the work of art to the universe and on the truth of the imitation that the work achieves. Mimetic theories maintained their force in criticism down to the end of the eighteenth century, had a lesser but still consequential existence in the nineteenth century, and are not without vitality today. In the nineteenth century they appear in the often highly polemical doctrines of realism and naturalism, which have chiefly to do with prose fiction and drama. At present they are most notably to be observed in the doctrine of "socialist realism," which constitutes the official aesthetic of the Soviet Union. And it is probably true that the mimetic assumption is at least one ground—perhaps the first ground —of artistic judgment of the majority of people who participate in Western culture. "Lifelike" and "true to life" are perhaps still the readiest and most common terms of praise of a work of art. It ought to be remarked that the diminished theoretical status of mimetic theories of art does not deny the genuineness of the pleasure that is to be derived from recognition, from perceiving the success of a work of mimetic art in representing what it intended to represent.

In the Renaissance another conception of art generated theories in a line which ran parallel with the mimetic. Professor Abrams calls them pragmatic theories because they look at the work of art "chiefly as a means to an end, an instrument for getting something done." The elements of the artistic situation that pragmatic theories concentrate on are the work of art and the audience: the end to which the work of art directs itself, the thing to be done of which it is the instrument, is to give pleasure to the audience. This, however, is not a final end but a means to yet another end, which is to instruct or edify the audience. The source of this conception of the right purpose of literature is the *Art of Poetry* of the Roman poet, Horace. "Poets," he said, "aim at giving either profit or delight, or at combining the giving of pleasure with some useful precepts of life." The beneficent moral effect of poetry was a chief preoccupation of criticism during the Renaissance; in England its most notable expression is Sir Philip Sidney's *An Apology for Poetry*. As a basis of critical judgment it survived with at least a degree of vitality into the eighteenth century—Dr. Johnson's essay on Shakespeare, the preface to his edition of the plays, attests to the interest it might still have for a powerful mind. By the nineteenth century its intellectual authority was at an end, although its social authority was still very commanding: that a work had a "high moral purpose" was a ready reason for praising it, and the reviewer or reader who could not discover such a purpose was likely to be disconcerted. Judgments of this kind were not commonly made by the highly developed literary minds of the age; Wordsworth, Shelley, and Matthew Arnold were firm in their belief that literature had a decisive effect for good upon the moral life, but they did not say that this influence was exercised purposefully and by means of precept. At the present time the idea that literature is to be judged by its moral effect has virtually no place in critical theory. In actual critical practice, however, it has a quite considerable vitality. Insofar as literature represents the relations between people, it deals with questions of morality, and a work is judged by the degree to which its treatment of moral situations bears in an enlightening way on moral actualities. This, to be sure, is not the same thing as judging a work by the criterion of its ability to inculcate correct moral principles.[6]

6 The English critic D. J. Enright, who has taught English literature in Thailand, reports on the high status that direct moral instruction has in the literary thought of that country: "The Thais display a strong and persistent tendency to moralize, or rather to expect other people to moralize, and they often feel unhappy if they cannot indulge this taste. Everything must teach a lesson, preferably a moral one; the lesson does not need to be a complex one, in fact complex moral lessons are suspect (doubtfully moral, that is). That the lesson is one you have learnt before does not detract from its value: in fact this serves to set the seal of approval on the moral—there are not many morals, either, in the world—and also on the

Pragmatic theory in its later stages tended to lighten the emphasis it placed on the moral effect of the work and paid increasing attention to the degree and kind of pleasure the work afforded and to the particular means by which pleasure is given. Horace's *Art of Poetry* had been written as a letter to two young friends of the poet who aspired to be poets themselves and it undertook to advise the aspirants as to what they ought and ought not do if they were to succeed in their ambition. The critics in the line of descent from Horace continue and develop his pedagogic intention: they are pragmatic not only in their assumption that a work of literature has a particular end in view—the giving of pleasure to the further end of giving moral instruction or edification—but also in their purpose of proposing to teach how this end is to be achieved.

The two elements of the artistic situation with which pragmatic criticism is concerned are, it will have been seen, the work of art and the audience. Of the two, the audience is the controlling one; the pragmatic investigation of the particular devices that were most advantageous to the poet took as its criterion the response of the audience: such effects as led the audience to respond in the desired way—which is to say, in the way that the audience itself was presumed to desire—were considered successful and the devices by

---

medium of the moral (that is, a poem with a good moral is a good poem). If everything is to teach us a lesson, then clearly lessons themselves, at school or at the university, must teach us a lesson. . . .

"Teachers in Thai schools were worried and embarrassed when Daphne du Maurier's *Rebecca* was set as an English reader. Finally one of them went to the Ministry of Education to make representations. The conversation unfolded along these lines:

Teacher: 'The pupils ask us what *Rebecca* teaches us, and we cannot give them an answer. What *is* the answer, please?'

Official: 'The book is intended to teach them English.'

Teacher: 'But that is not enough. It is a book and a book must convey a lesson of some sort. It must *teach*. If it doesn't teach a lesson, then they want to know why they have to read it.'

Official (sophisticated above the average): 'There are some books which we read just for pleasure.'

Teacher: 'Pleasure?'

Official: 'Yes, pleasure. We derive pleasure from reading it.'

Teacher: 'But we can't tell our pupils that! They wouldn't respect us any more!' "

—" 'Reading Poetry Makes You Nice and Neat,' " *Transition* (Kampala, Uganda), Vol. 7, No. 37, October 1968, page 25.

which these effects were secured were to be recommended. In short, the measure of artistic success was the approval of the audience, with this proviso only, that the audience must be an enlightened one, its taste properly trained and refined by habituation to the best in art.

The judicial hegemony of the audience was not to last. The focus of criticism gradually shifted from the work of art to its maker, who came to be seen as something other than a maker. Since one of its intentions had been to show how poetry should be written, pragmatic theory necessarily had the poet somewhat in mind, chiefly in his willingness to submit his natural energies to the rational control of precept and tradition. As the eighteenth century advanced, however, criticism became increasingly interested in the natural energies themselves, in the genius with which the poet had been endowed, which came to be identified with the spontaneity of his feelings and the force of his imagination. In the preceding age Ben Jonson, writing in the spirit of Horace, had supplied English pragmatic criticism with the maxim that summarizes its pedagogic mission: "A good poet's made as well as born." Now it became the critical tendency to invert the famous line, to lay the greater stress on the innate abilities of the poet. And in the degree that the interest in the poet grew, the attention paid to the audience and its demands diminished. The more authority criticism assigned to the poet, the less it granted to the audience.

During the late years of the eighteenth century this tendency accelerated dramatically. ". . . All good poetry is the spontaneous overflow of powerful feelings"—Professor Abrams quotes the famous statement of Wordsworth in the 1800 Preface to *Lyrical Ballads* as signalizing in English criticism the displacement of the mimetic and pragmatic theories of art by what he calls expressive theories.[7] In these the elements of the artistic situation that are

---

[7] It should always be kept in mind that Wordsworth's statement continues: "but though this be true, poems to which any value can be attached, were never produced on any variety of subjects but by a man who being possessed of more than usual organic sensibility had also thought long and deeply."

considered are the work of art and the artist. As Professor Abrams puts it, "The first test any poem must pass is no longer, 'Is it true to nature?' or 'Is it appropriate to the requirements either of the best judges or the generality of mankind?' but a criterion looking in a different direction; namely, 'Is it sincere? Is it genuine? Does it match the intention, the feeling, and the actual state of mind of the poet while composing?' The work ceases then to be regarded as primarily a reflection of nature . . . ; the mirror held up to nature becomes transparent and yields the reader insight into the mind and heart of the poet himself."

Here it should perhaps be said that the insights that the work yields are into the mind and heart of the poet himself *as poet*. When we ask of a poem whether it matches the actual state of mind of the poet while composing, we limit the range of our question to that part of the poet's state of mind which he has chosen to express. The *whole* state of his mind while composing will include, alas, much else—the discomfort of the rash on his neck, his dislike of the smell of the cabbage that is cooking, his anxiety over his child's persistent sore throat, not to mention all the unconscious but afflicting anxieties and conflicts that psychoanalytical theory says are always at work in us. The "actual state of mind" that we are aware of has been selected and even summoned; in some fairly simple sense of the word and in no pejorative sense, it is histrionic. The sincerity we discern and respond to is not only a function of the poet's intention but also—and perhaps chiefly—an effect of his art. His poem is sincere not only because he means it to be but also because he has a genius for sincere utterance, for using language that has, as we say, the accent of sincerity.

And of course the criterion of sincerity comes into significant use only when the work to which it is applied is judged to be in some way interesting and important. It is after all possible to recognize the sincerity of a work that does not engage our interest, and in such a case the sincerity is thought of not as a quality of art but as a quasi-moral quality; when we remark its presence in a work which we do not admire, we are in effect saying of the poor man who wrote it that at least he did not undertake to deceive us. Perhaps, indeed, the word sincerity is not the most fortunate one to denote the quality that expressive theory makes salient. In any work that does engage our interest it is taken for granted, and perhaps the least likely explicit positive judgment on a successful work that a critic will make is that it is sincere.

To perceive some awkwardness in the word sincerity as denoting the congruity between the poem and the poet's state of mind in the act of composing is not to question the importance that the congruity has in expressive theories. But perhaps an even more important characteristic of these theories is the authority with which they invested the poet. So far from requiring him to submit to the judgment of the audience, they conceived the reverse to be the appropriate state of affairs: the poet made the criterion by which the audience was to be judged. Even the critic approached him with awe; so far from presuming to suggest to the poet how he should go about his business, the critic conceived it as his function to serve the purposes of the poet, to learn to read him, divesting himself of the prejudices and predispositions that stand in the way of comprehension. The poet becomes a law unto himself which he hands down to the audience and critic, if they but have the humility and grace of spirit to receive it.

The latest-developed theories of art, those which Professor Abrams calls the objective theories, transfer to the work of art itself the authority and autonomy that the expressive theories had given to the artist. The objective view of art began to emerge in the late eighteenth and early nineteenth centuries and has had a very considerable influence on the literary thought of our own time. Unlike earlier theories—but Professor Abrams makes exception of "the central portion of Aristotle's *Poetics*"—it does not go about its work with reference to any other of the four elements of the artistic situation than the work itself: neither the audience, the artist, nor the universe is taken into account, only the work of art, which is to be dealt with only in terms of the formal relationships that are to be perceived among its parts. We may conjecture that the objective view of art came into being in response to, or at least concomitantly with, a new attitude among many advanced artists—their desire to liberate themselves from what they thought of as the bondage of personality, their distaste for the idea that they were expressing a state of feeling, which, after all, suggests communication to someone and submission to the conventions that make communication possible. The object that the artist created is understood to have no limiting relation to his own state of feeling, let alone to the audience or the universe; it exists in and for itself. In Joyce's novel, *A Portrait of the Artist as a Young Man,* Stephen Dedalus's remarks on what he calls "didactic" and "pornographical" art—art that seeks to inculcate a moral attitude and art that stimulates desire of any kind—and his celebrated description of the God-like imperturbability of the artist will serve to suggest the personal aesthetic of the attitude. It may be questioned whether, in final effect, any artist is capable of carrying out the program to the letter, and Professor Abrams notes the tendency of critics to depart from the strict objective concern with the literary object which they profess. Yet both the artistic program and the critical theory are salutary in reminding us that the work of art in and for itself has a first claim on us.

III

The intention of judgment is a salient motive of all critical theories. They undertake to say what literary excellence consists in and how discriminations between various degrees of excellence are to be made. But if criticism were confined to its judicial function, it would be a far less engaging activity than in fact it is. Actually, however, as has been seen, criticism is anterior to any particular act of judgment in that it defines the nature of the object to be judged and lays out the grounds on which judgment is to proceed. And criticism continues after judgment has been passed, if by judgment we mean simply the attribution to a work, or a canon of work, of a certain degree of excellence. For example, the peculiar excellence of Shakespeare's plays was very fully recognized in their own time and the first superlative judgment has really never been questioned in a decisive way. Yet the body of Shakespeare criticism that has come into being in the intervening years is of such magnitude that it is scarcely to be encompassed by any reader in a lifetime, and there is no likelihood of a falling off in its rate of increase.[8] What is all this activity about?

It is certainly true that much of it is devoted to judgment—to reaffirming in new and particular ways the general judgment made four centuries back. But judgment thus reiterated in ever-renewed ingenuity is not judgment in any ordinary sense. It is judgment as celebration. Or it is judgment as love. Spinoza spoke of the "intellectual love of God," by which he meant the unremitting activity of mind which ought to be directed to the comprehension of the totality of the universe which, in Spinoza's conception, is one with God. The criticism of Shakespeare may be thought of as just such an activity: its assumption is that the effort to understand its great object is to be perpetual, that it cannot come to an end, that there is always more for it to perceive. What is observed and concluded by one mind does not wholly satisfy another; the discernment that seems sufficient at one time seems inadequate or mistaken a few decades later. About the permanent interest of the object there can be no doubt.

Criticism does not always discharge its function of what might be called simple and primary judgment quite so expeditiously as in the case of Shakespeare, although on the whole it works with reasonable dispatch. Once it has done so, the larger part of its activity of understanding begins. This activity manifests itself in a variety

---

[8] "Over the sixty-year period following the two-volume Variorum Edition of 1877, and covered by the *Hamlet Bibliography* of A. A. Raven it is computed that twelve days have not passed without witnessing the publication of some additional item of Hamletiana."—Harry Levin, *The Question of* HAMLET (New York: Oxford University Press, 1959), pp. 3–4.

of particular forms and purposes, each of which is an expression of what criticism is, the intellectual love of literature.

The scientific implications of Spinoza's original phrase have some relevance to our paraphrase. Criticism in its relation to literary phenomena bears comparison with science in its relation to natural phenomena. The comparison is permissible only if it is not carried beyond a certain point. Aristotle said that "it is the mark of an educated mind to seek only so much exactness in each type of inquiry as may be allowed to the nature of the subject-matter," and certainly the degree of exactness to be sought in criticism is not equal to that sought in a natural science. It should also be said that comparison between the processes of the two disciplines will be valid only if the science referred to is at a relatively early stage of development. These provisos accepted, the connection between the two activities seems a useful one for our purpose.

A first undertaking of criticism in dealing with a work of literature is to describe the object of its interest. This may be expeditiously begun by saying—after an examination which usually, if it is made by a practised eye, need not be more than cursory—what genre of work it belongs to: it is an epic, a certain kind of long poem; or it is a lyric, a certain kind of short poem; or it is a novel, a prose narrative of a certain length setting forth fictive events; and so on.[9] The naming of the genre to which the work seems to belong is in itself not very enlightening (and sometimes it darkens understanding by raising false issues), but it serves to initiate the next step in description, the observation of the particularities of the work.

[9] "Just as every animal belongs to a species," José Ortega y Gassett says, "every literary work belongs to a genre (the theory of Benedetto Croce who denies the existence of literary forms in this sense has left no trace in aesthetics)."—"Notes on the Novel," in *The Dehumanization of Art* (Princeton, N.J.: Princeton University Press, 1968), p. 54.

A recently established scholarly journal describes itself as follows: "*Genre* is a quarterly publication devoted to generic criticism. It publishes articles which fall into the following categories: (1) theoretical discussions of the genre concept, (2) historical studies of particular genres and genre debates, (3) attempts to establish and define genres, (4) interpretations of works of literature from the genre point of view."

Milton's *Paradise Lost* is like the *Iliad* and the *Aeneid* in being a long poem about events of high import in which divine beings play a decisive part, and it is like its predecessors in certain linguistic respects. The effect of the work does not, it is true, wholly depend upon the reader's acquaintance with the earlier epics. But Milton obviously intended that it should be thought of in connection with them—to some extent he counted on the connection being apparent, and part of the descriptive work of criticism is to further the reader's consciousness of the tradition in which the author composed. And the noticing of similarities inevitably involves the remarking of differences: the reader and the critic will be at one in their curiosity about what in the work is new.

Here it should be said that the status of the quality of newness in art is an ambiguous one. Probably in all times certain people and groups of people have been made anxious and irritable by artistic novelty. In some cultural epochs the society as a whole is resistant to it. At other times it is one of the chief *desiderata* of art. This seems to be the case in our own time, when new styles and modes are likely to be readily accepted and quickly exhausted. As one writer has put it, "For modern art in general, and for avant-garde in particular, the only irremediable and absolute artistic error is a traditional artistic creation, an art that imitates and repeats itself." But even in cultural epochs much more conservative than ours, art, however traditional in intention, does not remain fixed and static but tends to change, even though sometimes almost imperceptibly. The awareness of its shifts in style, whether these be gradual and slow or radical and sudden, is part of the developed consciousness of any art, and it is one of the purposes of criticism to intensify this consciousness. To be aware of what a particular style evolved from or of what has evolved out of it is to become more sensitive to what in itself it is.

Early in his enterprise of description the critic will take account of the form or structure of the work he is dealing with. He perceives this, and seeks to make us perceive it, both as a shape, interesting and perhaps beautiful in itself, and also as the means by which the reader's emotions and thoughts are organized toward the effect the work intends.

Sometimes the description of form can proceed without difficulty and with the fairly confident expectation that it will be objective. Dante planned *The Divine Comedy* to have a form that would be readily apprehended. The poem is in three parts, each devoted to one of the three states of the after-life, Hell, Purgatory, and Paradise. The verse is *terza rima,* triple rime, i.e. stanzas of three verses, riming in the pattern *aba, bcb, cdc,* etc. Each book consists of thirty-three cantos, except the first, which has thirty-four; the total is thus 100. The structure of the poem, it is plain to see, intends a symmetry of a precise kind, one that, we know, was controlled by Dante's belief in the aesthetic and symbolic properties of certain numbers, of which 3 and 10 and certain of their multiples are pre-eminent, although he also attached special value to 7. There is no doubt a peculiar pleasure to be had from a structure so exact and symmetrical as this. And in general it can be said that readers are likely to respond in a positive way to a work whose component elements are arranged in a form that is rigorous and economical. The perception of unity in diversity is one of the gratifications of the experience of art; a unity made readily manifest, as, for example, in *Oedipus Rex,* may be supposed to give the pleasure of reassurance, as if it implied a thoroughly well-ordered and rational universe even though the substance of the play seems to suggest that the universe is incomprehensible.

But not all unity is readily manifest, often it must be discerned by effort, sometimes by controverting the received ideas of what constitutes unity. To Voltaire, who constructed his own plays according to the quite precise rules which governed French drama for a considerable time, *Hamlet* appeared to be virtually inchoate, and his opinion was long shared by the great majority of French readers, who were accustomed to a different conception of form than that which organizes *Hamlet.* Until relatively recent years, *A*

Winter's Tale made many of even the most ardent admirers of Shakespeare uncomfortable; it seemed to lack unity because its action falls into two parts, the second separated from the first by an interval of sixteen years. This dichotomy is nowadays generally thought to be of no account in view of the invincible integrity of the play's thematic development and style. For a considerable time *Ulysses* was said by its detractors to be formless—one notable critic called it "an explosion in a cesspool"; now the precision with which it is structured is generally recognized and there are even those who hold that the precision is too great, to the point of its being mechanical! The shifting opinions on questions of form will suggest the extent to which judgment in this matter is likely to be subjective and conditioned by prevailing taste and fashion. The coherence of a Gothic cathedral is now a thing taken for granted, but for a quite considerable period it was a perception beyond the competence of most educated people.

Up to a point, the description of a literary work can proceed with a considerable degree of objectivity. Certain of the elements of description can even be quantitative. Quantified data about literature are in rather bad repute as being contrary to the spirit of literature, but they have their uses. How one poet's management of a given kind of verse differs from another's can be expressed numerically, for traditional English verse is based on the ratio of accented to unaccented syllables, and the act of *counting* once seemed so important to it that the word "numbers" was a common synonym for verse. (*Noble Numbers* is the title of one of Herrick's collections of poems; Pope, speaking of his poetic precocity, said, "I lisped in numbers, for the numbers came.") Iambic pentameter normally has five stresses to a line; if it is observed of a poet who uses this form that he inclines to write lines which, if read "for sense" rather than being "scanned," have only four fully stressed syllables, we have learned something about why his verse sounds as it does. It is observed of Yeats that birds figure frequently in his poems. This seems pertinent to our effort to understand his symbolism and, in general, the processes of his imagination. Doubtless there is something absurd in determining that x number of birds appear in the poems and that among them there are this many curlews, that many herons, swans, or hawks. Still, the quantification makes the observation rather the more significant, and it might lead the critic to remark that birds figured more in Yeats's imagination at one period than at another, from which conclusions of some interest might be drawn. Marcel Proust, writing about Stendhal's novel *The Red and the Black,* says that the "loftiness of soul" of its hero, Julien Sorel, is "linked to actual height"; he has in mind the circumstance that the incidents in which Julien is shown on, or climbing to, a high place run to a quite considerable number—eight by my count. Once we have been put in mind of this repetition, each of these incidents comes into a sharper focus and is seen as a sort of epitome of the whole story of Julien's commitment to a life which will rise above the mediocre and the commonplace. Caroline Spurgeon remarks on the group of grandiose images in *Antony and Cleopatra* which, she says, is peculiar to this play.[10] They are "images of the world, the firmament, the ocean and vastness generally." And she goes on: "This vastness of scale is kept constantly before us by the word 'world,' which occurs forty-two times, nearly double, or more than double, as often as in most other [of Shakespeare's] plays, and it is continually employed in a way which increases the sense of grandeur, power and space."

The usefulness of quantitative description can be of only limited extent and the objectivity of description is not to be measured by the degree to which it relies upon quantification. As for objectivity itself, although it is indeed a quality which we look for in criticism and prize when we find it, Aristotle's *caveat* against demanding more exactness than the subject-matter permits is here most relevant. We expect of the critic that he will make every possible effort,

---

[10] *Shakespeare's Imagery and What It Tells Us* (New York: Cambridge University Press, 1958), p. 352.

in Matthew Arnold's famous words, "to see the object as in itself it really is" and to describe it accordingly. But we know that what is seen by one critic with the best possible will to see accurately is likely to be different from what is seen by another critic with an equally good will. There comes a point at which description becomes interpretation. There is no help for this failure of perfect objectivity, if that is indeed what we ought to call it. It is in the nature of the case that the object as in itself it really is will not appear wholly the same to any two minds. Perhaps this is properly a cause for rejoicing. Mozart as interpreted by Toscanini is not the same as Mozart interpreted by Munch, but both interpretations give us pleasure and win our admiration. And if, apart from either interpretation, there is a Mozart as in himself he really is, we shall never know him: there can only be other interpretations.

Which does not in the least mean that one interpretation of a musical work through performance or one critical interpretation of a literary work is as good as another. Laurence Olivier's screen production of *Hamlet* was introduced by a descriptive statement which won for itself an unhappy fame. A portentous voice was heard to say, "This is the tragedy of a man who could not make up his mind." On its face, this description of the play is absurd, conjuring up as it does the sad fate of a man who, on being asked, "Vanilla, chocolate, or strawberry?", found it impossible to fix on one flavor in preference to the others and was in consequence destroyed. Yet a certain dim cogency is lent to the description by the influential line of criticism it can be seen to have descended from. In the nineteenth century, critical comment on the play concentrated on Hamlet's not having carried out his quick-conceived intention of killing the King, his uncle and stepfather, in vengeance for the King's having murdered Hamlet's father, the former King. Why did he fail of his purpose? In Goethe's novel *Wilhelm Meister's Apprenticeship,* the play is a presiding presence, often referred to and discussed. At one point the protagonist Wilhelm undertakes to explain why Hamlet did not do what he had resolved to do. After a long description of the young prince's traits which stresses his gentleness and magnanimity, Wilhelm says:

Figure to yourselves this youth, . . . this son of princes; conceive him vividly, bring his state before your eyes, and then observe him when he learns that his father's spirit walks; stand by him in the terrors of the night, when the venerable ghost itself appears before him. A horrid shudder passes over him; he follows it, and hears. The fearful accusation of his uncle rings in his ears; the summons to revenge and the piercing oft-repeated prayer, Remember me!

And when the ghost has vanished, who is it that stands before us? A young hero panting for vengeance? A prince by birth, rejoicing to be called to punish the usurper of his crown? No! trouble and astonishment take hold of the solitary young man; he grows bitter against smiling villains; swears that he will not forget the spirit, and concludes with the significant ejaculation:

> The time is out of joint; O cursed spite,
> That ever I was born to set it right!

In these words, I imagine, will be found the key to Hamlet's whole procedure. To me it is clear that Shakespeare meant, in the present case, to represent the effects of a great action laid upon a soul unfit for the performance of it. In this view the whole piece seems to me to be composed. There is an oak-tree planted in a costly jar, which should have borne only pleasant flowers in its bosom; the roots expand, the jar is shivered.

A lovely, pure, noble and most moral nature, without the strength of nerve which forms a hero, sinks beneath a burden which it cannot bear and must not cast away. All duties are hard for him; the present is too hard. Impossibilities have been required of him; not in themselves impossibilities, but such for him. He winds, and turns, and torments himself; he advances and recoils; is ever put in mind, ever puts himself in mind; at last does all but lose his purpose from his thoughts; yet still without recovering his peace of mind.

Coleridge's view is consonant with Goethe's:

[Shakespeare] intended to portray a person, in whose view the external world, and all its incidents and objects, were comparatively dim, and of no interest in themselves, and which began to interest only when they were reflected in the mirror of his mind. Hamlet beheld external things in the same way that a man of vivid imagination, who shuts his eyes, sees what has previously made an impression on his organs. [He learns from his father's ghost of his uncle's crime.] What is the effect upon the son?—instant action and pursuit of revenge? No: endless reasoning and hesitating—constant urging and solicitation of the mind to act, and as constant an escape from action; ceaseless reproaches of himself for sloth and negligence, while the whole energy of his resolution evaporates in these reproaches. This, too, not from cowardice, for he is drawn as one of the bravest of his time—not from want of forethought or slowness of apprehension, for he sees through the very souls of all who surround him, but merely from that aversion to action, which prevails among such as have a world in themselves. . . . All that is amiable and excellent in nature is combined in Hamlet, with the exception of one quality. He is a man living in meditation, called upon to act by every motive human and divine, but the great object of his life is defeated by continually re-solving to do, yet doing nothing but resolve.

Hazlitt is in the same vein:

The character of Hamlet stands quite by itself. It is not a character marked by strength of will or even of passion, but by refinement of thought and sentiment. Hamlet is as little of the hero as a man can well be: but he is a young and princely novice, full of high enthusiasm and quick sensibility—the sport of circumstances, questioning with fortune and refining on his own feelings, and forced from the natural bias of his disposition by the strangeness of his situation.

All three writers concentrate on Hamlet's not doing what he has resolved to do. And they are in agreement in saying that the reason he does not is that he is averse to action, because he is too gentle and delicate and because he is too much committed to thought. They do not quite say that he does not make up his mind, and indeed Coleridge says the contrary. Still, if someone wanted to sum up the general drift of the three descriptions of Hamlet for a large popular audience, he might fasten on the circumstances that Hamlet had a mind, that it was very active and complicated, that it seemed to get in the way of his doing what he meant to do, and come up with "This is the tragedy of a man who could not make up his mind."

How far the brutally dull sentence betrays the marvellous complexity of the play it presumes to describe will be plain not only from actual experience of the play but also from what is said by Goethe, Coleridge, and Hazlitt, all of whom succeed in conveying something of the excitement that *Hamlet* generates. But modern Shakespeare critics are by no means content with these statements, charged with responsive feeling though they be. Indeed, the modern tendency of criticism is to say that the view the Romanticist critics took of *Hamlet* was all too heavily charged with responsive feeling of a certain kind. They did not sufficiently resist the temptation that the character of Hamlet surely does offer, to identify ourselves with him—"it is *we* who are Hamlet," Hazlitt said—and in consequence they focus their thought upon the protagonist rather than on the play itself. As Professor Harry Levin puts it, *"Hamlet* without Hamlet would, of course, be altogether unthinkable; but Hamlet without *Hamlet* has been thought about all too much."[11]

Yet when a modern critic of Shakespeare has explained why the Romanticist interpretation of *Hamlet* is at fault, he has no disposition to believe that what was said by Goethe, Coleridge, and Hazlitt is of no account. "Wrong" it may be, but in criticism it is of consequence who is being wrong and in what way. The Romanticist view of *Hamlet* is not ours but it has become part of our awareness of the play. No teacher would permit a serious student of Shakespeare to be ignorant of it. At a certain time, for the best minds of Europe, *Hamlet* existed in this way; this *was* the play. It now exists differently, but who would wish to assert that its past is not implicated in its present?

No one nowadays is likely to agree with Dr. Johnson's view of *Lycidas* which led to his total condemnation of the poem, or with his judgment that Donne and the so-called metaphysical poets are absurd in their far-fetched imagery. Yet for many readers these opinions have become part of the existence of the works to which they were directed. They are kept in mind because they are, in all

11 *The Question of* HAMLET, p. 5.

that we now think their wrongness, an aid to understanding: these judgments are made on premises so forthrightly stated that they have the effect both of stimulating and of organizing our controversion of then, of shaping the view that we think right.

A couplet of Blake's lays down the principle on which wrongness in criticism is to be dealt with:

> The errors of the wise man make your rule
> Rather than the perfections of a fool.

This, of course, is advice to the reader of criticism, not to the critic himself, who can scarcely proceed with his task on the assumption that he is one of the wise men whose errors will be of the enlightening kind. He must believe, however aware he may be of the extent to which his perception is conditioned and limited, that it is possible for him to see the object as in itself it really is.

IV

If we pursue the limited analogy that may be made between criticism and science, we observe that criticism, like science, occupies itself with questions of causation. In the modern period, criticism has in large measure committed itself to the belief that the comprehension of a literary work can be advanced by knowledge of the conditions under which it came into being, which may be supposed to explain why it is what it is.

The belief does not go unchallenged. There are critics of notable authority who take the position that a work of literature is an autonomous and self-determining entity and that its nature is violated if it is dealt with in any other terms than those which in itself it proposes. They maintain further that to adduce considerations extrinsic to the work itself inevitably diverts from it some part of the attention it should receive. These objections are not without cogency and to them others might be added. Yet the resistance is but a rearguard action; the belief that causation is a valuable and interesting category of criticism is now pretty firmly established.

The idea that literature, or any art, is a conditioned thing would seem to have taken its rise in the eighteenth century with the striking development of historical thought that occurred at that time. Historical investigation proliferated at an ever-increasing rate and concerned itself not only with the great manifest events of nations, with wars and the succession of rulers and dynasties, but also with social and economic arrangements, with religion and the moral code, with manners and customs, with philosophy and art. The historians' growing sensitivity to these elements of a national life could not but lead to the perception that they were vitally interconnected, that they formed an organic whole which was a controlling condition of the nature of any one of its components. This way of looking at a people's history was but one expression of an idea that was beginning to command the mind of Europe—the idea of *society*. It might seem absurd to speak of this as a new idea, since men have always lived in society and from time immemorial have reflected on this definitive circumstance of their existence. But never before had society been conceived of as having a distinct and substantial being which was susceptible to investigation and predication. Before long it became possible to propose a study, conceived on the model of the physical sciences and to be called sociology, which envisaged the comprehension of the laws by which society lived and moved and had its being; comprehension was eventually to lead to rational control, for part of the conception of society was that it had an autonomous life whose purposes were not in all respects beneficent. The extent to which the idea took dominion over men's minds may be judged from the great novels of the nineteenth century, of which there is perhaps not one in which society is not a presiding presence, commonly thought of as adversary to human happiness and virtue.

In the late nineteenth century certain implications of the concept of society were given sharper focus by the use of the word *culture*. A precise definition of culture in the sense that is now most usually intended must perhaps be despaired of—in 1952 two eminent anthropologists, A. L. Kroeber and Clyde Kluckhohn, thought it worth their while to bring together the diverse and often contradictory definitions that had been advanced up to that date; the compilation, together with its commentative apparatus, makes a sizable volume.[12] In its most inclusive meaning, the word denotes all of society's activities, from the most necessary to the most gratuitous, as these are conceived in their observed, or assumed, integrality. Sometimes, however, the meaning is narrowed by the exclusion from its purview of economic and political activity; what then is left is the society's technology, its religious beliefs and organization, its moral code, its manners and customs, its intellectual and artistic pursuits, its systems of valuation, whether expressed or implicit. A considerable part of the attraction of the concept of culture is the credence it gives to the *implicit,* to those conventions and assumptions that the members of a cultural entity share without being conscious of them.

The concept of culture is of decisive importance in contemporary thought. As Kroeber and Kluckhohn put it in the introduction to their book, "In explanatory importance and in generality of application it is comparable to such categories as gravity in physics, disease in medicine, evolution in biology." It permits us—even invites, perhaps requires, us—to think of any one element of a given culture as being conditioned by the other elements and as being appropriate to them all. The perception of the appropriateness to each other of all the elements finds expression in a quasi-aesthetic judgment, that among the elements there is a continuity of *style.* The same spirit seems to have set its mark on each of them.

If anything is definitive of the concept of culture, it is this idea of a unitary spirit at work. Taine, the nineteenth-century French historian who did much to propagate the idea of cultural causation, speaks in the opening sentence of his *History of English Literature* (1863) of the transformation of history that has taken place "within

---

12 *Culture: A Critical Review of Concepts and Definitions,* Vol. XLVII—No. 1 of the Papers of the Peabody Museum of American Archaeology and Ethnology, Harvard University; also New York: Random House, 1963 (Vintage Books).

a hundred years in Germany, within sixty years in France." He attributes this great change to the study of literature, not as it had been traditionally carried on but in a new way. "It was perceived," he says, "that a literary work is not a mere individual play of imagination, the isolated caprice of an excited brain, but a transcript of contemporary manners, a manifestation of a certain kind of mind," by which he means the habits of thought which differentiate the people of one culture from those of another. "It was concluded that we might recover from the monuments of literature a knowledge of the manner in which men thought and felt centuries ago."

The conclusion was momentous not only for history but also for literature. On first inspection, the new way of thinking about literary works might seem to degrade their status to that of mere documents in evidence. It is scarcely a recognition of the true nature of, for example, the *Iliad* to say of it that it is not a mere individual play of imagination, the isolated caprice of an excited brain, but a transcript of contemporary manners, a manifestation of the mind of the people among whom Homer lived and for whom he composed his poems. But such maltreatment as literature might seem to have suffered is very quickly redressed and the achieved purposes of history are seen to have served literature. For to perceive a work not only in its isolation, as an object of aesthetic contemplation, but also as implicated in the life of a people at a certain time, as expressing that life, and as being in part shaped by it, does not, in most people's experience, diminish the power or charm of the work but, on the contrary, enhances it.

It needs no special knowledge or intention to see a work in this way. Any reasonably practiced reader, in his experience of the literature of another time, is likely to bring the category of cultural causation into play as a matter of course. In reading, say, Molière's *Misanthrope*, he will be divided between a feeling of familiarity and a feeling of strangeness. He has, for example, no difficulty in responding to the question the play asks: Although sincerity is indeed an admirable trait and to be urged on everyone, is it not possible to set excessive store by it? The question is an engaging one, worth trying to answer. As it figures in the play, it implies an ideal of human behavior and a conception of man's life in society which deserves serious consideration. Still, the reader feels that as a question presumed to be of large public import it would not be posed in our present time; it could not be the subject of a contemporary play, certainly not in the terms that Molière devised, for his protagonist's overvaluation of sincerity expresses itself in a contempt for good manners and in rude behavior, and an audience of our time could scarcely be expected to take a grave view of this. But as the subject of a play in France in 1666 it seems wholly appropriate. In order to make that judgment the reader does not have to be learned in the details of French culture at that time. The play itself provides him with a considerable amount of information. The characters, with the exception of servants, are all aristocrats, and presumably the play was written for a predominantly aristocratic audience. Not all aristocracies set store by elegant manners, but this one is represented as doing so. The author would seem to have counted or gambled, on his audience being intelligent enough to know that his hero, Alceste, is right in thinking that elaborate good manners make a pleasant façade behind which triviality, stupidity, malice, and injustice have their ugly way, and in judging that life in society is ignoble. This is manifestly Molière's own opinion. Yet his play at its conclusion seems to say that despite all the ignobility that may be discovered in it, society must be accepted as a necessary and essentially beneficent circumstance of human existence; its peace and order, though dependent on lies, must not be disturbed. Alceste is doubtless noble in his rage against social falsehood, yet it is suggested that his commitment to sincerity and his scorn of those who lack it spring from something less admirable than the simple love of virtue, that pride and self-love have their part in the disgust that leads him to alienate himself from society. There is every likelihood that the reader, perhaps to his surprise, will not take this conclusion to be a recommendation to acquiescence and "conformity," that he will understand the play to be saying something grave and difficult and that what it says is part of the effort of the men of its time to realize the idea of society in the terms that were available to them.

The awareness of cultural causation which I have ascribed to the reasonably practiced reader in his experience of *The Misanthrope* comes simply from his having the abstract idea of culture as part of his intellectual equipment. With no more fully substantiated awareness than this he generally does very well in most of his reading.

But perhaps he does even better when the abstract concept of culture is given a degree of substantiation. If, for example, the reader learns the simple historical fact that *The Misanthrope* was not very successful when it first appeared, something is pretty sure to happen to his perception of the play. He must at once complicate his idea of what it means for a literary work to be called the product of its culture, the expression of the mind of the people at the time. *The Misanthrope* is now often said to be Molière's greatest play, yet when it was first produced, opinion went against it. This is not to say, however, that it was given no admiration at all; many thoughtful people, some of great intellectual authority, held it in the highest regard. Such a division of opinion might seem to bring into question the idea of the unitary nature of culture. Actually, of course, the cogency and usefulness of that idea depend exactly upon its being discovered in a manifest diversity, and, indeed, in the disputes that, in any highly elaborated culture, go on between diverse preferences and opinions. A culture has its being in activity, in its complex response to possibilities, as these are offered by external circumstances or as they are conceived by the culture itself, and perhaps the most characteristic form of its activity is the opposition which one group in the culture offers to another. *The Misanthrope* represents such an opposition—between, on the one hand, a body of opinion, perhaps amorphous but later to be more articulated, which holds Alceste's view that society is an affront to rationality and virtue, and, on the other hand, a body of opinion which resists this radical conclusion and which, without making any claims for the rationality and goodness of society affirms its necessity and the wrongness of judging it by absolute moral standards. *The Misanthrope,* in representing this conflict of opinion, participates in it, although not, as at first we have been led to think, by giving credence only to the moderate view. The mockery of Alceste for his intransigence and the hint that it springs from motives not wholly worthy do not finally negate the force of his condemnation of society; the play's resolution in a counsel of moderation and acceptance is no doubt sincere and not merely formal, yet it does not prevent the supposition that, to have imagined Alceste's revulsion from society, Molière must himself have felt it and that he was inviting his audience to share it or at least to acknowledge its validity. The reader who has learned that the play was coolly received will scarcely fail to conjecture that the reason for its having been resisted was its intention of affecting the culture by bringing it under a scrutiny which was in some degree adverse. The single extrinsic fact has suggested to him something more than he might at first have imagined of the extent to which the play is implicated in its culture, and in doing so has made the more likely his recognition of the living *will* of the play, its energy of intention. The intention is an ambiguous one, which is one reason why *The Misanthrope* is the saddest of comedies.

It is a tribute to the cogency of the idea of cultural causation that it won the assent of the eighteenth-century philosopher, David Hume, much of whose fame rests on the doubts he raised about causation in the physical sciences. He found it reasonable to suppose that the culture stood in a causal relation to individual works of genius the reason being that geniuses—"choice spirits"—arise from and are related to the mass of people of their time. "The question, therefore," he said, "is not altogether concerning the taste, genius, and spirit of a few, but concerning a whole people; and may, therefore, be accounted for, in some measure, by general causes and principles." But before he gave this license for the use of the category of cultural causation in dealing with the arts, he warned of its dangers.

"There is no subject," he said, "in which we must proceed with more caution than in tracing the history of the arts and sciences; lest we assign causes which never existed and reduce what is merely contingent to stable and universal principles." And he goes on: "Chance, therefore, or secret or unknown causes must have great influence on the rise and progress of all refined arts."[13]

By and large, cultural criticism as it has developed over the intervening years shares Hume's view that a culture is an entity so complex that the category of causation used in relation to it can be of but limited potency. Part of the common conception of culture is that, although predications about it can indeed be made, it is in many respects a mystery, perhaps a sacred one, and to be treated with a degree of intellectual diffidence. One line of cultural thought, however, is characterized by its intransigent confidence in the category of causation. It holds that contingency can indeed be reduced to stable and universal principles, that nothing in culture need be attributed to chance, that such causes as are secret and unknown will not remain in the darkness forever. This is the line of thought that derives from Karl Marx and goes by his name.

Like other theorists of the subject, Marx conceived culture as an integral whole, as the necessary interrelationships of all the elements that comprise it. What differentiates his view from others is that he grants culture virtually no autonomy at all; its nature, so far from being self-determining, is strictly conditioned. For Marx the determining condition of a culture is the particular mode of economic production with which it is associated. Marx's statement of the case is succinct and uncompromising: "In the social production which men carry on they enter into definite relations that are indispensable and independent of their will. . . . The sum total of these relations of production constitutes the economic structure of a society—the real foundation on which rises a legal and political superstructure to which correspond definite forms of social consciousness. The mode

[13] *Essays Moral, Political and Literary* (New York: Oxford University Press, 1966), pp. 114–115.

of production in material life determines the social, political, and intellectual life-processes in general. It is not the consciousness of men that determines their being, but, on the contrary, their social being that determines their consciousness."[14] Of equal importance with the idea of economic determinism in Marx's theory of culture is the idea of the antagonism between social classes which is intensified in periods when changes occur in the economic structure. The conflict of classes finds expression in "legal, political, religious, aesthetic, or philosophic—in short, ideological—forms" and serves to explain the succession of cultures.

Marx's theory of culture has had a considerable influence on contemporary criticism. Most critics are not willing to make the political commitment it seems to demand, not so much in itself as in its connection with the revolutionary intention of the whole of Marx's thought. Yet any critic who thinks about literature in relation to society and culture cannot fail to be aware of it as a formidable presence. What I have called its intransigent confidence in the category of causation exerts an unremitting pressure on those who use the category more diffidently. It is hard not to feel that there is a large potential for criticism in the Marxist theory. By the same token, it is hard not to be surprised at how little this has been realized. *The Hidden God,* by the French scholar and critic, Lucien Goldmann, an elaborate study of the tragic vision of Pascal and Racine in relation to the religious thought of their time which in turn is seen in relation to the developing ideology of certain social classes, suggests how much can be done with the Marxist assumptions when they are used by a sufficiently complex mind. But of comparable works there have been none in America and England and few in Europe. For the most part Marxist criticism seems to be ignorant of the intellectual possibilities of the doctrine to which it gives lip-service and contents itself with a simplistic moralizing

14 Preface to *A Contribution to the Critique of Political Economy.* Translated by N. I. Stone (New York: International Library, 1904), p. 11. The work first appeared in 1859.

about literature: having taken for granted the badness of capitalist society, it conceives its chief enterprise to be the demonstration of how the social turpitude manifests itself in the corruption of the artistic consciousness.

V

In highly developed cultures an admired work of literature has always been associated with the man who wrote it and its qualities accounted for by his temperament.[15] Buffon's famous statement, "Style is the man himself," made in 1753, was perhaps, in its being made at all, a portent of the emphasis that Romanticism was to place on the personality of the author, but it expresses what readers have always felt without saying so. For the earlier readers, however, the equation of man and style was a satisfying tautology; for later readers it settled nothing—on the contrary, it opened the way to questions. If the style is the man himself, how did the man become himself, the person who is signalized by this style and no other? And since style is at the service of, and controlled by, the man's emotion seeking expression, would not the emotion be the better understood if its occasion in the author's actual experience were known?

The belief that biography provides a basis for the fuller understanding of a work of literature meets with substantially the same objections as are offered to the belief that such a basis is to be found in culture. A concern with the author's life is said to usurp the attention that should be given to the work itself. And it is held that knowledge of the biographical circumstances of the work's genesis not only is irrelevant to the work as an autonomous aesthetic object but serves to prevent its being seen in this way.

Such validity as these objections have is limited by the consideration that much of our experience of literature is not of single isolated

---

[15] I specify highly developed cultures because there are simpler cultures in which the author of an admired work is not known and his identity is of no moment, as, for example, the culture in which the ballads of Scotland and northern England were composed.

works but, rather, of some sizable number of the items that make up an author's whole production. If in an anthology we read a story by, say, Henry James, we incline to be aware of it only in itself and to have but little concern with the author's personal existence. But if the story engages and pleases us, we will probably wonder whether the person who made this particular aesthetic object did not make others that would similarly please and engage us. We discover that this is indeed the case, that Henry James wrote a great many stories, in addition to his many novels, enough to fill twelve sizable volumes, and that most of them are very good. We will not have gone far in our reading of them before we recognize that, although each story does indeed have its own peculiar existence as an aesthetic object, it also has an existence in its relation to the other stories. They all have something in common, a characteristic tone or style and characteristic social and moral assumptions. We come to think of them as not merely stories but as Henry James stories. And it is because of, and in reference to, what they have in common that we remark the differences among them. In accordance with modern editorial practice, the stories are arranged in the order in which they were written, and if we read them in this order, we are conscious of the continuity between those that James wrote at twenty-one and those he wrote in his late sixties, but we are no less conscious of the respects in which they are unlike. As the stories proceed from the early to the late, they show not only an increasing sureness of execution but also an increasing boldness, complexity, and weightiness. We observe, that is to say, a development. Try as we will at the behest of those critics who warn us of the irrelevance and distraction of biography, we do not see this as the development of autonomous aesthetic objects—the stories are Henry James stories, the development we are conscious of is that of the creative powers of Henry James. We cannot suppress the knowledge that a person, a young man, addressed himself to mastering an art which has as one of its criteria of success the ability to evoke interest and deep feeling by telling the truth about life and that to this end he gave the energies of nearly fifty working years. Try as we may, we cannot down our consciousness of Henry James the man, the man-writing—he becomes part of our experience of his work, which we see not as a collocation of particular aesthetic objects but as an intention, the enterprise of a lifetime, which has its own coherence and form and is thus in itself an aesthetic object of a kind.

As I have suggested, the involvement of our consciousness of the writer in our experience of his work is a relatively new way of experiencing literature. No biography of Shakespeare was undertaken until nearly a century after his death. We of our time would feel at a loss if we did not believe that we could determine at least in a general way the successive stages of Shakespeare's artistic and intellectual development, but the editors of the First Folio, the earliest collection of his plays, published seven years after his death, had no such interest to satisfy and printed the plays without regard to the chronology of their composition. For us the artist is an element of his art, an element so important, indeed, that we call his art by his name—we say that we read *King Lear* but we also say that we read Shakespeare, and *Madame Bovary* but also Flaubert—and we want to see him as intensely as we can to know "what he is like," what his temperament was, and his moral character, and the circumstances of his career.

Thus described, the interest in the biography of writers may be thought of as essentially aesthetic. There is a pleasure, cognate with the pleasure we take in the work itself, in discerning a consonance between the work and the personality and life of its author. But perhaps inevitably we go beyond the discernment of consonance to look for causal connections. A work of literature is not an exception to the conditioned nature of all things: it is what it is by reason of the circumstances of its genesis, which are the circumstances, both external and internal, of the man who made it; and he in turn, no less than the thing he creates, is a conditioned being susceptible to explanation in terms of the circumstances that determined his nature. His parentage, his social class, the mode of his rearing and education, the surroundings and events of his early years all contribute to making him the person he is, with the mind and imagination he has. Sometimes he will say so himself, for writers have licensed our personal interest in them and our impulse to explain them by themselves doing that very thing in their autobiographies. Wordsworth, for example, undertook to explain himself in considerable detail in his long autobiographical poem *The Prelude* (which has for its subtitle *The Growth of a Poet's Mind*) by adducing exactly those circumstances that have just been mentioned—he was the man and poet he was because his mother was the woman she was, because the society of his native Cumberland was simple and democratic, because he was allowed great freedom to range the beautiful and somewhat dangerous countryside, because he attended Hawkshead School, because he went to live in France at the age of twenty-one, having two years before witnessed with sympathy the early days of the French Revolution. The explanation is very full and nearly successful—Wordsworth, who believed, correctly, that he was a genius, undertakes to explain how he came to be a genius and almost convinces us that he has done so. Actually, of course, he has not. He gives us a full account of his emotional development, of the steps by which he came to have the view of the world that infuses his great poems, and of his dedication to poetry, but he tells us nothing of how he came to possess the power to write the poems that so deeply affect us. He explains a mind and a temperament that are appropriate to his genius, but the genius itself he does not explain.

And because genius would seem to be beyond the reach of explanation, the attempts to account for Wordsworth's strange loss of genius carry no conviction. Although Wordsworth lived to be eighty and was productive through this long life, virtually all the work for which he is remembered was written within a period of ten years, the "marvelous decade" of 1797–1807. Thereafter, although there are infrequent brief moments when the old magic revives, the work, although not without interest, is not of the same order as that which makes him one of the great poets of the world. This sudden evanescence of genius is a phenomenon that arouses a natural and legitimate curiosity. One proposed explanation is that the beginning of Wordsworth's great period coincided with the beginning of his close friendship with Coleridge and that the end came when the two men quarrelled. Another refers to his relations with Annette Vallon, the French girl by whom he had an illegitimate daughter and whom he would have married had not the outbreak of war prevented his return to France from what was to have been a short visit to England; it is said that Wordsworth's guilt over this affair destroyed his genius. Yet another explanation is that Wordsworth's genius was the effect of his sensory acuity which is said to have deteriorated materially and abruptly at the age of thirty-seven. And still another is based on Wordsworth's disenchantment with and opposition to the French Revolution, to which he had at first given his enthusiastic assent.

All the explanations offered have a superficial plausibility (except the last which is contradicted by chronology and Wordsworth's own testimony, a consideration that has not kept it from being the most enduring and popular). None of them, however, bears substantiation and all of them make a false assumption: that Wordsworth wrote great poetry by means of a certain faculty whose existence depended on and therefore in some sense was defined by the presence or absence of one particular emotional circumstance. Nothing that we know of the nature of poetic genius lends credibility to this simplistic assumption.

The tendency to speculate about the determinants of genius was given strong impetus by the development of psychoanalysis. Sigmund Freud had not proceeded very far in the shaping of his theory of the mind before he expressed the belief that the technique used in his therapeutic work might disclose something of the nature of the mysterious processes of art. The basic assumption of psychoanalysis is that certain forms of mental illness are the result of painful threatening emotions which the patient entertains without being conscious of them. When these emotions are brought—usually with great difficulty—into the light of consciousness their force is mitigated. A further assumption is that these threatening emotions were established in the unconscious part of the mind in the patient's early childhood. With the help of the psychoanalyst, the patient conducts a research into his past and present life by talking about his conscious feelings as truthfully as he can and, so far as possible, without regard either to coherence or to propriety: he is to say whatever comes into his head, and the hope that unexpected and untoward things will make their entrance there is usually realized. The products of this "free association," together with the patient's remembered dreams, supply the clues to the workings of his unconscious mind, which are interpreted for him by the psychoanalyst.

Freud, of course, was not the first to propose the idea that something other than, or in addition to, the conscious mind was the agent of artistic creation. Plato had called poets "mad," meaning to say that they were "inspired," that their minds were under some other control than that of the conscious intellect, and this conception of the creative process was variously formulated in succeeding times, although it remained for psychoanalysis to develop it in a positive way and to claim that its method could accomplish two things—explain the personality of the artist and discover and explicate in the work of art meanings which were not consciously intended and which, though not manifest, are integral to the nature of the work.

The success of the first enterprise has been of a limited kind. The use of psychoanalytical concepts does indeed lead us to scrutinize more closely and with an enhanced sense of their significance the details of an artist's life and to be more aware of the complex and subtle ways in which personality is determined. But when the psychoanalytical method is used with the degree of elaborateness and systematization to which it can be brought—and to which psychoanalysts often bring it in their studies of literary figures—it all too often obscures what it attempts to explain, and, what is worse, reduces a personality to the sum of its neurotic manifestations. And whatever else the psychoanalytical method may account for in the personality of the artist, it cannot, any more than traditional biography, explain his genius. It is beyond the power of psychoanalysis to say why one artist is great while another is not. The late Ernst Kris, who was one of the most respected theorists and practitioners of psychoanalysis and distinguished for his knowledge of the arts, was explicit on this point.[16] "We do not at present," he said, "have tools which would permit us to investigate the roots of gift or talent, not to speak of genius." And he goes on to remark another limitation of the psychoanalytical method—it is not able to explain the artist's style, the peculiar way in which he uses the material that his cultural tradition gives him. As Dr. Kris put it, ". . . The psychology of artistic style is unwritten." That it may yet be written is not beyond the range of possibility.

In its other enterprise, that of interpreting the meaning of the work itself, psychoanalysis has been more successful and its concepts have exerted no small influence on literary criticism. Even those critics who do not accept the whole of psychoanalytical doctrine can find something essentially congenial to literature in the complexity, secrecy, and *duplicity* that Freud ascribes to the human mind. They have been quick to respond to the psychoanalytical assumption that in any human expression more goes on than meets the eye, that something more is being said than first appears, that the "manifest content" of a literary work, like that of a patient's dream or free association, is qualified, sometimes contradicted, always enriched, by the "latent content" that can be discovered lying beneath it.

VI

What I have said about the intentions and processes of criticism does not undertake to be a complete account of them, only a first view. As such, it requires that one further word be added to it. This relates to what might be called the natural amity between literature

---

[16] *Psychoanalytic Explorations in Art* (New York: International Universities Press, 1952), pp. 20–21.

and the criticism of literature. I put the matter in this way because it is impossible not to be aware of the opinion—it never prevails but neither does it ever wholly die—that criticism is of its nature essentially alien to the art which is its concern and, in fact, harmful to it. Literature, the opinion goes, directs itself to the feelings while criticism is an activity of the intellect, and therefore, in undertaking to serve literature, can only betray it, interfering with the exercise of its function, diminishing the immediacy with which, if left to itself, it can affect the reader. It would be wrong to say that, as a matter of occasional experience, this is never true. The ineptness or officiousness of a particular piece of criticism may make it true. The mood of a moment may make it true for the moment—there are times when criticism seems beside the point of literature and it is literature beyond the reach of criticism that we want, just as there are times when literature itself seems beside the point of life and it is life itself beyond the reach of literature that we want. But it is not true in principle. And to its not being true in principle the creators of literature itself offer testimony by being themselves practitioners, often especially distinguished ones, of the art of criticism. When, in 1922, the novelist and critic André Gide wrote in homage to the poet and critic Paul Valéry, he prefixed to his essay as an epigraph a passage from the poet and critic Baudelaire which puts the situation succinctly: "Through a natural development, all great poets eventually become critics. I pity those poets guided by instinct alone; for they seem incomplete to me. In the spiritual life of the former, infallibly there comes about a crisis that makes them want to reason out their art, to discover the obscure laws by virtue of which they have created."

Mind in the Modern World

[Delivered as the first Thomas Jefferson Lecture
in the Humanities of the National Endowment for
the Humanities, 1972, Viking Press, 1973]

I

IN 1946, in the last year of his life, H. G. Wells published a little
book which is surely one of the saddest and possibly one of the
most portentous documents of our century. Much of its sadness lies in how far it is from being a good book. Wells was old
and ill and sunk in despair over the Second World War; he still
wrote with his characteristic assertiveness, but he no longer commanded the lucidity which had marked his prose for fifty years,
and this last utterance is neither orderly in its argument nor per-
spicuous in its expression. Yet it does communicate its informing
idea, which is as heartbreaking as the incoherence in which it is set
forth. Actually, the whole import of the essay is contained in its
title, *Mind at the End of Its Tether*. With that weary and desperate
phrase Wells repudiated his once passionately held belief that the
human race might find salvation, which is to say happiness, in the
right exercise of its mental powers.

The creed had been simple and unequivocal. If mind were cleared
of its inherited illusions and prejudices, if it put itself to two tasks,
that of perceiving the physical universe as it really is and that of
comprehending its own nature, then what had long been accepted

as the inevitable rule of harsh necessity might be overthrown and mankind would achieve the felicity which was both its immemorial dream and its clear evolutionary destiny. This expectation, once the root and ground of his thought, was now said by Wells to be false. He had come to see that the power of mind which mankind required not only for the winning of felicity but even for survival was not to be counted on. Mind was at the end of its tether.

It need scarcely be said that Wells's little book made no place for itself in the intellectual life of the quarter-century after it appeared. Nor would it have done so if its mode of discourse had more nearly approached a persuasive coherence. The war, which had led Wells to abandon all hope for mind and the human race, did not have a similar effect generally. In the face of the dreadful suffering the war had entailed, in the face, too, of the close approximation to success that had been made by the brutish antirational doctrine of Nazism, as well as of the unimaginable destructive power of the new weapons that mind had brought into being, the prevailing mood was one of chastened optimism, which involved the expectation that mind would play a beneficent part in human existence.

Yet now, in this year of 1972, as I say the title of Wells's book, *Mind at the End of Its Tether,* there will, I think, be some among us, and perhaps many, who will hear it with the sense that it has a chill appositeness to our present time. Of those who entertain an apprehension about the future of mind, there may be those who do so on Wells's absolute ground, that the tasks which are now imposed upon mind are beyond its inherent capabilities. Some will locate the cause of their anxiety in the paradoxes about the nature of mind which seem to be proposed by mind itself through the realization of its powers. Others are made uneasy by what they discern of a complex tendency of our contemporary culture to impugn and devalue the very concept of mind. Whichever way the foreboding points, I venture to believe that there will be no difficulty in understanding how it might happen that, as I first contemplated speaking under the bright aegis of the name and spirit of Thomas Jefferson, there should have arisen out of the depths of memory the dark portent of Wells's phrase.

Between Thomas Jefferson and H. G. Wells there was no affinity of personal temperament or of class tradition, and certainly none of political view. And although both men put the pursuit of happiness at the center of their speculations about man's existence, the meanings each of them attached to that enterprise were widely disparate. But they were at one in the firm confidence they placed in mind, Jefferson until his dying day, Wells up to his last years. Historically speaking they stood in the same line.

In some respects this is a very long line indeed. It goes back to the philosophers of ancient Greece both in what might be called its aesthetic appreciation of mind, its admiration of the mental faculties almost for their own sake, apart from what practical ends they might achieve, and also in its assumption that mind can play a decisive part in the moral life of the individual person. In other respects its extent is relatively short, going back only to the Renaissance in its belief that what mind might encompass of knowledge of the physical universe has a direct bearing upon the quality of human existence, and also in its certitude that mind can, and should, be decisive in political life. In the eighteenth century, this belief established itself so firmly and extensively as to become the chief characteristic of the intellectual culture of the age.

When we consider the enthusiasm with which Jefferson assented to this master belief of his time and the assiduity with which he implemented it in the conduct of his own life, it is possible to make too much of his own mental endowment and by doing so to obscure one of the most important significances he has for us. Thus, if we apply to him the word *genius,* we ought to use it, as he did, in the quiet, unassertive sense that prevailed in the eighteenth century, to mean distinguished ability, rather than in the sense it later came to have, that of a unique power, an originating power, which puts the person who possesses it into a class apart. A unique originating power of mind Jefferson did not in fact have. He was, for example, a devoted student of philosophy, and it is possible for scholars to write learned books on the philosophy of Thomas Jefferson, yet none of them asserts that Jefferson was, in the modern sense of the word, a genius of speculative thought. He did not give new answers to old questions or propose questions never asked before. He possessed himself of the ideas of the philosophical originators of his own time and of the past; he chose among these ideas and made use of them.

I make this point, it will be plain, not to depreciate Jefferson's native gifts of intellect but to describe their nature as he himself understood it. We may say that it was on the basis of this understanding that he conceived the place of mind in the future of the United States. He held the view, which was characteristic of the eighteenth century, that men were essentially equal in their mental faculties. This is not to say that all men have the same speed, or agility, or strength of mind, only that all men have reason and that the intellectual resources of a nation are invested not in a few but held in common.

Jefferson's estimate of the intellectual capability of the whole people is part of the fabric of American history. A great scholar of our past has traced in detail the long unhappy course of anti-intellectualism in American life, but Richard Hofstadter also made it plain to us, through his studies of higher education in the United States, how strong in our culture is the opposite tendency, to conceive of intellect as a cherished element of democracy. Of this tendency Jefferson is the presiding spirit. A sense of what he expected of the American people in the way of intellect may be readily gained from one detail of the plan of popular education which he set forth in 1783 in his *Notes on the State of Virginia*. He is speaking of the instruction that is to be given in the earliest of the three stages of schooling he proposed, not the primary skills of reading, writing, and figuring, which he takes for granted, but the substantive matter by which the minds of children are to be formed. This is to be, he says, "chiefly historical"—the memories of the pupils are "to be stored with the most useful facts of Greek, Roman, European, and American history." Consider what he understands to follow in the way of intellectual process: "History by apprising them of the past will enable them to judge the future; it will avail them of the experiences of other times and nations; it will qualify them as judges of the actions and designs of men."

I shall not pursue in further detail Jefferson's views on education as they illustrate his confidence in the mind of the people but shall allow this one project to speak for the whole. It can tell us much about the fortunes of mind in the course of two centuries. Jefferson hoped that most of the children who were to receive the instruction he envisaged would become farmers or be engaged in occupations connected with agriculture, and it seemed to him natural and right that men in this walk of life should have had their memories stored with "the useful facts of the past" against the day when, as citizens responsible for their own happiness, they would bring them to bear upon the events of their own time and place. The facts of the past were useful because they gave rise to ideas, and in ideas Jefferson perceived a power which would countervail the power of property and thus make for social equality in the Republic.

Scarcely anybody nowadays will judge Jefferson's plan to be beyond debate. Our contemporary pedagogic theory will be distressed by the idea of storing what it would call the mere memories of children with what it would call mere facts and, at that, facts about the conduct of the alien race of adults in far distant times and places, having nothing to do with the desires and instincts of children. And searching questions are sure to be raised about the present state of the subject which Jefferson makes pre-eminent in elementary education. It will be asked, for instance, whether his view of history was not, as compared with ours, a naïve one. He did, of course, understand that history might be biased, that party-interest might obscure or distort the facts. But he did not doubt that the facts were to be known and that the narrative of them, which they themselves would dictate to any honest mind, would be the truth and, as such, unitary and canonical. This belief the historiography of our day teaches us to regard with skepticism.

It can be said of Jefferson that his sense of the past was definitive of his intellectual life. From earliest youth into his old age the intense imagination of the past gave impetus to his mind—as, of course, it gave impetus to all the shaping minds of the eighteenth and nineteenth centuries. Voltaire, Diderot, Rousseau, Goethe, Hegel, Darwin, Marx, Freud—all were rooted in their sense of the past, from which derived the force with which they addressed themselves to the present. None of them could have imagined that event of our day which one eminent historian, Professor J. H. Plumb, has called the "death of the past," that mutation of culture, represented by Professor Plumb as following inevitably from the full development of industrial society, which makes the idea of the past supererogatory and, for many, nothing but limiting and obstructive.[1] This profound alteration of our culture is explicit in the ever-diminishing place that history is given in the curriculums of our schools and colleges. The efflorescence of mind in the two centuries before our own seems so closely bound up with the vivid imagination of the past that we are led to conclude that the urgent recollection of what man has already done and undergone in pursuit of his destiny is a necessary condition of comprehending and intending mind. And if now we may be aware of a diminished confidence in mind, of a disposition to withdraw our credence from it, we might conjecture that this is, if not a consequence, then at least a concomitance of our diminished awareness of the past, of our disaffection from history.

II

What mind is, and what it should be, and what part it ought to play in human existence became an issue of public policy at least as

---

[1] *The Death of the Past* (Boston: Houghton Mifflin, 1969).

early as the eighteenth century. If we regard the history of Europe between the Puritan revolution of the seventeenth century in England and the yet more drastic revolution in France at the end of the eighteenth century, we cannot fail to be aware of a new element in the life of mankind—the ever-growing power of ideas. Professor Michael Walzer has said of the Puritan clergymen of England in the seventeenth century that they were "the first instance of 'advanced' intellectuals in a traditional society," that is to say, the first of a class of men who bring ideas, publicly expressed, to bear upon the nature of the polity, making it a question for debate how society should be constructed.[2] With the French Revolution this new element in human life reached a further development. Hegel said of the French Revolution that it was the first time in history that mankind recognized the principle that "thought ought to govern spiritual reality."

An early consequence of this new expectation of mind was that it gave rise to a certain coarseness of intellectual procedure—to what we call, with some adverse force, rationalism. To be rational, to be reasonable, is a good thing, but when we say of a thinker that he is committed to rationalism, we mean to convey a pejorative judgment. It expresses our sense that he conceives of the universe and man in a simplistic way, and often it suggests that his thought proceeds on the assumption that there is a close analogy to be drawn between man and a machine. This analogy, if for some it guaranteed optimism about the possibility of the control and direction of life, was for others the cause of an intense anxiety, as seeming to limit the freedom and dignity of man. To the principle of the machine the antagonists of rationalism opposed the principle of the organism, the view that man and his institutions are not designed and contrived but have their autonomous existence through the inherent laws of their growth and development.

The powerful cultural tendency to which we give the name Ro-

2 *The Revolution of the Saints* (New York: Atheneum, 1965).

manticism is defined by its effort to correct the theory of the mind which had become dominant in the eighteenth century. Opposing itself to what Pascal had called the "spirit of geometry," that is to say, the programmatic isolation of the cognitive process from feeling, imagination, and will, Romanticism insisted that these faculties were integral to any right conception of mind. Wordsworth's great auto-biographical poem *The Prelude* gives the classic account of the damage done to the mind of the individual, to its powers of cognition no less than to its vital force, by the scientistic conception of mind that prevailed among intellectuals at the time of the French Revolution. The explanatory subtitle of the poem is "The Growth of the Poet's Mind"—for Wordsworth, the poet's mind was the normative mind of man. It grew, he said, not through the strengthening of its powers of analysis and abstraction but through the development of feeling, imagination, and will.

Wordsworth's attitude toward science has a peculiar pertinence to any canvass of the situation of mind in our own culture. One of the best remembered things about Wordsworth is the antagonism to science he expressed, but it is scarcely less characteristic of his thought that he did not consent to see the poetic mind and the sci-entific mind as being in final opposition to each other. On the con-trary, he asserted that there was a natural affinity between them. "Poetry," he said, ". . . is the impassioned expression which is on the countenance of all science," and he predicted that the day would come when the discoveries of scientists would be "as proper objects of the Poet's art as any which can be employed." There was, how-ever, one condition which he said must prevail before this happy state of affairs could come about—that the substance of science should become familiar to those who are not scientists. No one will suppose that this familiarity has been achieved. Physical science in our day lies beyond the intellectual grasp of most men. The news-papers inform us in a loose, general way of its great dramatic events. We have our opinions of its practical consequences, but its operative conceptions are alien to the mass of educated persons. They generate no cosmic speculations, they do not engage emotion or challenge imagination. Our poets are indifferent to them.

The old humanistic faith conceived science, together with mathematics, to be almost as readily accessible to understanding and interest as literature and history. Jefferson took this for granted. The belief that the fully developed man—the "whole man," as the phrase goes, or went—must have, and would want to have, *some* knowledge of science and mathematics was until recently taken for granted in the American theory of higher education and was implemented in the requirements of the curriculum. These requirements, it is well known, are undergoing severe attrition and in many colleges have been abolished. No successful method of instruction has been found, and the need for finding one no longer seems pressing, which can give a comprehension of science in its present state of development to those students who are not professionally committed to its mastery and especially endowed to achieve it.

This exclusion of most of us from the mode of thought which is habitually said to be the characteristic achievement of the modern age is bound to be experienced as a wound given to our intellectual self-esteem. About this humiliation we all agree to be silent, but can we doubt that it has its consequences, that it introduces into the life of mind a significant element of dubiety and alienation which must be taken into account in any estimate that is made of the present fortunes of mind?

But surely, it might be said, when it comes to the actual living of life this exclusion from science is not of decisive consequence. When Adam in *Paradise Lost* says that he wants to understand the mysteries of the cosmos, the archangel Raphael tells him not to puzzle his head over these abstruse matters and assures him that the "prime Wisdom" is to know "that which before us lies in daily life." The good sense of the angelic advice is confirmed when we consider that our scientific friends and colleagues do not seem any further advanced in the prime Wisdom than any of the rest of us. They see no more clearly than we do what lies before us in daily life.

But this reassurance loses some of its efficacy when we observe that, as compared with the relation in which we stand to physical science, most of us do not come any closer to the contemporary intellectual disciplines which address themselves to the affairs of daily life. Economics may serve as an example. In 1848, John Stuart Mill published his *Principles of Political Economy.* The book was at once a great popular success; over the next fifty years thirty-two editions of it appeared in England alone. The most widely read author of the day, whom Mill referred to as "that creature Dickens," wrote a novel, *Hard Times,* which undertook to demonstrate how deplorable were the human implications of Mill's views. John Ruskin, until then known only as a critic of art, attacked the assumptions of the work in a great series of essays which Thackeray published in his *Cornhill Magazine* until the outraged subscribers threatened to cancel. That is to say, Mill's treatise on economics entered into the general culture of its time; it was an object of the general intellect of the nation. We know that in our day no work of economic theory comparable to Mill's in completeness and authority could be similarly received, that any contemporary economist must think and write in terms which by their abstractness and technicality put his subject at a hopeless distance from the layman. In one or another degree this is true of the practitioners of the other social sciences.

In the humanistic disciplines the situation is similar. I have already spoken of the deteriorating status of history. Philosophy would appear to have become a technical subject for specialists and no longer consents to accommodate the interest and effort of any reasonably strong general intelligence. With my own discipline of literary study the case is somewhat more complicated. Over recent decades much of the study of literature has proceeded on the assumption—how it would have astonished Jefferson!—that literary works are not so readily accessible to the understanding as at first they might look to be, and there have developed elaborate and sophisticated methods for their comprehension which cannot but have tended to make literature seem an esoteric subject available only to expert knowledge. As long as twenty years ago some literary critics of high repute complained that the hyperactivity of criticism and scholarship had come to stand as a barrier between the ordinary reader and the literary work. This objection did not question the usefulness of literary study itself. On the contrary, it affirmed the faith in the inherent instructive power of literature which had long characterized American higher education. At the present time, however, that faith is being brought into ultimate question. Within the literature-teaching profession itself there is now a significant body of opinion which holds that literature, so far from having an educative power, can only obscure truth and impede virtue.

This view has been put forward by a person no less eminent in the profession than a recent president of the Modern Language Association, Professor Louis Kampf, who in his presidential address of 1971 assured his colleagues that the teaching of literature in American colleges is now virtually at its end, having lost all rational justification. Professor Kampf made reference to what he correctly takes to have been Matthew Arnold's shaping influence upon the literature-teaching profession in America. But he did not locate that influence in the part of Arnold's theory of literature where it truly resides, in the continuing force of the famous characterization of literature as "a criticism of life" and in Arnold's definition of criticism as the effort "to see the object as in itself it really is," the objects upon which it directs itself being not literature alone but also ideas in general and most especially ideas about society. Professor Kampf characterizes literature in a way that is at an opposite pole from Arnold's—literature, he says, is nothing but "a diversion and a spectacle," it exists wholly in what he calls the "realm of aesthetics" and thus stands at an ultimate remove from "practical activity." That is to say, it has no possible bearing upon the matters which must be the chief or only objects of concern, the anomalies and injustices of American life. Why, if the dereliction of literature from seriousness is this absolute, the totalitarian countries are so fearful of it Professor Kampf does not tell us. He is prepared, however, to name the exact moment when, after generations during which teachers were animated by their faith in the educative powers of literature, they came at last to understand that theirs was a commitment to a corrupting frivolity—the year was 1968, the occasion was the campus uprisings which, in Professor Kampf's view, at long last forced social and political reality upon the consciousness of students and teachers alike. Since 1968, Professor Kampf says, "the young go into the profession with dread; the old can scarcely wait for retirement; and those of the middle years yearn for sabbaticals." He speaks as the elected chief officer of the professional association of teachers of literature: in his estimate of the morale of his constituency there must be some quantum of truth. We can therefore say that in our time the mind of a significant part of a once proud profession has come to the end of its tether.

III

I have touched upon certain developments in the organized intellectual life of our day which may be thought to make an individual person's participation in it difficult or fruitless. But if it is indeed the case that an uneasiness has come into our relation to mind, we ought to consider whether this might not be something other than a response to particular alienating circumstances, whether it is not rather the expression of an attitude toward mind which is more nearly autonomous, an adverse judgment passed upon mind in its very essence.

It is a commonplace of our day to speak of crises of authority, and the glibness with which we use the phrase does not derogate from the salient actuality of what it denotes. One such crisis of authority, we might suppose, is taking place in relation to mind. Certainly a chief characteristic of mind is the claims which it makes, or which are made for it, to a very high authority indeed. Of these claims one goes so far as to identify mind with divinity itself, and it was once

usual to express the idea of intellectual authority in terms which
were explicitly analogous with social authority and the status per-
taining to it. The classic example is Plato's account of mind, which
asserts the superiority of thought to all other activities and represents
it as free and noble while condemning physical occupations, however necessary and skilled, as mechanical and servile; in Plato's ideal
polity all authority is vested in men of mind, the Philosopher-Kings.
Aristotle can imagine the right development of individual mind as
taking place only in men of high rank. The association of mind
with social authority continues into modern times, when, however,
the emphasis is placed upon the aggressive activity by which
authority is achieved and asserted—in the nineteenth century the
received way of praising mind was to connect it with the aristocratic-
military ideal: we hear of "the march of mind," of "man's uncon-
querable mind," of "the imperial intellect," of "heroes of thought."

But at the end of the nineteenth century a voice was raised to say
that mind in its traditional authoritative and aggressive character
was so far from being in the service of mankind as actually to constitute a principle of social evil. The voice was that of William Morris in *News from Nowhere,* the enchanting romance in which he
envisioned a society of perfect felicity. Two ideals were to be realized in Morris's utopia: one was equality; the other was rest, the
cessation of all anxious effort. To this end Morris excluded science,
philosophy, and high art from his community. His happy people
occupy themselves with what he had elsewhere called the "lesser
arts," those modest enterprises of the hand which produce useful
and decorative objects of daily life. Morris wanted neither the aggressivity of comprehension and control which highly developed
mind directs upon the world nor the competitiveness and self-
aggrandizement which obtain among those individual persons who
commit themselves to the life of thought and creation and which he
associates with the worst traits of capitalist enterprise. He wanted no
geniuses to distress their less notable fellows by their pre-eminent
ability to tell the truth or be interesting, and to shine brighter than

the general run of mankind, requiring our submission to the authority of their brilliance, disturbing us with novel ideas and difficult tastes, perhaps tempting some few to emulate them by giving up rest in order to live laborious days and incur the pains of mental fight. As Morris's young friend William Butler Yeats was to put it, mind says, "Thou fool," and Morris wanted no such divisive anti-egalitarian manners in his society. He would not even allow teachers into it, justifying their exclusion by his certitude that anybody could learn all by himself all that he wanted and needed to know.

News from Nowhere has always been regarded with a sort of affectionate condescension—most readers have been charmed by its vision of unvexed life but have felt that its attitude toward mind made it impossible for them to take it seriously. We in our time will be less disposed to condescend to the book which eight decades ago stated the case against mind that is now being openly litigated in our culture. This adversary proceeding represents mind as having two maleficent effects. One is that the authority accorded to mind leads to the negation of social equality. The other is that mind works a personal deformation in those who commit themselves to its service.

That mind could be thought to make a principle of inequality would once have bewildered any man of good will and advanced views. Jefferson thought that it was virtually of the essence of mind that it pointed toward equality, and his system of education had the specific goal of countervailing the power of property by the power of ideas, which he assumed to be accessible to all men equally. Yet we must see that whatever inherent antagonism there may be between ideas and property, they are not in all respects dissimilar. Between ideas and one form of property, money, there is actually a close analogy to be drawn. At a certain point in history money began to play a part in society which can be thought of as ideational—in England in the late Renaissance, in a society in which the aristocratic land-owning class was prepotent, money had a disintegrating effect upon the nation's class structure and hence upon its moral and intellectual assumptions. As Shakespeare said in the famous speech in *Timon of Athens,* which Karl Marx found so apt to his own purpose, money has the power to bring into question every certitude and every piety. It was the ever-growing power of money that proposed and propagated equality as a social ideal. And then, to carry the analogy further, it can be said of ideas that they are, like money, a mobile and mobilizing form of property. They are, to be sure, accessible to all and held in common, but as they come to have power in the world, it is plain that a peculiar power or, at the least, status accrues to the individuals who first conceive them, or organize them, or make them public. Men of ideas, perhaps even more rapidly than men of money, move toward equality with men of birth. Voltaire, Rousseau, and Diderot appear on the eighteenth-century scene as sovereign princes of intellect.

This, of course, was not what Jefferson meant when he spoke of ideas as making for equality, nor was it what the French Revolution meant when it emblazoned the word on its banners. But with the exception of equality before the law, it was all that established society was ready for. Napoleon's maxim, "Careers open to talents," seemed in its time a quite sufficient, even a bold, definition of social equality. In 1856, Alexis de Tocqueville, the great historian of the modern ideal of equality and of its developing force in the world, judged England to be notably advanced over France in egalitarianism because in England it was not required that a man be of gentle lineage in order for him to be received into good society and full participation in the political and cultural life of the nation. In England there had long been growing up a strong mercantile, middle-class culture which celebrated the kind of man it called "self-made," who rose from humble or simple origins to wealth, status, and influence through his talents and efforts alone, beholden to no one. The careers of men of mind might follow the same course; the necessitous childhoods of such imposing figures as Michael Faraday, Thomas Carlyle, and Charles Dickens were part of their legend of glory. And as the professions proliferated and their practitioners grew in number, more and more careers were opened not only to transcendent talent but even to ordinary competence.

No one said that this was equality, only that it was equality of opportunity. In England it had created the class of gentlemen which Tocqueville admired because it seemed so effectual a means of preventing the revolutions which plagued France, but there was no disposition of English society to go further. Carlyle and Ruskin in their impassioned demands for social justice were quite explicit in excluding equality from its conception. In 1876, when Arnold gave his famous lecture on equality before the Royal Institute, he observed that everyone in England repelled the idea of equality, and he went so far as to say that the English had "a religion of inequality," which accounted for what he judged to be the poor tone and style of the national life. Expectably enough, Arnold saw the cause of equality as being best served by the improvement and spread of the education available to the lower-middle and working classes, and in England in relatively recent times this has become an avowed national purpose, although its realization proceeds slowly by American standards. In America for more than a century higher education, to speak only of that, has spread among the population at an ever-accelerating rate, and nothing has so much confirmed the nation's happy certitude of its commitment to equality.

We know, of course, that this sanguine view of the equalizing potential of higher education no longer prevails in its old force. Indeed, in some quarters, it has given place to a view which holds that higher education is one of the citadels of social privilege. This change in opinion has led to a radically revised conception of the nature and function of our colleges and universities.

Up to a few years ago, when our colleges and universities were still generally thought to be a successful means of upward social mobility, this one of their imputed functions was allowed to remain at least partially tacit and they could still be viewed in the light of the ideal intellectual and cultural purpose which they traditionally avowed. Everyone was perfectly aware of their being a way to social advancement, but much of the complex interest they had for the American people, much of the esteem and even affection in which they were held, derived from the purposes of general enlightenment and humanization which they claimed, from their conceiving themselves to be in the service of disinterested mind. Now, however, with the rapidly developing opinion that our colleges and universities do not further equality to the extent that was once supposed, their equalizing function is being made fully explicit and the tendency grows ever stronger to say that they must be wholly defined by the function in which they are now said to fail. It is coming to be taken for granted that they are primarily agencies of social accreditation. They may still claim, though they do so ever less often and less firmly, that they are in the service of those ideals which are announced by the Latin mottoes on their corporate seals, ideals of "light" and "truth," but it is increasingly believed that their real duty is to enable as many people as possible to pass from a lower to a higher position in society. By an inevitable inference, the intellectual disciplines in which they give instruction are to be regarded not as of intrinsic value, but, at best, as elements of a rite of social passage and, at worst, as devices of social exclusion.

I think I do not exaggerate a view of our academic institutions which in recent years has become widely established. It scarcely need be said that such a view can lead to no practicable program of change, that serious thought about the nature and function of education in our society cannot proceed from its cynicism and intellectual nihilism. Yet we cannot fail to take gravely the extremity of its negation, understanding it to be the index of how bitterly felt is the *de facto* situation of inequality which does indeed exist in our system of higher education. If higher education is, among other things, an institutionalized means of upward social movement, it must be recognized that many members of our society are debarred from its process by reason of an ever more galling circumstance of their disadvantaged position, a limited acculturation and an early schooling of extreme inadequacy.

The redress of this state of affairs is imperative. To all appearances, our society's commitment to the correction of the inequality is genuine, even if, like all large commitments of any democratic society, it is not perfectly single-minded. And I think there can be no doubt that our colleges and universities themselves are especially active in moving toward it. Yet if we consider some of the assumptions on which the effort of redress has so far been made by our society through its government, we must see that they constitute telling evidence of that uneasy or ambivalent or actually disaffected relation to mind which has come to mark our culture. And no less significant in this respect is the silence of our colleges and universities about what is implied for their continuing life by the particular means our society has chosen to remedy the injustice.

I have in view the posture toward colleges and universities which of recent years has been taken by the Department of Health, Education, and Welfare. This, of course, does not bear directly upon the inaccessibility of higher education to the members of disadvantaged ethnic groups but upon the social situation that follows from it, the low representation of these ethnic groups in the academic profession. To this the Department of Health, Education, and Welfare has responded with its directive that institutions of higher education which receive government funds shall move at once toward bringing about a statistically adequate representation on their faculties of ethnic minority groups.[3] The directive does not pretend that this purpose is to be accomplished without

---

3 The affirmative action program, as it is called, applies not only to certain ethnic groups but also to women. In the text of my lecture as it was delivered, the latter stipulation was included in my paraphrase of the program's directive. I omit it here because what I go on to say about the effect of the program on academic standards does not bear immediately upon it. At the present time the number of trained academic women is perhaps large enough to support the frequently expressed belief that no lowering of academic standards can result from the requirement that women be proportionately represented on faculties. Doubtless it will eventually be possible to say the same thing of the disadvantaged groups, the sooner the better. When that time comes, the anomaly of prescribed social or sexual representation in the life of the mind will perhaps seem necessary to no one.

change in the standards of excellence of the academic profession. Since it is of the essence of the situation which is being redressed that certain ethnic groups, by reason of circumstances beyond their control, have not yet produced any large number of persons trained for the academic profession, the prescribed representations— the word "quota" is strenuously resisted by HEW—are to be achieved by the appointment of persons who are not competitively qualified but only equal in professional attainments to the least qualified person who in a given past period has been appointed to the academic unit in question.

To the general and ideal goal of this directive every person of good will is bound to give happy assent. And it is perhaps possible to find in its particular stipulations an arguable merit. It might be argued, for example, that if certain ethnic minorities are to enter the full stream of the nation's cultural life, a good way of bringing this about is simply to put them there. It might also be contended that for members of ethnic minorities who are students in colleges and universities, the process of their education will go better if members of their own groups, even if they have been appointed without particular regard to their academic qualifications, have some decisive part in it, offering by their mere presence a needed reassurance and hope. As against such cogency as these positions may be thought to have, it must nevertheless be urged that there will be serious adverse consequences for the academic profession if it is required to surrender an essential element of its traditional best sense of itself, its belief that no considerations extraneous to those of professional excellence should bear upon the selection of its personnel.[4] These consequences, we must know, will be felt not within the academic community alone but within the cultural life of our society as a whole, not least, we may

---

[4] I would not wish to be understood as saying that the academic profession has invariably acted on this belief or that, even when it has, its selection of its personnel has been unimpeachable. I mean to say only that, whatever the profession's inadequacies may be, the requirement that it act as if professional excellence is not of first importance is certain to have a drastically deteriorating effect upon its ethos, which, taking one thing with another, has hitherto been a reasonably good one.

be sure, by that part of it to which the disadvantaged ethnic groups will themselves look for sustenance.

This issue I do not now mean to debate; my point is only that the academic profession does not debate it. The profession must have noted that, by way of justifying the drastic sanctions which are being invoked against it, its traditional standards of training and achievement have been explicitly and as it were officially impugned, actually charged with having no other purpose than that of discriminatory exclusion. Surely it says much about the status of mind in our society that the profession which is consecrated to its protection and furtherance should stand silent under the assault, as if suddenly deprived of all right to use the powers of mind in its own defense.

The diminished morale which marks the academic profession in its official existence is, we may suppose, of a piece with the growing intellectual recessiveness of college and university faculties, their reluctance to formulate any coherent theory for higher education, to discover what its best purposes are, and to try to realize them through the requirements of the curriculum. And no observation of the decline in academic confidence can leave out of account the effect of a tendency which of recent years has established itself within the academic community, among teachers as well as students, the ideological trend which rejects and seeks to discredit the very concept of mind. This adversary position is now highly developed and its influence is of considerable extent. However specious we may judge the position to be, we must see that it is not merely captious—those who hold it are persuaded that the concept of mind which is traditional to Western civilization is an informing principle of modern culture in those of its aspects which are most dehumanizing and life-denying.

One ground for this opinion I have already touched on: the analogy that may be drawn between the authority claimed by mind, or for it, and an exigent and even repressive social authority. Implicit in the concept of mind is the idea of order, even of hierarchy, the subordination of some elements of thought to others. And in the carrying out of the enterprises of mind a hierarchy of persons prevails—those who are recruited to such undertakings must rise from the ranks, usually by slow stages, although some are inequitably privileged to rise faster and higher than others. In the institutionalized training of mind, some persons are given, or arrogate, the right to prescribe to others a certain degree of proficiency, to specify the means by which they are to attain it, and to test the extent to which they have done so. Such personal gratification as mind affords is likely to be of the postponed kind. Sometimes, it is true, the mind makes exhilarating leaps, but not often, and if its ethos has at times been associated with the aristocratic-military ethos, which, though deplorably aggressive, is at least spirited, a more common association is with another ethos of later growth and less vivid character, the work ethos of early capitalism, whose defining virtues are patience, the taking of pains, and the denial of spontaneous impulse.

The resentful view of mind cannot be wholly new, else the word *docile,* which originally meant only teachable, would not have long ago come to mean submissive. In our time, however, the social compensations for the sacrifice of personal autonomy which mind is presumed to exact have been drastically devalued, and, as a consequence, resentment of the authority of mind has grown to the point of becoming a virtually political emotion.

Another ground, a more comprehensive one, on which mind is now impeached is its commitment to the ideal of objectivity. What has been called the myth of objective consciousness[5] is held to be pre-eminently responsible for the dehumanizing tendency of our culture. It is said that objectivity has come to control and pervert our mental life through the agency of technology, which has established as a model of mental process in general the quite special psychology implicit in the method of science. The consequences

[5] The phrase is used by Theodore Roszak in *The Making of a Counter-Culture* (Garden City, N.Y.: Doubleday, 1969), which is perhaps the best-known and also the best-tempered defense of the ideologized antagonism to mind.

imputed to the domination of the psychology of science over our way of perceiving the world are readily identified, for, except that they are more extreme, they are those which the Romanticists saw as following from the ascendancy of scientific thought. One of these consequences is said to be the devaluation of the objects of our perception—even if these objects are human beings or human situations, the objective consciousness is accused of not permitting them to exist in their full integral being but only so far as they can be known in abstract and quantifiable terms. Another consequence is that because the psychology of science postulates that all the human faculties shall be subordinate to the one faculty of abstract cognition, we who as perceivers are under the sway of that psychology suffer a deformation of our personal existence, an acute diminution of our humanity. Our instinctual life is curtailed; joy becomes ever less available to us; our natural impulse of sympathy with our fellow men and with the universe we inhabit is thwarted.

No one, I think, can fail to take seriously this description of the mental life of our society. The anxiety it expresses has been with mankind for more than two centuries, at some times less overt than at other times but always there. In 1856, when the technological dispensation was as yet nothing like so encompassing as it has since become, Emerson saw it as having a malevolent power over mental life—"A terrible machine," he said, "has possessed itself of the ground, the air, and the men and women, and hardly even thought is free." The consciousness that some alien power has taken possession of human existence is now of the very substance of our life in culture. In one or another degree we all share it, we all are aware of some diminution which technology works upon our humanity.

But when we have given this much assent to the common characterization of the mental life of our time, we must see that what distresses us has nothing whatever to do with the intellectual ideal of objectivity as that has traditionally been understood and striven for. Objectivity is by no means an invention of science. It is by no means a limitation upon the range of perception. It does not imply the devaluation of the object that is perceived, its characteristic purpose is not reductive.

Actually the opposite is so. The aim of what we properly call objectivity is the fullest possible recognition of the integral and entire existence of the object. It has always seemed to me that the simplest and best definition of objectivity is contained in that phrase of Matthew Arnold's which I quoted earlier—objectivity is the effort "to see the object as in itself it really is." The object, whether it be a phenomenon of nature, or a work of art, or an idea or system of ideas, or a social problem, or, indeed, a person, is not to be seen as it, or he or she, appears to our habitual thought, to our predilections and prejudices, to our casual or hasty inspection, but as it really is *in itself,* in its own terms, in these alone. Objectivity, we might say, is the respect we give to the object as object, as it exists apart from us. Eventually we will probably, and properly, see the object in more terms than its own—what in itself it is seen really to be will make it an object of admiration, or an object of affection or compassion, or an object of detestation. This way of seeing the object, as something we move toward or away from, even as something we wish to destroy, is not precluded by the ideal of objectivity, which requires only that, before the personal response is given, the effort to see the object as in itself it really is be well and truly made.

It is an effort which can never wholly succeed. That it must at least partially fail, that the object as in itself it really is can never finally be known, is guaranteed by the nature of individual persons, by the nature of society, even, the philosophers tell us, by the nature of mind itself. In the face of the certainty that the effort of objectivity will fall short of what it aims at, those who undertake to make the effort do so out of something like a sense of intellectual honor and out of the faith that in the practical life, which includes the moral life, some good must follow from even the relative success of the endeavor.

We know that these reasons for making the effort of objectivity have never been universally compelling. And we can scarcely fail to be aware that at the present time their moderateness confirms the belief that mind is discredited because it cannot be in an immediate relation to experience, but must always stand merely proximate to it, that through mind we can never know the world in a way which is, to use a favorite modern word, authentic—that is to say, real, true, wholly to be relied on. These are, of course, the qualities of experience which mind itself cherishes. But as authenticity is conceived by those who take an adversary position toward mind, it stipulates that only those things are real, true, and to be relied on which are experienced without the intervention of rational thought. And it is on the basis of this judgment that the contemporary ideology of irrationalism proceeds, celebrating the attainment of an immediacy of experience and perception which is beyond the power of rational mind. The means to this end are not new; they are known from of old. They include intuition, inspiration, revelation; the annihilation of selfhood perhaps through contemplation but also through ecstasy and the various forms of intoxication; violence; madness.

The impulse to transcend rational mind would seem to be very deeply rooted in man's nature. Before modern anthropology taught us not to despise or condescend to it, the highest literary and philosophical tradition of Western civilization took sympathetic cognizance of it, together with the various means by which it is thought to be realized. Madness, for example, figures memorably in the work of Plato, Shakespeare, Cervantes, Nietzsche, and Yeats, all of whom represent it as a condition productive of truths which are not accessible to our habitual and socially countenanced mode of perception and constitute an adverse judgment upon it. No one is ever in doubt that their representation of madness is of the profoundest and most cogent import, yet no one ever supposes them to be urging it upon us that madness, because of the heuristic and moral powers they ascribe to it, is a state of existence which is to be desired and sought for and, as it were, socially established. To say that madness is for them merely a figure of speech would not, I think, state the case accurately. But while their representation of the powers of madness is doubtless something more than a metaphorical construct, it does not ask for credence as a practicable actuality. In our day it has become possible to claim just such credence for the idea that madness is a beneficent condition, to be understood as the paradigm of authentic existence and cognition. This view is advanced not only by speculative laymen but also by a notable section of post-Freudian psychiatric opinion with wide influence in the intellectual community. The position is argued on grounds which are quite overtly political. The line is taken that insanity is directly related to the malign structures and forces of society, not as a mere passive effect but, rather, as an active and significant response to society's destructive will. Insanity is represented as a true perception appropriately acted out—society itself is insane, and when this is understood, the apparent aberration of the individual appears as rationality, as liberation from the delusions of the social madness. From individual madness, its heartbreaking pain, isolation, and distraction blithely ignored, is to be derived the principle by which society may recover its lost reason and humanity. The project may be taken as the measure of how desperate is the impulse to impugn and transcend the limitations of rational mind.

IV

In what I have said this evening I have tried to canvass the situation in which mind stands in our nation at the present time. My emphasis has been on the vicissitudes of the situation, on those circumstances of several kinds which might be thought to limit a free, general participation in the activities of mind or to baffle its intentions and fatigue its energies.

As we look back over history, it is difficult to say what part mind has played in the life of nations. A nation's life gets carried on by many agencies, of which conscious and self-conscious mind has seldom over the long past seemed the most salient. Mere habit and inertia are powerful elements of a national life, as are old pieties, as are commitments to particular social interests or classes. And intelligence has always been of moment, what we call practical intelligence, which, in the degree to which it is effectual, is probably more than simply practical. But at a point in relatively recent history, about four centuries ago, there would seem to have developed some obscure unarticulated idea that mind, in the sense in which I have been speaking of it, ought to have a place in the national enterprise. I refer to a phenomenon of English life in the sixteenth century which Professor J. H. Hexter describes in an interesting essay[6]: the sudden movement of the aristocracy and gentry into the schools and the two universities. These had hitherto been the preserve of boys and young men of the lower classes who were preparing for careers in the Church. But now, to an extent which in some quarters was thought to be scandalous, their places were pre-empted by young gentlemen. The new tendency was the more surprising because it went against the settled tradition of aristocratic education, which had concerned itself wholly with manners and graces and had quite explicitly excluded all intellectual training as unsuitable to a man of gentle birth. Professor Hexter discovers no documented reason for the sudden change; he speculates, however, that it was brought about by the growing intention of the upper classes to take a more immediate and active part in the government of the nation. What their sons would learn at Winchester and Eton, at Oxford and Cambridge, the disciplines of theology and

6 "The Education of the Aristocracy in the Renaissance," in *Reappraisals in History* (Evanston, Ill.: Northwestern University Press, 1961).

classical philology in which they would be schooled, could of course have not the slightest bearing upon what they might actually do in governing the nation, but this seems to have caused no dissatisfaction; no one said that the curriculum was not relevant. Apparently the upper classes had somehow got hold of the idea that mind, not in one or another of its specific formal disciplines but in what any one disciple might imply of the essence of mind, was of consequence in statecraft and in the carrying on of the national life. What they would seem suddenly to have identified and wanted to capture for themselves was what nowadays we might call the *mystique* of mind—its energy, its intentionality, its impulse toward inclusiveness and completeness, its search for coherence with due regard for the integrity of the elements which it brings into relation with each other, its power of looking before and after. In some inchoate way these ambitious upper-class parents of the sixteenth century sought the characteristic traits of mind which they might incorporate into the activities of government; and in so doing, in pursuing their inarticulate intuition that mind made the model of the practical activity of society, they proposed the ideal nature of the modern nation-state.

With the passage of time that dim perception has achieved a fuller consciousness—we now judge societies and their governments by the same criteria we use in estimating the rightness of the conduct of mind. We judge them by their energy, their intentionality, their impulse toward inclusiveness, by their striving toward coherence with due regard for the integrity of the disparate elements they comprise, by their power of looking before and after. Plato, when he undertook to say what the right conduct of mind should be, found the paradigm in the just society. We reverse that procedure, finding the paradigm of a just society in the right conduct of mind.

In describing some of the special vicissitudes which at the present time attend the right conduct of mind, it has not been my intention to suggest that these, though disquieting, are overwhelming. I have not meant to say that mind, in Wells's phrase, is at the end of its tether. In my account of its present situation I have represented mind through its ideal purposes and through the procedures and attitudes by which it moves toward the realization of these ends, through its criteria of order, inclusiveness, and coherence. To speak of mind only in this way is not to describe the life of mind in its full actuality as a human phenomenon. Seen in its totality, seen historically, the life of mind consists as much in its failed efforts as in its successes, in its false starts, its mere approximations, its very errors. It is carried on, we may say, even in the vicissitudes it makes for itself, including its mistrust or denial of its own ideal nature. All these are manifestations of the energies of mind, and William James, a philosopher in whose peculiar largeness of spirit we may perceive an affinity with Jefferson's, was at pains to remind us that they, in all their ill-conditioned disorder, are actually a function of mind's ideal achievement. Mind does not move toward its ideal purposes over a royal straight road but finds its way through the thicket of its own confusions and contradictions.

This thought must always be with us as we make our judgment of the intellectual temper of a culture. Yet we know that when we cast up the fortunes of mind at any given moment in history, what makes the object of our concern is mind as it defines itself by its ideal purposes, by its power to achieve order, inclusiveness, and coherence. It is when we take mind in this sense that I believe there is reason for disquietude about its future, discerning as I do within the intellectual life of the nation, and not of our nation alone, a notable retraction of spirit, a falling off in mind's vital confidence in itself. The history of mind has of course never been a bland continuity. There have always been periods when mind shines forth with a special luminosity and periods when it withdraws into the shadows. In the past, when a retraction of mind took place, it might well seem to affect only such specific and discrete intellectual life as a society had developed: what was thought of as an ornament of the general life was no longer there and yet the general life went its habitual way. In our time this cannot be the case. When mind, far from being ornamental, part of the super-structure of society, is the very model of the nation-state, as now it is for us, any falling off of its confidence in itself must be felt as a diminution of national possibility, as a lessening of the social hope. It is out of this belief that I have ventured to urge upon you the awareness that mind at the present time draws back from its own freedom and power, from its own delight in itself. That my having done so is not a counsel of despair is assured by one characteristic of mind, its wish to be conscious of itself, with what this implies of its ability to examine a course it has taken and to correct it.

Art, Will, and Necessity

[Rewritten version of a lecture first delivered at Cambridge University, 1973]

I

IT IS one of the defining characteristics of our contemporary civilization that in the degree we cherish art and make it the object of our piety we see it as perpetually problematical. From the eighteenth century onward, enlightened opinion has held that art plays an important part in the life of the individual and of society, some would say a decisive part. But although art is regarded as momentous in its function, which is sometimes said to be no less than that of providing the significance of life, nothing is more typical of our cultural activity than our periodic discovery that art is not so serviceable as it was supposed to be or that it has lost some measure of the power it once had. Art, we might say, exists for us through our crises of belief in its potency. We experience it not through pleasure, as men did in former times, but through anxiety—through our uneasiness over its status and over its chances of survival, and through our sense that we do it injury by holding false ideas about its nature and about the ways in which it works for our good.

Sometimes we are saddened that our devotion to art finds no mode of expression more carefree than this. But it does not. Our gray, moralistic relation to art appears to be an element of the modern fate. And this fate I submit to when in my talk here this evening I undertake to speculate about our cultural situation at the present time by remarking on the part that is played in art, and in our experience of art, by the faculty—as once it was called —of the will.

The concept of the will no longer figures significantly in the systematic psychology of our day. Those of us who are old enough to have been brought up in the shadow of the nineteenth century can recall how important the will was once thought to be in the conduct of the personal life, how confidently our parents and teachers pointed to the practical as well as the moral advantages of having a will of developed strength and discipline. Nothing could be more alien to the contemporary style of rearing and teaching the young. In the nineteenth century the will was a central and controlling topic in psychological and ethical theory—as how could it not be, given an economic system in which the unshakeable resolve of the industrial entrepreneur was of the essence, and given the temperaments of its great cultural figures? Goethe, Byron, Balzac, Dickens—to name just these few practitioners of the single art of literature is to suggest how salient was the will in the personal life of individual artists and the extent to which it preoccupied the moral imagination of the age. A chief subject of the literature of the nineteenth century was the physiology and hygiene of the will, what its normality consisted in, what were its pathologies of excess or deficiency, what were its right and wrong goals.

For us, as I say, the will has lost virtually all this former standing. This does not mean, however, that it can no longer be thought about, if only anonymously. And in fact I am going to talk this evening about two recent critical documents which seem to me to be of high significance in what they imply of the present state of our artistic culture and in both these documents the will, though not spoken of by name, is plainly a chief matter of concern.

One of these documents, the first I shall touch on, is a recent book by Harold Rosenberg, who for some two decades has been the most widely read critic of the visual arts in this country. The book is called *The De-Definition of Art* and it presents in unhappy detail its author's sense of a crisis which now obtains in the visual arts, perhaps threatening their very existence.

The other document is an essay published two years ago in *New Literary History* by Robert Scholes, an American scholar and critic of literature, who advances the view that the contemporary novel in its best manifestations is transforming the aesthetic of fiction in such a way as to promise a beneficent change, an actual mutation, in the moral and political life of mankind.

This summary description of the two documents makes them out to be dissimilar almost to the point of contradicting each other, yet I think it will eventually appear that they are in essential accord with each other in what they tell us of the attitude toward the will which at the present time informs our high culture.

II

An understanding of the dramatic significance of Mr. Rosenberg's book should perhaps begin with a reference to the provenance of the essays of which it consists. With one exception, all the essays first appeared in *The New Yorker,* the magazine for which Mr. Rosenberg writes regularly about art. From the beginning of its nearly half-century of existence, *The New Yorker* has directed itself to that section of the affluent middle class of America which, while not committed to the most urgent aspects of the cultural life, yet wishes not to be philistine. In its early days the magazine was commonly described by an adjective which has since fallen into disrepute: it was said to be "sophisticated." Actually *The New Yorker* soon transcended this description and achieved a kind of bright, modest, decent awareness. This was signalized by the good-tempered wryness of its witty cartoons and by its famous prose style, which was obsessively concerned to be correct, lucid, and level, resistant to the intensities as well as the vagaries of current American writing. In its critical departments it was committed to an ideal of cool intelligence which confronted the vanguard of any of the arts with a grave amenity, a curiosity which was at once diffident and imperturbable.

But then in the Sixties the advanced culture began to press harder upon the middle-class consciousness than it had formerly done and *The New Yorker* bestirred itself to respond to this new exigency. The expression of its always liberal political views became more highly charged, and for its critical columns and major articles it increasingly recruited serious writers of note, many of whom had come to reputation as exponents of left-wing views both in politics and art.

Of these Mr. Rosenberg was one. It was exactly his intransigent dedication to the most extreme tendencies of modern painting that *The New Yorker* was honoring when it called Mr. Rosenberg to its staff.

As art critic of *The New Yorker* Mr. Rosenberg continued to put his strong and agile mind at the service of—to use the phrase with which his name came to be associated—"the tradition of the new." As Mr. Rosenberg saw it, this tradition had never been anything but exigent. In modern art, each succeeding instance of the new entails its own peculiar difficulty, which is not to be overcome merely by habituation. Taste and what it implies of learning to be comfortable with a new mode of art have very little to do with the understanding of modern art, which is not, Mr. Rosenberg tells us, to be regarded as exclusively a visual experience; it is also, and perhaps more decisively, a conceptual experience. The individual work of art can be rightly known only if we grasp the theory that brought it into being. Which is to say, as Mr. Rosenberg does say, that our response to the *words* that express these concepts is no less essential to our experience of the tradition of the new than is sensory perception. "The basic substance of art" (I quote Mr. Rosenberg) "has become the protracted discourse in words and materials, echoed back and forth from artist to artist, work to work, art movement to art movement, on all aspects of contemporary civilization and of the place of creation in it. . . ." He continues: "Begin by explaining a single painting (and the more empty of content it is the better) and if you continue describing it, you will find yourself touching on more subjects to investigate—philosophical, social, political, historical, scientific, psychological—than are needed for an academic degree."

The effort is indeed an arduous one and perhaps it needs to be justified by what Mr. Rosenberg goes on to tell us of art's beneficence, its unique redemptive power. The arts, he says (I quote him again), "have never been more indispensable than they are today. With its accumulated insights, its disciplines, its inner conflicts, painting (or poetry, or music) provides a means for the active self-development of individuals—perhaps the only means. Given the patterns in which mass-behavior, including mass-education, is presently organized, art is the one vocation that keeps a space open for the individual to realize himself in knowing himself."

In the virtually Victorian eloquence of Mr. Rosenberg's profession of faith in art's high function you will perhaps have discerned a note of conscious pathos. If so, you will have heard aright. Mr. Rosenberg's statement comes at the end of the first essay of his book and it is in this essay, which is in effect the manifesto of his developing position, that he expresses his belief that art at the present time is being deprived of its redemptive power and that it may even be threatened with extinction. This, I need scarcely say, is a grimly significant statement to come from the prophet of the tradition of the new.

The danger in which Mr. Rosenberg believes art to stand derives from none if the circumstances which are commonly known to be hostile to art. There is no question of a repressive government forbidding what is new or strange or likely to subvert conformity. Nor does Mr. Rosenberg suggest that the survival of art is being endangered by the indifference of a materialistic society. Even mass-

behavior and mass-education aren't the source of the threat. No—
the present plight of art derives, according to Mr. Rosenberg, from
art itself. And herein lies the drama of his book: the threat to art
of which Mr. Rosenberg warns us is a development of its own
nature. It is the logical outcome of its own chosen relation to
society.

How that logic has unfolded I shall try to say as briefly as possible. The account begins with the coming into vogue, in the early
nineteenth century, of the word *philistine* to suggest the character
of society and why art stands in opposition to it. Confronting bourgeois society in the materialism of its aims and the insensibility of
its power are those persons who, by creating art or by giving it their
loyalty, become the new Chosen People. These Children of Light
set at naught the objects worshipped in the crass life of bourgeois
capitalism. But bourgeois society, it turns out, is not so Goliath-like
as at first it appears to be. It does not wish to be philistine if it can
help it—it is not inaccessible to shame. Beginning in the nineteenth
century, at first tentatively, then more boldly, eventually by official
action, society set out to claim art for its own. And in fact it was
precisely those paintings which were most overt in their antagonism
to society and which had once been refused by the Salon which
came to have the highest value for bourgeois collectors, for mu-
seums and ministries of culture.

Certainly, as Mr. Rosenberg makes plain, no work of art in our
day is so extreme in the outrage it offers to society as to prevent its
being given social canonization. Almost in the degree that art expresses its contempt of all that is established and official, it is
sought and paid for—which is to say: taken into camp and deprived
of its antagonistic force. The readiness of capitalist society to accept the art that avows its antagonism to capitalist society is
therefore anything but the evidence of art's power; it is exactly the
means by which art is made impotent. The expectation that art
will supply the principle by which society can be redeemed is
little more than a self-congratulatory fantasy. No redemption has

occurred; all that has happened is that the highest achievement of the free subversive spirit has been co-opted to lend the color of spirituality to the capitalist enterprise.

To this situation the profession of painting—of the visual arts in general, but I follow Mr. Rosenberg in speaking most particularly of painting—has had but a single response: to step up the rate of its inventiveness, style succeeding style and theory superseding theory in an ever more urgent attempt to outstrip society's relentlessly accelerating accommodation to it. But the heightened rate of inventiveness has proved to be of no avail. Such has become society's appetite for new art that it will gag at nothing, and indeed in the last few years it has reached the point where not only the output of individual painters but the very idea of painting has been appropriated by society. To this the response of painting has been as nearly ultimate as possible: it is as if art would sooner negate itself than be gulped down in this fashion. Mr. Rosenberg puts the matter with a terrifying succinctness; "Painting today," he says, "is a profession one of whose aspects is the pretense of overthrowing it." That is to say, painting is in the process of "de-defining" itself, of denying the attributes of its former identity. And as Mr. Rosenberg proceeds with his exposition, he puts less emphasis on the element of pretense in art's overthrow of itself—in Mr. Rosenberg's judgment the de-definition of art will in all probability issue in the actual extinction of art.

In the course of outlining this belief, Mr. Rosenberg speaks of our present situation as one in which art is no longer thought to consist of specifically *created* objects. In a striking phrase he refers to "the heroic concept of masterpieces"—it is no longer the intention of the vanguard artist, Mr. Rosenberg tells us, that his effort should be controlled by "the heroic concept of masterpieces." The word *masterpiece* has traditionally suggested the exercise of the creative will in its highest and purest form. It implies that the creative will freely elects to meet resistance, not only that which is inherent in whatever genre is being explored but also that which the will, in its happy consciousness of its powers, seeks out or invents. It is from the kind of difficulty which the creative will acknowledges, or chooses, or invents, and from its manner of mastering this difficulty that the value of a masterpiece derives. Through the overcoming of resistance the masterpiece is produced and then itself becomes an object which offers resistance to the will of the viewer. For Mr. Rosenberg this process is a paradigm of what he characterizes as virtually the essential undertaking of human existence, the overcoming of passivity, the realization of self through self-knowledge, the forming of an autonomous personal character.

I need scarcely say that Mr. Rosenberg doesn't believe that it is inevitably in the nature of vanguard art that it should reject the idea of masterpieces. Nothing could be further from his thought. The great "tradition of the new" with which Mr. Rosenberg's name is associated, the movement of American vanguard art in the Fifties of which the pre-eminent figures were Gorky, Pollock, Rothko, Newman, Gottlieb, and de Kooning, was assuredly extreme, perhaps even outrageous in its practice, but it never lost its commitment to the heroic concept of masterpieces. Whatever hostility it directed to the bourgeois social principle, it was in this far social, and in this far traditionally humanistic, that it invited the individual viewer to enter into a complex transaction with its works. Implicit in its programs was the expectation that the product of its creative will would speak to persons who similarly valued the will and who too were intent upon overcoming their passivity to the social environment.

By Mr. Rosenberg's account, it is precisely this transaction that the vanguard art of recent years seeks to disrupt. We have not the time to follow Mr. Rosenberg in his adverse characterization of the particular schools of contemporary art he refers to—Pop art; miminal art; *arte povera;* earthworks; World Game; the staging of autonomous events which go under the name of happenings; art in which the project is described rather than executed. What all these artistic modes have in common is the wish to deny the validity of the traditional aesthetic experience. Which is to say that their ultimate goal is to deny the will as we traditionally know it.

This animus against the will, we must understand, does not always present itself explicitly and directly. Sometimes it takes the form of a paradox of a most extravagant kind, for nothing is more typical of contemporary vanguard art than the enormous claims it makes for the power of the will of the artist. Mr. Rosenberg tells us that (I quote him) "an excited view, recently become prevalent in advanced artistic and academic circles, holds that all kinds of problems are waiting to be solved by the magical touch of the artist. . . . So intense is this enthusiasm for what the artist might accomplish that mere painting and sculpture are presented as undeserving of the intention of the serious artist. . . ." And he goes on: "In contrast to the meagerness of art, the artist is blown up to gigantic proportions. . . . The artist has become, as it were, too big for art . . .": the only undertaking that is now thought to be appropriate to his status and function is, as Mr. Rosenberg puts it, "a super-art presumably able to encompass all experience." One does not need to be deeply instructed in the contradictions of the unconscious to understand that the surest negation of the potent will is the fantasy of the omnipotent will.

The situation which Mr. Rosenberg describes can have, he is certain, but one outcome. He tells us that "except as a figure of popular nostalgia," a mere fiction, the "post-art" or "beyond-art" artist is fated for dissolution. And of the art which transcends art he says that such existence as it may continue to have will (I quote) "blend into the communications and entertainment media."

To most of us, even those who are ambiguous in their relation to vanguard art, the prediction is a dire one. We cannot be surprised, however, that there are those who are anything but distressed by it, among them, for example, Douglas Davis, who is the art critic of *Newsweek,* a magazine whose readers are numbered in the millions. In reviewing *The De-Definition of Art* in *The New York Times Book Review* Mr. Davis acknowledges the intimacy that has developed between vanguard art and the public media and he finds it nothing but beneficent. He puts the case with a passionate intensity which obscures his precise meaning but not his general purport. "The media," he says, "the pulse of rapid information, is a fact of life. We cannot expect artists to labor at inclusive tasks for generations. They find and meet problems more quickly now because the rhythm of the aesthetic dialogue demands it. The media have plunged us not into Post Art but into Total Art." By Total Art Mr. Davis means an art which is momently present to the public consciousness and which we do not confront and contemplate but of which we are an element.

A similar response to the idea that art is moving away from aesthetic discreteness to a generalized state which approximates extinction is taken account of by Mr. Rosenberg himself in the essay he devotes to a French book called in translation *Art and Confrontation,* a symposium occasioned by the student uprising in Paris in the spring of 1968, in which, as you will recall, artistic culture was a salient topic. The contributors to the symposium were all of them Marxists, which perhaps makes it curious that they found it impossible to imagine that the creative will could any longer express itself to some good human purpose—several of them took the view that art, in any conception of it whatever, is so hopelessly compromised by its social acceptance that it had best be liquidated. In this they echoed and supported the animus against humanistic culture which the insurgent students expressed in their posters and graffiti, in which they rejected the whole tradition of personal development which is represented in Mr. Rosenberg's characterization of art as "the one vocation that keeps a space open for the individual to realize himself by knowing himself." According to the insurgent French students, art thus conceived, so far from being the agent of freedom, constitutes a tyranny: the will of the individual is being coerced by the will of art. What they oppose to art's traditional function of advancing self-realization is a concept of art as simultaneously a total environment and a total participation. As one contributor put it: "Art doesn't exist. Art is you."

III

I turn now from Mr. Rosenberg's book about the visual arts to Professor Scholes's essay about the destiny of the novel, with which I shall deal far more briefly. To make this move is to pass from the darkling plain of crisis to what is presented to us as the bright up-land of order and confident hope. While the visual artists have been desperately de-defining their profession, the new novelists—so Mr. Scholes tells us—have quietly jettisoned the old idea of the novel and, without any polemical fuss, have got on with the de-velopment of an entirely different order of creation, as firmly de-fined as its predecessor and apparently no less committed to the heroic concept of masterpieces. This new genre seeks no help from systematic theory. But it stands, if not under the banner, under the aegis of the mode of thought known as structuralism, whose im-plications for the moral and political life of our time are, as Mr. Scholes sees it, of the very greatest positive value.

To all appearances, that is, no two situations could be more unlike than those to which our two authors turn their thought. Yet quite as much as the situation in the visual arts which distresses Mr. Rosen-berg, the situation in the novel about which Mr. Scholes is so sanguine proposes the idea which concerns me this evening: the devaluation of will in our present-day high culture.

I am afraid that I must begin what I say about Mr. Scholes's essay by explaining that I am implicated in its argument. The essay is called "The Illiberal Imagination" and this may suggest to some of you that Mr. Scholes states his position by reference to a book of mine. *The Liberal Imagination* was published in 1950; it is a collection of critical essays which I wrote over the preceding decade. Mr. Scholes finds the book convenient to his purpose of explicating the new novel because he feels that it sums up the assumptions and values which once informed fiction but which fiction now repudiates.

Mr. Scholes's transaction with my book calls for no defensiveness on my part not only because Mr. Scholes characterizes my views with unfailing generosity but also because the issue between us plainly transcends personal opinion. That issue, which I believe must occupy the consciousness of our culture for a long time to come, is whether life is the better or the worse for putting a high valuation on the will. It is my position that it is the better. Mr. Scholes takes the opposite view.

The essays of *The Liberal Imagination* were not concerned exclusively with literature and those that did deal with literature were not only about the novel, but Mr. Scholes is justified in concentrating upon what I said about that genre. What I said was not remarkable for its originality. I spoke of the novel as an especially useful agent of the moral imagination, as the literary form which most directly reveals to us the complexity, the difficulty, and the interest of life in society, and which best instructs us in our human variety and contradiction. All this had been said many times before and if any particular interest attached to my saying it in the decade of the Forties, it was because I said it with a polemical purpose and with reference to a particular political-cultural situation.

At our distance in time the significance of this situation is perhaps not easily recalled. I speak of the commitment that a large segment of the intelligentsia of the West gave to the degraded version of Marxism known as Stalinism. No one, of course, called himself a Stalinist; it was the pejorative designation used by those members of the class of advanced intellectuals who were its opponents. At its center was the belief that the Soviet Union had resolved all social and political contradictions and was well on the way toward realizing the highest possibilities of human life. The facts which refuted this certitude were not hard to come by but the wish to ignore them was resolute, which is to say that the position of the Stalinist intellectuals of the West was not, in any true conception of politics, a political position at all but, rather, the expression of a settled disgust with politics, or at least with what politics entails of contingency, vigilance, and effort. In an imposed monolithic government they saw the promise of rest from the particular acts of will which are needed to meet the many, often clashing requirements of democratic society. The Stalinists of the West were not commonly revolutionaries, they were what used to be called fellow-travellers but they cherished the idea of revolution as the final, all-embracing act of will which would forever end the exertions of our individual wills. Failing the immediate actuality of revolution, their animus against individual will expressed itself in moral and cultural attitudes which devalued all the gratuitous manifestations of feeling, of thought, and of art, of all such energies of the human spirit as are marked by spontaneity, complexity, and variety.

All my essays of the Forties were written from my sense of this dull, repressive tendency of opinion which was coming to dominate the old ethos of liberal enlightenment. The opposition I offered to it was of the simplest kind, consisting of not much more than my saying to people who prided themselves on being liberals that liberalism was 1) a political position and 2) a political position that affirmed the value of individual existence in all its variousness, complexity, and difficulty, and that, since this was so, literature had a bearing upon political conduct because literature, especially the novel, is the human activity that takes the fullest and most precise account of variousness, complexity, difficulty—and possibility.

Well, I wrote at the mid-point of our century, and in the years that have intervened the novel has undergone a mutation which manifestly makes my old characterization of it obsolete. To Mr. Scholes the change is a welcome one. Its best and most significant aspects result, he says, from the novel's having come under the influence of structuralism, which he speaks of as "the most vigorous current of thought in modern life." Structuralism, according to Mr. Scholes's description, is a mode of thought defined by the emphasis it puts upon "the universal and systematic at the expense of the individual and idiosyncratic." Its effect upon the novel is most clearly revealed in the way in which the characters who figure in fictional narrative are conceived. The novel in its traditional form confirmed the liberal ethos by its loving and enthusiastic account of individual characters, by the attention it paid to the particularities of individual personality—to what, with a certain condescension, Mr. Scholes calls individual *quirkiness*—even though this principle of individuation went along with another and opposite principle, that of typification—the representation, that is, of certain categories of humanity. The novelists of today, however—and Mr. Scholes refers to Iris Murdoch, Barth, Pynchon, Fowles, Coover— are no longer interested in individual fates, but only in one or another mode of typification, and as an aspect of this programmatic preference they represent human existence not as a series of contingencies but as a *structure,* a discernible pattern of reiterated destinies in which personal intention is but one of several formal elements.

And it is in this concentration upon the pattern of events and circumstances and in the subordination of personal intention that Mr. Scholes discovers the momentous moral implications of the new novel. He does not put it so, but we cannot fail to see that what gratifies him in the new fiction is its desire to purge itself of its old concern, its undeviating nineteenth-century concern, with the will of its characters, who want so much from life—money, rank, achievement, fame, each other—and with the will of the reader who wants these things too and seeks to learn what are his chances of getting them and at what cost; and not least with the will of the novelist himself, so all too imperious, Mr. Scholes tells us, in encompassing and directing his world, controlling his characters, assigning them their fates, instructing his readers in the way life goes and in how they ought to feel about it and what they ought to do about it.

And how much it all was thought to matter! Pain was momentous, so also were relief and joy, because it was believed that each person happened only once and would never recur—which is to say, each life, like the culture in which it was lived out, was a history. It began, it developed, it came to an end. And in this history what was decisive was its end—for it was the end that suggested the extent to which things mattered and the reason why the will had better exert itself to the fullest extent of its power.

But if things are not singular, as once was believed and as the traditional novel urged us to believe, if a life is not to be seen as a history, then the end, if we are to conceive it at all, is not decisive. Things do not matter to the degree that we once supposed and the will need not exert itself as was once expected. In other words, if I read Mr. Scholes aright, what constitutes the tremendous moral significance he attributes to the new novel is the diminished demand it makes upon the will. Indeed, so great is his estimate of the redemptive power of the structuralist vision that it permits him to speak of the new novel as portending a "politics of love," thus licensing the hope—did we not make its acquaintance some decades ago, in the program of Stalinist liberalism?—that the conflict of wills may be brought to an end and order made to prevail in the conduct of human affairs.

IV

There is a point in *The De-Definition of Art*—it is in the essay on the French symposium to which I have referred—where Mr. Rosenberg uses a phrase with which I should like to lead to my conclusion. He has been speaking of the importance which is now commonly attached to eliminating the distance between audience and art-object or art-event; he refers particularly to the success in this regard of American rock festivals. The store that is nowadays put upon merging the audience with the art-object or art-event he explains as arising from the wish to (I quote him) "dispense with ego-values." In the context it is unmistakable that he is using the word *ego* in its precise Freudian meaning.

According to Freud, in the very earliest stages of infancy, the self is not experienced, let alone conceived, as separate from its environment. In the first months of life the universe is, as it were, contained within the infant's sensory system. Only by gradual stages in the process of maturation does the infant come to perceive that the world is external to it and independent of it, and learns to surrender the omnipotence of its subjectivity. Recognizing the imperative nature of the objectified universe, the infant acquires the ability to deal with the external world in individual acts of will. Thus it survives, and to the agency of its survival, to that element of the psychic economy which has guided the infant in making this necessary differentiation between itself as subject and the world as object, Freud gave the name of ego.

The development of the ego is a process of infinite complexity, of which one aspect is its periodic reluctance to go forward in its growth. Sometimes it is tempted to regress to a less active and effectual stage, even to turn back to the comfortable condition of subjective omnipotence, to the megalomania of infantile narcissism. Yet, typically, of course, the positive tendency of the ego is strong, so strong, in fact, that the ego goes well beyond its primary function of seeing to the survival of the individual and comes to define itself in activities—art, sport, speculation, invention, play of all kinds—which are not dictated by necessity but are, as we say, gratuitous, undertaken only for the sake of the ego's delight in itself.

We assess these gratuitous undertakings of the ego more complicatedly than we are readily aware of. In general, we value them highly: they make the substance of our imagination of freedom and happiness. Yet at the same time we regard them with a certain disquiet because, while the ego does indeed find delight in going beyond necessity, it also looks to necessity for the assurance of its integrity and authority, which necessity had evoked and continues to affirm. We happily assent to Schiller's idea that "man is most fully human when he plays," yet we have but to read about an imagined society, such as William Morris depicts in *News from No-*

where, where there is almost no necessity and where virtually every.
activity is a form of play, to know from the anxiety that is aroused
in us by this state of affairs how much we count on necessity to assure us that the ego is actual and authoritative. Nietzsche, speaking
of the condition of mind which would follow from the realization
that God is dead, said that for some time to come men would experience the uncomfortable state which he called *weightlessness.*
The word may be used to describe the similarly unhappy state
which is associated with the sense that necessity has lost its imperative force.

It is possible, I think, to write the psycho-cultural history of the
nineteenth century in terms of its anxious concern over the threat to
the ego when necessity is diminished in power. The issue was tersely
stated by William James as the nineteenth century drew to its close.
"If this life be not a real fight," James wrote, "in which something is
eternally gained for the universe by success, it is no better than a
game of private theatricals from which we may withdraw at will."
James was not able to say with certitude that life *was* a real fight,
though what he could say seems to have served his purpose: "But it
feels like a fight." His culture made it possible for him to affirm
necessity in at least this far: that *something* demanded of him the
exercise of his will and that therefore his ego had the traditional
evidence that it was actual.

The careful balance between will and necessity which the nineteenth century undertook to maintain was no mere psychological
construct. It reflected realities of the culture, in particular the technological situation of the time. Although it was a day in which the
practical requirements of life were met with confidence and ingenuity, there could be no promise that the attainment of goals was inevitable. Too, although society had become measurably more open
and the rate of mobility, at least within the middle class, had increased, the making of a career was still far from something that
even a member of the middle class could take for granted. There
were far fewer professions than we know today, and those there

were were not rationalized. Society was penetrable only by the few, and even by these only with great effort. A life had to be shaped, devised, battled for. Necessity, in short, made the actual condition of human experience.

But of course it still does, however we may try to persuade ourselves to the contrary—except that we no longer believe that it *should*. A perfecting technology, a growing confidence in rational system, a new drama of social mobility—all these elements of modernity have had their effect on us. And, in consequence, necessity figures in the modern imagination as only contingently necessary, in fact as an anomaly which continues in existence not because it cannot be mastered but only because we have not yet put ourselves with sufficient energy to getting rid of it. What would be the human outcome were necessity indeed obliterated and there were no fight in which the ego took shape and then went on to gratuitous activity— this is a question we have no wish to ask ourselves.

Perhaps, however, the two documents I have talked about this evening force the question upon our unwilling attention. Both tell us, if we read them with due awareness, of the really quite dramatic degree to which the contemporary ego is baffled by the diminishing credence we give to the idea of necessity. At the beginning of this lecture I said that the older members of this audience would have the remembrance of a time when our parents and teachers held the training of the will to be a chief concern of their pedagogy. What I had in mind in using the word *will* in this context was that element of character which we mobilize to meet the demands of necessity— it is the *will* of that now discredited phrase *will-power*. But there was, of course, another form of will to which the old pedagogy was addressed, negatively: that is, will as willfulness, or will associated, most familiarly in very young children, with the narcissistic fantasy of omnipotence and thus constituting a counter-force to the will we associate with the developed ego. The prepotency of will which is asserted by the present-day artists of whom Mr. Rosenberg writes plainly belongs in the narcissistic category; it is the will of the undeveloped ego, unresponsive to necessity. From Mr. Rosen-berg's book we learn of the possibility that in the present state of vanguard art the effectual will, the will of ego, has in fact so far neutralized itself that art has been brought to meaninglessness and that it is even moving toward extinction. And from Mr. Scholes's essay we similarly learn of the reduced condition of the will of de-veloped ego: Mr. Scholes invites us to a world where, indeed, the will is to be so thoroughly abrogated that life will virtually cease to have meaning except in its formal aspects. In both documents we confront the evidence of a regressive impulse which may be of some considerable significance in the human destiny.

Aggression and Utopia

A Note on William Morris's
News from Nowhere

[A paper for a panel on the Role of Aggression in Human Adaptation at a meeting jointly sponsored by the American Psychoanalytic Association and the American Association for the Advancement of Science, Section on Psychology, Philadelphia, December 26, 1971; first published in *The Psychoanalytic Quarterly,* April 1973]

WILLIAM MORRIS'S great Utopian romance, *News from Nowhere,* is a work I once knew quite intimately but had not re-read for something like a decade. Recently, however, I turned to it again. My latest experience of the work was surprising in that it was marked by a mild distress, a degree of anxiety. When I tried to discover a reason for this, I seemed to find it in the book's attitude toward aggression. A salient element of *News from Nowhere* is its certitude that aggression can be rooted out of human nature. And when I went on to ask why this latest reading of the book should produce untoward feelings which had not occurred on any of my several previous readings, the answer that proposed itself was that a recent development of our culture had made this a different book from the one I formerly knew. It had changed the relation which the book's fantasies bore to actuality.

Over the last decade many people, young people especially, have come to share Morris's certitude about the feasibility of extirpating aggression and this circumstance presumably gave it a new immediacy and force when I encountered it in the book. I was therefore led to the supposition that my disquiet was the result of confronting the possibility of a life in which aggression plays no part.

I shall begin my discussion of *News from Nowhere* by saying a word about its author. The peculiar power and charm of William Morris are suggested by the deep admiration in which he was held by two great writers of the generation after his own, William Butler Yeats and George Bernard Shaw. The dissimilarity of these men is legendary. Yeats was committed to the idea of an archaic class-bound society which alone, he believed, made it possible for life to be instinctual, significant, and beautiful. Shaw in his day was the exemplary exponent of the reorganization of society on rational lines. Antithetical as they were in their hopes for life, both men acknowledged Morris as master. The young Yeats was encouraged in his dreams of an authentic existence by Morris's celebrations of the old cultures of Northern Europe. In the socialism which was the central concern of Morris's later years, Shaw found confirmation of his own vision of a society that would be the perfection of rational order and peace.

Of all the great Victorians, Morris came closest to being a happy man. His adaptation to life and the joy he took in it are almost unique in modern times and are deeply inspiriting. Whatever he put his hand to, he did well and to his own satisfaction, and with entire absorption and no strain. How he did so much is a perpetual wonder. He was a poet, a writer of prose romances, a translator; he was a brilliant designer and the most influential theorist of design of his time; he was an efficient businessman; he was a great printer and publisher; he was a tireless and cogent lecturer on social questions; he threw himself into political activity with passionate energy. The master doctrine of his thought, that work must be a joy to the worker, had been formulated by Ruskin, whose influence upon him was decisive, yet we cannot doubt that Morris derived it in the first instance from his own experience.

There was, to be sure, one discernible ground for unhappiness in his mature life—his wife, who was famous for her beauty, was indifferent to him and gave her affection to his close friend, Dante Gabriel Rossetti, with whom for many years her relation was most intimate although probably not adulterous. While this was a cause of great pain to Morris, and although he was capable of terrible outbursts of rage, he responded to the situation with restraint and amenity. I mention this circumstance because it bears upon one aspect of the ethical program of *News from Nowhere*—that which gives expression to Morris's explicit and intransigent antagonism to the Victorian sexual code and his insistence on freedom in the erotic life.

Even from this brief description, it is evident that Morris was a man on a very large scale indeed. His thought was large, was ultimate: its informing idea was the goodness of life, and its end in view was nothing less than making that goodness universally apparent and universally accessible. As much as anyone ever did, Morris really believed that this end could be brought about and he was ready to go to all lengths to do so; his revolutionary faith was entire. And perhaps not the least revolutionary element of his program was his willingness to jettison an assumption which is integral to high Western culture: that man's nature and destiny are fulfilled not through his success in achieving pleasure but through setting himself goals which are beyond pleasure—though not, of course, beyond gratification—and pursuing them with unremitting energy, with ceaseless devotion in the face of defeat and frustration. It is from this "effort and expectation and desire"—the phrase is Wordsworth's—that man's highest value to himself is commonly thought to derive; that is to say, his sense of his largeness of spirit, his dignity, his transcendent significance. *News from Nowhere,* which may fairly be taken to summarize Morris's social creed, wholly repudiates this assumption. It is overtly hostile to conceptions of largeness and dignity. It rejects the line of thought which connects transcendence with the putting forth of superlative effort and with the risk of defeat and frustration that this entails. Its conception of man's nature and destiny is informed by what might be called a calculated modesty.

This principled limitation of ambition had characterized Morris's thought from the beginning. The most decisive step in his life was taken when, disgusted by the domestic furnishings commercially available in his day, he designed cabinets, tables, and chairs for his own home and then went on to make the designing of objects for daily use his profession. By his furniture, by his marvelous wall-papers and printed fabrics, he intended an assault on Victorian taste. He did not take the badness of that taste to be adventitious: he believed it to be the expression of deprived and therefore morally sordid life, of personal existences deteriorated by a society based upon commerce and industry. The ugly and vulgar objects made to gratify the aesthetic preferences of well-to-do Victorians were not merely indices of depraved sensibility but also the agents of its perpetuation: their deadness made fullness of life less possible.

This was the rationale of what Morris called the "lesser arts," those arts which shade imperceptibly into what we call crafts, the making of charming and beautiful things for use and decoration rather than for the more momentous purposes commonly attributed to the high arts. Morris's feeling for the lesser arts went along with a measured but strong antagonism to high art. We cannot quite say that he preferred the craftsman to the artist, but certainly he preferred the modest and anonymous artist to the artist of unique individual genius. This preference accounts for his animus against the Renaissance and his admiration for the Middle Ages. He took a dim view of the great individual artist and of the pains and crises of creative striving.

In one of the several arts that Morris practiced, this doctrine served him ill. When, as a young man at Oxford, his friends praised his first attempts at poetry, he said, "Well, if this is poetry, it is very easy to do." He found it easier and easier to do, and although nothing that he wrote is without interest and charm, his later poetry cannot be highly rated. If he had realized this, he would not, I think, have changed his method of composition. It has been said, I believe correctly, that Yeats had Morris in mind when he wrote the famous last stanza of *Among School Children* which begins, "Labour is blossoming and dancing where / The body is not bruised to pleasure soul," which is to say, labor is blossoming and dancing where ego is not bruised to gratify superego. To the cruel demands that the superego makes in the psychic economy of genius, Morris offered a principled opposition. He believed that these demands went along with the externally directed aggression of genius, with its impulse to be pre-eminent and dominant which, in his view, put the nature of genius all too much in accord with the ruthless ethos of capitalist competition. There are no geniuses in *News from Nowhere*.

The book appeared in 1890, seven years after Morris had openly declared himself a socialist. The word "nowhere" has been translated into Greek by St. Thomas More to yield the word we commonly use for ideal societies, and Morris translated "Utopia" back into English in the title of his peculiarly English imagination of an achieved perfection of human existence. Although only an Englishman—perhaps only an Oxford man!—could have written this enchanting romance of summertime and river parties, of sweet meadows and great trees and houses that are as natural as trees, of frank, hearty fellowship, the quality of the book is by no means wholly encompassed by its particular national, and class, tone. It is a deeply moving book for it embodies an ancient and universal dream.

The people of *Nowhere* are certain that they have realized, and now momently experience, the goodness of life. The violent, but not especially bloody, revolution which led to this condition had brought private property to an end. This entailed the abolition of industry and the factory system, as a consequence of which the environment —a matter of great concern to Morris—is once again rural and everlastingly clean and beautiful. The Thames, whose pollution was notorious in the Victorian era, runs fresh and bright and salmon-thronged. Money is unknown and, indeed, there is no system of exchange: there is plenty of everything and the maxim of distribution is to each according not only to his needs but according to his desires, even his whims, which can be depended on not to go against the good of all. Because economic necessity no longer takes its physical and psychic toll, the people become beautiful in face and form, a state of affairs which makes it easy for the individual to love mankind. Longevity, though not extreme, is yet considerable and youth lasts beyond what we call middle age, with the result that life is lived without urgency and without anxiety. It is lived for itself alone, for its own delight in itself. In the life of each individual, the past now exercises no tyranny and the future is not exigent. The present is all, and it is all-satisfying.

The particularities of life's goodness under the new dispensation are easily enumerated. First, there is the consciousness of one's own being, of one's physical and emotional endowment and its adequacy and appropriateness, the experience of its appetites, all of which are innocent, and of their gratification. Cognate with this is the consciousness of one's fellow beings, the sense—the sensation—of community with one's neighbors and the confidence of their regard. Then there is love for a person of the opposite sex. (The sexes are equal but markedly different.) This emotion can be quite intense and it is recognized as a source of pain if it is not reciprocated: in the general felicity it is the only source of pain. It is also the unique basis of aggression that the people of *Nowhere* comprehend. They are grieved but not appalled when it leads to actual violence: it is not unknown that a man should be overcome by jealousy and kill his rival in love. Such acts are not dealt with punitively because it is certain that the murderer, as we should call him, will be moved to deep remorse and will never repeat his act. Punishment, it is believed, can serve no useful purpose and can only make its object resentful and hostile.

Then there is the pleasure of work. Morris, who read Marx and was influenced by him, could not, of course, have known the now famous early manuscripts in which Marx dealt with the alienation of the worker from his work and, in consequence, from his own being. But Morris's views on the subject are in close accord with Marx's, and his feelings no less intense. In *Nowhere* there is no alienated or alienating work. Some work is necessary, such as building, weaving, harvesting; some is wholly gratuitous, such as mathematics and scholarship. However, the line between the two is thin, and many people alternate between necessary and gratuitous work. Everyone does some sort of physical work; no one does work he does not like; hopelessly unpleasant and dehumanizing work is relegated to a certain few highly sophisticated machines which have a kind of secret existence, and there is no residual necessary work that someone does not find pleasure in doing. Even garbage removal gives gratification to some people. One such person figures in the story; he is an engaging man who also writes novels. Certain kinds of work, like harvesting and road building, are referred to as "easy-hard" work and are thought of as we think of sports. The most highly cherished kinds of work are those which require a combination of manual skill and aesthetic taste, such as ornamental stonecutting, ceramics, and the making of decorative metal objects.

No work is represented as offering difficulties of either conception or execution, or as making a demand upon the worker's reserves of energy and will. No situation requires the putting forth of more effort than is immediately and consciously enjoyable. It is never suggested that gratification is something to be postponed or that it will follow upon an end which is achieved despite, and through, frustration. No one conceives a situation of obduracy or intractability, let alone proposes that such a situation might be of peculiar interest. In short, no value whatever is assigned to that expression of will which we call aggression—that is, the expression of the will which is directed outward upon resistant or challenging objects or situations.

The state having withered away, there are no politics with their inevitable implication of personal aggressivity. Such questions of policy as do exist—for instance, where a bridge shall be built—may arouse debate, but never a passionate commitment to one's own views. Although conversation is not in short supply, there is no intellectual activity as we would define it: the world is an aesthetic object, to be delighted in and not speculated about or investigated; the nature and destiny of man raise no questions, being now wholly and finally manifest. The prophecy that Trotsky was to make, that when all the problems of necessity have been solved, men would attach their strong emotions to ideas about art, has not come to pass: in Morris's vision of the future, the judgment having once been made that grandiosity in art is not conformable with happiness and that Sir Christopher Wren had exemplified radical error in designing St. Paul's, the race has settled upon a style for all its artifacts that is simple and modestly elegant, and no one undertakes to surprise or shock or impress by stylistic invention.

Perhaps by now you understand the discomfort to which I referred, and perhaps have even begun to share it. Morris was by no means unaware of the possibility of his readers' being made uneasy by the representation of a felicity that depends upon the eradication of virtually all impulses of aggressivity. Indeed, he takes quite explicit cognizance of it as the one possible ground for some discontent with the redeemed life. At three points in the narrative this discontent is expressed, mildly by two well-disposed persons, more vehemently by a person whose disaffection with felicity amounts to an aberration. One of the well-disposed persons is the garbage-removal man who is also a novelist. He performs his public duties in a beautiful costume of his own devising; it is elaborately embroidered in gold and for this reason he has been given the nickname of Boffin. Mr. Boffin, you will recall, is one of the chief characters in Dickens's

novel, *Our Mutual Friend;* he is referred to as the Golden Dustman
because he has made a fortune out of his great piles of refuse, which
the English call dust. Dickens was quite conscious of the symbolic
equivalence of dust, or excrement, and money. This foul element,
with all the anomalies and unhappiness of which it is the cause, has
been eliminated from the existence of regenerated man. But so has
Dickens. Neither the characteristic subject of his art, the personal
fates of those who resist or endure the anomalies of society, nor that
competitive aggressivity of his genius which led him to refer to himself as "The Inimitable" is compatible with the perfection of communal happiness which Morris envisages. That poor Boffin of
Nowhere emulates his great master and writes what his friends call
"reactionary" novels about people who have fates through suffering,
but his books can at best be "antiquarian." He has no material for
his art from his own experience and observation, and when he tries
to learn about suffering from a visitor from the unregenerate past, he
is genially mocked and interrupted by his friends who think that his
concern with the "interesting" is a foolish idiosyncrasy. Morris takes
it with a degree of seriousness, yet he is at one with Boffin's friends;
he means to say in effect that human felicity does indeed entail the
surrender of that ideal upon which the humanistic tradition puts so
high a value—the imaginative will of genius in aggressive adversary
relation to the world as it is, shaping the intractable stuff of error-
laden and suffering humanity into high art.

Midway in the tale, the idea that regenerate life yields no interesting subjects for art is uttered again by a sweet young woman named
Clara. She gently complains that the people of the present are never
represented in contemporary art—"I wish," Clara says, "we were
interesting enough to be written about or painted about." And as
the story draws to its end, the complaint is uttered with a quite
bitter force and is met with an explicit and impassioned resistance.
An old man praises the former time—which is of course our time—
for the good effects which adversity and competition had upon the
human character, doing so with a querulous energy which justifies

his being severely dealt with. His own daughter is among his opponents in the extended dispute and she ends her argument with a statement of ultimate momentousness: "I love life better than death." To which the father replies, "O, you do, do you? Well, for my part I like reading a good old book . . . like Thackeray's *Vanity Fair.* Why don't you write books like that now?"

It is with this petulant, small-minded response that Morris ends the debate and seeks to bring into contempt an idea which is definitive of the high culture of humanism: that a chief value of life lies in its ability to make itself, and especially its various forms of aggressivity, the object of its own admiring contemplation. Keats formulates the idea memorably in one of his great letters: "Though a quarrel in the streets is a thing to be hated, the energies displayed in it are fine; the commonest Man shows a grace in his quarrel." And he goes on: "This is the very thing in which consists poetry. . . ." In the humanistic tradition, the aggressive energies, even when they are defeated, constitute the ground of man's dream of his transcendence, of his projection of his being into the permanence of the future, into what he calls "immortality" and "glory" or at least "dignity," which is to say "worth."

Morris rejects this ancient and compelling idea partly because he is acutely aware of its corruption in the ethos of the capitalistic enterprise, partly because in its uncorrupted form it is not accessible to the mass of mankind, nor conducive to its well-being. He replaces it with an ideal of life which, in my description of it, I have chiefly referred to as felicity, a word chosen to emphasize the immediacy and simplicity of its hedonism. Morris himself characterizes it in two ways which are more particular. Both ways suggest his consciousness of the boldness of what he is doing, the extent of the defiance he offers to accredited cultural assumptions. And both lead us to understand a little more precisely why *News from Nowhere* might generate a degree of anxiety. Morris says of the new dispensation that it is the regaining of childhood, and he says that it is the epoch of man's rest.

Childhood and rest. Not maturity and activity but childhood and rest are represented as making the ideal condition of man. It would scarcely become a layman to explicate to this audience the ambivalence with which these two states of being are regarded, the attraction they have, and the anxiety the attraction generates.

As I said earlier, the anxiety had not been in evidence on my previous readings of the book. As I recall my response to *News from Nowhere* some ten years ago, there was in it a large element of genial condescension: what a very pleasant dream! As an ideal of life certainly not appropriate to a fully developed member of Western culture, but as an afternoon's dream how very pleasant is this ancient imagination of the golden age, the pastoral tradition before Milton spoiled it with all that business about fame, and laborious days: life being what it is and must be, how natural and salubrious a dream to have.

So one might speak of the book a decade ago, but at the present moment it is not only a dream, it is also an active ideal. Even if B. F. Skinner had not published *Beyond Freedom and Dignity,* we could not fail to be aware of the deep animus against the presuppositions of the humanistic tradition that has established itself in our culture. By something of the same logic that moved Morris, hostile aggression, the aggression of man against his fellow, has been assimilated (perhaps not without reason) to that manifestation of aggression which presumably goes into creative achievement. The day has passed when William James's project of finding a "moral equivalent to war" can be warmly responded to. James hated war but he loved the idea of fighting: "If this life be not a real fight," he said, "in which something is eternally gained for the universe by success, it is no better than a game of private theatricals from which one may withdraw at will. But it *feels* like a fight." To an increasing number of people the moral life not only does not feel that way but ought not to feel that way. That special kind of fighting in which, as Keats puts it, consists poetry—in which consists high art in general—is now looked at with a skeptical eye; the pre-eminent genius is less likely to be thought of as having gained something for the universe and is now open to the charge of having sequestered for his own purposes the creative force of the race, of being an illicitly dominating figure. I think it can be said that there is, in general, a tendency to identify with the aggression imputed to nationalism and capitalism that element of "fighting" which, in the cultural tradition of the West, has been thought essential to the artistic life, the intellectual life, and the moral life, and thus to reprobate and reject it.

Whether this tendency has for its end a regenerate peaceableness or a new and ingeniously clandestine mode of aggression will scarcely fail to be a subject for future speculation. To suggest the likelihood of the second alternative, I refer you to Skinner's book.

The Uncertain Future of the Humanistic Educational Ideal

[A paper delivered at a conference on the Educated Person in the Contemporary World, Aspen Institute for Humanistic Studies, Summer 1974, *The American Scholar*, Winter 1974–75]

I*N the summer of 1974 the Aspen Institute for Humanistic Studies held a two-week conference on education, or, to be more particular and cite the phrase by which the conference was announced, on* The Educated Person in the Contemporary World. *It was planned that the first four meetings of the conference should address themselves to certain specific topics which bore upon the general subject and that the discussion at these meetings should be initiated by prepared papers. I was asked to deal with the question of what were the factors in contemporary society which worked for or against the likelihood that, in the late twentieth century, there would emerge an effectual ideal of education which would be integrally related to the humanistic educational traditions of the past. What follows is my effort to respond to this all too momentous question.*

Partly for Socratic reasons, but chiefly because it is my actual belief, I shall take the view that at the present time in American society, there are few factors to be perceived, if any at all, which make it likely that within the next quarter-century there will be articulated in a convincing and effectual way an educational ideal that has a positive and significant connection with the humanistic educational traditions of the past. At the moment, it seems to me that the indications point the opposite way and urge upon us the conclusion that our society will tend increasingly to alienate itself from the humanistic educational ideal.

Yet, although I would argue the necessity of this conclusion from the evidence before us, I think it necessary to stipulate, as I have done, that the state of affairs to which I refer is one that exists "at the moment." I wish, that is, to express my sense of how readily the winds of American educational doctrine shift, and that they do so at the behest of all manner of circumstances which are hard to discern, let alone predict. It is true that as I look toward the future, it appears improbable that the present situation will change; I do not think that circumstances are likely to arise that will call into being an ideal of education closely and positively related to the humanistic educational traditions of the past. And by this prognostication I am saddened, the more so when I consider how very little time has gone by since the humanistic educational traditions of the past were invoked in the formulation of an educational theory that seemed to have established itself very firmly in our culture, winning at least the passive assent of the educated middle class and the general approval of the intellectual class, as well as the profound loyalty of some of the best elements of the academic profession. Yet I reflect that the authority of this admirable theory of education was won as swiftly and as unpredictably as it was lost: that this was possible restrains, in some small degree, the impulse of pessimism.

A Columbia man is perhaps in a particularly good position to comment on the impermanence of educational theory, especially of such theory as takes account of the traditional humanistic conceptions of what education properly is. The history of my university over most of the last hundred years might be told in terms of its alternations of attitude toward these conceptions, and perhaps it will serve our purpose if we have before us a brief summary of its career of ceaseless backing and filling.

In 1889 the Columbia trustees deliberated over the expediency of abolishing Columbia College—that is to say, of doing away with the undergraduate school which was the original part of the rapidly proliferating institution and which was still its core. Because of the accelerating tendency of the College toward becoming a university (which it did at last by statutory charter in 1896) the undergraduate school was increasingly referred to by the absurd phrase, "the College proper"; sometimes it was called the School of the Arts. The proposal to abolish the College proper had been made by the then president, Frederick Barnard. He wanted his institution to get on with its new commitment to scholarly and professional graduate education, which was being shaped more or less on the then much-admired German model.

Had President Barnard succeeded in getting rid of the undergraduate college, it cannot be said that the loss to learning would have been a grievous one. And perhaps even the loss to education could not have been thought momentous. The College was a small, old-fashioned school, its curriculum limited to Latin, Greek, mathematics of an outmoded sort, a little metaphysics, a very little natural science. Looking back at it now, perhaps the best that can be said for it was that it was not committed to early professionalism and specialization.

In the event, Columbia College, the College proper, was not abolished. But it was kept under constant suspicion and constraint, and in 1902 Nicholas Murray Butler put forward in his presidential report his belief that "four years is too long a time to devote to the college course as now constituted, especially for students who are to remain in University residence as technical or professional students." And in his report of 1903, he proposed that a Columbia student be required to do only two years of college work before going on to a graduate school. In 1905 Butler was able to announce with pride that this "professional option," as it came to be called, had actually been made available to undergraduates. He summed up the meaning of the new arrangement in the following words: "The Faculty of Columbia College say that to prescribe graduation from a four year college as a *sine qua non* for the professional study of law, medicine, engineering, or teaching is not a good thing but a bad thing."

Why was it not a good thing but a bad thing? Butler was in no doubt about the answer. In those days what we call liberal education or, even more commonly nowadays, general education, often went under the name of "culture," and Butler said flatly that "any culture that is worthy of the name . . . will be increased, not diminished, by bringing to an end the idling and dawdling that now characterize so much of American higher education."

But, as I say, the winds of American educational doctrine are never steady. No sooner had "idling and dawdling" been brought under control by cutting down the number of college years through "professional option" than Butler began to wonder whether he quite liked the new efficiency after all. In his report of 1909 he offers dark reflections on what he now calls the "cult of the will," which, he says, "has gone far enough just now for the good of mankind." Suddenly it seems to him that young men are in too much of a hurry to become lawyers, doctors, engineers, and teachers, and he recalls nostalgically that the four-year undergraduate college did after all make possible what he no longer speaks of as "idling and dawdling," but, rather, as "the generous and reflective use of leisure." He is explicit in saying that it is not enough to be a lawyer, a doctor, an engineer, or a teacher; one must be something else in addition—a cultured man. We understand that he really wants to say that one ought to be a cultured *gentleman,* but he is canny enough to know that the time has already gone by when one might conjure with that word.

Butler's change of heart did not immediately revise the Columbia situation. But a decade later, after the First World War, for a variety of reasons which we must not take time to consider, "professional option" became much less popular than it had formerly been, and the "generous and reflective use of leisure" established itself as a proper mode of life for the young men of Columbia College. It was John Erskine, a scholar of Renaissance English literature, who gave it its most effectual form by initiating what elsewhere came to be known as the Great Books Program; at Columbia, the Great Books were read in a rather exigent two-year course for juniors and seniors which was called General Honors and remembered with gratitude and pride by everyone who was permitted to take it. (Not the least attractive aspect of the course was what would nowadays be called its "format"—it was organized in groups of about fifteen; two instructors presided over the discussion and were under tacit obligation to express their own differences with each other; the groups met, with a touch of ceremoniousness, once a week, on Wednesday evening, presumably for two hours but usually for longer than that.) Erskine was not a person of the finest intellectual temper; he stood on the edge of flamboyance and at a distance from significant achievement in his undertakings as poet, novelist, musician, and critic. But he was genuinely committed to the idea of intelligence; he wrote an essay which was famous in its day, its whole substance lying perhaps in its title, "The Moral Obligation to Be Intelligent." He believed that the best way to make oneself intelligent and thus to prepare oneself to function well as a citizen or as the practitioner of one of the professions was through a happy and intimate acquaintance with the great intellectual and artistic works of the past, books chiefly, but music and the visual arts as well.

Erskine put his mark on Columbia, and, indeed, on educational theory throughout the country. Mortimer Adler as a very young graduate student was one of the first teachers in that enchanting General Honors course that Erskine had devised, and the mention of his name will suggest the response to the Great Books idea at the University of Chicago and at St. John's College and at the innumerable other schools that were led to believe, though of course with varying degrees of intensity, that the study of the pre-eminent works of the past, chiefly those in the humanities, with what this study implied of the development of the "whole man"—no one then thought of the necessity of saying the "whole person"—was the best possible direction that undergraduate education could take.

It is not my intention to review in anything like full detail the career of the ideal of general education in this country over the last half-century, an ideal which, as I have said, was consciously humanistic in its emphasis and which insisted in the traditional humanistic way that the best citizen is the person who has learned from the great minds and souls of the past how beautiful reason and virtue are and how difficult to attain. The purpose of my historical reference has been only to put us in mind of how recently it could be conceived that a traditionally humanistic education had a bearing upon contemporary American life and deserved to be given an honored place in it. I recall my experience as a college teacher through the Thirties, Forties, and Fifties as having been a peculiarly fortunate one: I inhabited an academic community which was informed by a sense not merely of scholarly, but of educational purpose, and which was devoted to making ever more cogent its conception of what a liberal and humane education consists in. I know how eager will be the impulse of many to match my experience at Columbia College with their own at their own places; it is indeed a striking and impressive circumstance that in our country in our time it has been possible for there to be so pertinacious a concern with questions of what is best for young minds to be engaged by, with how they may best be shaped through what they read—or look at or listen to—and think about. It was a Columbia colleague of mine who wrote the classic account of the part played in American society by its tendency to anti-intellectualism, but Richard Hofstadter knew that this made a paradox, that in American society there is also a strong, if complex, disposition to admire and sustain the life of knowledge and thought.

I speak of the Thirties, the Forties, and the Fifties. But by the Sixties, something had happened to reduce the zeal for such education as set store by its being general, and defined its purpose as being the cultivation of general intelligence in the young. For reasons which, to my knowledge, have not yet been formulated, but which I cannot doubt to have been of great cultural moment, this concern lost its characteristic urgency. At Columbia College, the consciousness of this change in our educational ethos was made explicit when, in 1964, the dean of the College, David Truman, asked Daniel Bell to look into the state of general education in the College and report on it to the faculty. I shall not touch upon the substance of Bell's brilliant report, which was later published under the title of *The Reforming of General Education*. I wish only to commemorate as a sad and significant event in the culture of our time the response of the Columbia College faculty to the questions the report raised and sought to answer. From my long experience of the College, I can recall no meetings on an educational topic that were so poorly attended and so lacking in vivacity as those in which the report was considered. If I remember correctly, these meetings led to no action whatever, not even to the resolve to look further into the matter. Through some persuasion of the *Zeitgeist,* the majority of the faculty were no longer concerned with general education in the large and honorific meaning of the phrase.

Nothing could be further from my intention than to say that they had become cynical about their function as teachers. Actually, indeed, it was in some part the seriousness with which they took their teacherly function that led them to withdraw their interest from the large questions of educational theory; periodically the answers to these questions become platitudinous and boring, mere pious protestations, and at such times a teacher might naturally and rightly feel that he does most for his students not by speculating about what shape and disposition their minds ought eventually to have, but by simply pressing upon them the solid substance and the multitudinous precisions of his own particular intellectual discipline. I think there can be no doubt, too, that the growing indifference to the ideals of general education was in some considerable part an aspect of the new mode of political anxiety that was manifesting itself at the time. The urgency of the problems, the sordidness of the problems, which pressed in upon us from the surrounding world made speculation on educational theory seem almost frivolous.

But no sooner have we taken note of how things stood in 1964 and in the years of violent disruption of university life that followed—in the brief compass of this paper I shall not dwell on the latter—than we have to observe that the doctrinal winds are shifting once more, that the feeling about general education is changing yet again: we perceive that in certain circles, the circumferences of which tend to enlarge themselves, general education is being represented as a subject of ultimate and urgent importance.

Among those who have a professional concern with education, there is now a strong inclination to make the humanities salient in the ideal curriculums they project. Of the three categories into which the American system of higher education divides all learning, we can scarcely fail to be aware that the physical sciences, in their relation to general education, have come to be regarded with at least ambivalence and perhaps in a more pejorative way than that; their own moral nature is thought of as at best highly problematical, and not much is expected of what they can do for the moral nature of those who study them. It is no less plain that there has been a marked diminution in the confidence that the social sciences commanded only a few years ago. But on all sides we witness a renewed commitment to the promise of the humanities. Of the three categories of learning, this is the one that lays least claim to immediate practicality, to being effectual in what we call problem-solving, yet among those who are prophetically concerned with education the feeling seems to grow, and to be affirmed in conference after conference, in seminar after seminar, that in the humanities is to be found the principle that must inform our educational enterprise, the principle that directs us to see to the development of the critical intelligence, of the critical moral intelligence, without which—so it is increasingly said— we shall perish, or at least painfully deteriorate.

I speak of our society as being at the present time animated by a renewed interest in the kind of higher education whose moral content will help us in the right ordering of social and political existence. This is the interest in and the conception of higher education that is entertained by the educated middle classes and made articulate by those among them—among *us*—who have a professional concern with the process and goals of education and who are habituated to connect them with the welfare of society at large. But we can scarcely fail to be aware that this large, ultimate, and ideal concern is concomitant with, and possibly a remonstrative response to, an interest in higher education that has both a different source and a different purpose. What I refer to is the interest in higher education of people for whom its salient characteristic is that they have not had any of it.

Of the resentment that this deprivation arouses, we are nowadays all aware, but perhaps we know less particularly than we might what it is that the grievance entails. We all recognize that in our society higher education is the most dependable means of upward social mobility. Through it may be acquired the technical knowledge and the conceptual aptitude that make it possible for a person to enter the professions and to enjoy the economic-social advantages that the practice of them entails. It is a distressing aspect of the situation that many members of disadvantaged groups have come to think of education, not as the means of acquiring technical training or the preparation for technical training, but merely as a process of accreditation, with an economic-social end in view, which has no relation to actual academic achievement. How much this is ignorance and how much cynicism is perhaps not immediately relevant here.

But the grievance of those who have been debarred from higher education is not wholly understood if it is thought of as having reference to economic deprivation alone. Those who feel the grievance—or at least many of those who feel it—are not merely saying that because they have not had college educations they cannot make as much money as those who have. Nor are they quite talking about their unsatisfactory social status only in the simple way that associates it immediately and directly with income. Their grievance is social in a more complex sense, in the sense that it is cultural. Its nature is vividly described in a book called *The Hidden Injuries of Class,* by Richard Sennett and Jonathan Cobb. The senior author of this work proposes the idea that, although all enlightened people abundantly understand that the division of any society into classes implies that some classes as compared with others are disadvantaged or deprived or (to use the term proposed by the book's title) injured, the range of the injuries extends further than is commonly supposed. The overt injuries of class are the short supply of goods, of sustenance, physical comfort, leisure, security, freedom from constraint, and so on. But there are other injuries of class of a less manifest kind: for example, Sennett suggests that increasingly members of the American urban working class feel themselves to be in an unsatisfactory relation to high culture. So that there will be no misapprehension of what Sennett means, I quote his strikingly explicit statement of the situation: "The changes in [the] lives [of these people] mean more to them than a chance, or a failure, to acquire middle-class *things*. For them, history is challenging them and their children to become 'cultured,' in the intellectual's sense of that word, if they want to achieve respect in the new American terms; and toward that challenge they feel deeply ambivalent."

Let us pass over the negative side of this ambivalence to consider only its positive component. These urban workers want to become educated persons; they believe that being educated is to their advantage. They do not exactly know why this is so, and Sennett, the professional observer and recorder of such desires and beliefs as they entertain, cannot say with any definiteness what the advantage might be. As I say, he rules out crass economic advantage and such social gains as follow directly from it. He seems to suggest that the desire to be educated is associated with the diminished force of the ethos of class, that the people who think it would be good for them and their children to be "cultured" feel that they have lost a class idiom and a class bond—they want to be "cultured" because they have been deprived of the community once provided by class. They think of themselves, that is, as postulants for membership in a new, larger, and more complex community to which they are as yet extraneous. They conceive education, higher education, as the process of initiation into membership in that community.

And to conceive of education in this way is perhaps not to conceive of education as fully as might be, but surely it is not a mistaken conception: we who are concerned to discover what it is that, in the contemporary world, makes a truly educated person, cannot be greatly at odds with the view of the matter taken by those members of the urban working class whom Sennett interviewed. If we consider, for instance, that the word *initiation* carries archaic and "primitive" overtones, bringing to mind tribal procedures and mystery cults, we may suppose that a great deal of what we will say in the discussion of our subject will disclose our assumption that the educated person is exactly an initiate who began as a postulant, passed to a higher level of experience, and became worthy of admission into the company of those who are thought to have transcended the mental darkness and inertia in which they were previously immersed. This assumption has always existed somewhere in the traditional humanistic ideal of education.

But if, following Sennett's lead, I suggest that there is an affinity between the way in which higher education is conceived by traditional humanism and the way in which it is conceived, instinctually as it were, by a significant group of uneducated people who want to be educated, have I not in effect said that the educational ideal of traditional humanism can count upon being ceaselessly sustained and renewed? And if I have done that, then how can I maintain the opinion expressed at the beginning of this paper, that there is but little likelihood that in our time there will be articulated in a convincing and effectual way an educational ideal that has a positive connection with the humanistic educational traditions of the past?

I have used the word *initiation* to suggest the ritually prescribed stages by which a person is brought into a community whose members are presumed to have attained to a state of being superior to his own. Such ritual procedures typically involve a test, which, by reason of its difficulty or danger or pain or hardship, is commonly called an ordeal. It is from this exigent experience that the process of initiation is thought to derive its validity. The ordeal is presumed to bring about a change in the postulant, a state of illumination and power. In the German word for education, *Bildung,* a word which is almost comically notorious for the multiplicity of its meanings, which make it the despair of translators, both the idea of initiation and the idea of the ordeal are among its significations. Hegel, for example, speaks of *Bildung* as a "terrible discipline" by which mankind is shaped toward its higher next stage of existence. It is of course true that *Bildung* can mean gentle and gradual things, such as *development, growth, generation,* and achieved things, such as *structure* and *organization,* and, going beyond these, *cultivation, culture, civilization,* but it also means *fashioning, forming, shaping,* and it means as well the state of *being fashioned, being formed, being shaped,* which, in the making of a human being, as in the making of a Tyger, if Blake is telling the truth, are processes in which there is a fashioner, a former, a shaper, who puts forth strenuous effort against the recalcitrance of the material he is dealing with, and that the material—which is to say the person—submits to being dealt with, consents to undergo the ordeal of being fashioned, formed, shaped.

If I am right in saying that humanistic educational traditions of the past were grounded in strenuous effort and that the idea of ordeal was essential to them, it will be obvious, I think, that our American culture will not find these educational traditions congenial. Perhaps other national cultures still follow their own traditions in being less distressed than ours by what the humanistic education of the past entailed in the way of strict sanction and required submission. In England, for example, *pupil* is still not a compromised word as it is in this country. The English use it quite neutrally except perhaps where it carries subtle overtones of celebration, as when an established scholar refers to the distinguished man who was his tutor at the university by saying, "I was a pupil of So-and-so," which is to say, "He taught me; I learned from him." But, in America, an excellent handbook of linguistic usage tells us that one should not refer to anyone over the age of (I think) twelve as a *pupil*. To apply the word to a person who has passed the canonical age can only be considered derogatory in that it implies being taught or being required to learn, and thus denies the autonomy made manifest in the word *student*.

Very likely this feeling on the part of many Americans that being taught or required to learn is an arbitrary denial of autonomy goes far toward explaining the state of primary and secondary education in our country. Everyone seems to act as if that cause is wholly and irretrievably lost and to conclude that the best way of dealing with this significant defeat of the democratic ideal is to put it behind us, to say nothing more about it, and to place our hope for education wholly in its higher branches. At the several conferences and seminars that I have attended through the past year, all of which put their emphasis on the humanistic aspects of education, it was taken for granted that the effectual process of education begins at age eighteen, upon entrance into college; any questioning of this assumption, any attempt to suggest that the quality of higher education might have some relation to the quality of primary and secondary education was unfailingly met with irritated resistance as being an obstructive irrelevance. This would have greatly surprised—would have appalled—John Milton or any theorist of humanistic education of the past.

Yet will we be fair to our society if we let those old theorists of humanistic education have the last word? Will we be doing justice to our system of education in its totality if we take the view that we fail in our duty to our young people because we do not see to it that they are really taught, that they are really required to learn traditional substantive subjects, that they are early and compulsorily subjected to such fashioning, forming, shaping as will prepare them for further *Bildung* at the university? As I have said, there is pretty wide agreement that this is not how our primary and secondary schools understand their function. But might it not be a question whether, in the light of precisely our most conscientiously forward-looking and hopeful cultural sentiment, there is any real need for them to regard their function in this way? Consider the following estimate of young people who have entered the universities after having had the presumably inadequate training our schools give: "The present generation of young people in our universities are the best informed, the most intelligent, and the most idealistic this country has ever known. This is the experience of teachers everywhere." I am citing the opening paragraph of the *Report of the Fact-Finding Commission Appointed to Investigate the Disturbances at Columbia University in April and May 1968*. It was written by the chairman of the commission, Professor Archibald Cox of the Harvard Law School. The statement, we may presume, was not carelessly made.

Although when I first read Professor Cox's statement my response was one of natural bewilderment, upon further consideration perhaps I have come to see how Professor Cox arrived at this remarkable judgment. Ours is a culture of which a chief characteristic is its self-awareness. Not only that aspect of our culture which we refer to as "high" is largely given over to enhancing this alertness to our condition—no less intense and overt in this effort is what we might call the institutional-popular sector of our culture, which includes advertising, television in its various genres, journalism in its various modes. Through the agency of one segment of the culture or another, there is unceasingly being borne in upon us the consciousness that we live in circumstances of an unprecedented sort. And through these agencies we are provided with the information and the attitudes that enable us to believe not only that we can properly identify the difficulties presented by the society but also that we can cope with them, at least in spirit, and that in itself our consciousness of difficulties to be coped with gives us moral distinction. The young share with their elders this alertness to our condition; and the consciousness, together with the moral validation it confers, appears in the young at an increasingly early age, the rate of social and cultural maturation having radically accelerated in recent years, doubtless as a consequence of extreme alterations in the mores of the family and in the mores of sexuality. The excitement about the problems of our world (perhaps not the less heady for being touched by apprehensiveness) and the emotions of mastery (perhaps not the less cherished for showing some color of factitiousness) that are so abundantly generated in our culture make a convincing simulacrum of a serious address to, and comprehension of, the society.

In his high estimate of the young, Professor Cox accepted the simulacrum for the real thing: he celebrated as knowledge and intelligence what in actuality is merely a congeries of "advanced" public attitudes. When he made his affirmation of the enlightenment of the young, he affirmed his own enlightenment and that of others who would agree with his judgment—for it is from the young and not from his own experience that he was deriving his values, and for values to have this source is, in the view of a large part of our forward-looking culture, all the certification that is required to prove that the values are sound ones. But surely more important than the deference to youth that was implicit in Professor Cox's high estimate of the attainment of this generation of students was his readiness to accept another of the master traits of our contemporary culture: its willingness—its eagerness—to forgo the particularization of conduct. Recognizing the great store now placed on selfhood and the energies of the self, Professor Cox met and matched the culture in its principled indifference to the intellectual and moral forms in which the self chooses to be presented.

If we consider the roadblocks in the path of a re-establishment of traditional humanistic education, surely none is so effectually obstructing as the tendency of our culture to regard the mere energy of impulse as being in every mental and moral way equivalent and even superior to defined intention. We may remark, as exemplary of this tendency, the fate of an idea that once was salient in Western culture: the idea of "making a life," by which was meant conceiving human existence, one's own or another's, as if it were a work of art upon which one might pass judgment, assessing it by established criteria. This idea of a conceived and executed life is a very old one and was in force until relatively recently; we regard it as characteristic of the Victorian age, but it of course lasted even longer than that. It was what virtually all novels used to be about: how you were born, reared, and shaped, and then how you took over and managed for yourself as best you could. And cognate with the idea of making a life, a nicely proportioned one, with a beginning, a middle, and an end, was the idea of making a self, a good self. Yeats speaks of women dealing with their outward selves as works of art, laboring to be beautiful; just so does Castiglione in *The Book of the Courtier* represent men laboring to come up to standard, to be all that men might reasonably hope to be, partly for the satisfaction of being so, partly for the discharge of rather primitive political functions.

This desire to fashion, to shape, a self and a life has all but gone from a contemporary culture whose emphasis, paradoxically enough, is so much on self. If we ask why this has come about, the answer of course involves us in a giant labor of social history. But there is one reason which can be readily isolated and which, I think, explains much. It is this: if you set yourself to shaping a self, a life, you limit yourself to that self and that life. You preclude any other kind of selfhood remaining available to you. You close out other options, other possibilities which might have been yours. Such limitation, once acceptable, now goes against the cultural grain—it is almost as if the fluidity of the contemporary world demands an analogous limitlessness in our personal perspective. Any doctrine, that of the family, religion, the school, that does not sustain this increasingly felt need for a multiplicity of options and instead offers an ideal of a shaped self, a formed life, has the sign on it of a retrograde and depriving authority, which, it is felt, must be resisted.

For anyone concerned with contemporary education at whatever level, the assimilation that contemporary culture has made between social idealism, even political liberalism, and personal fluidity—a self without the old confinements—is as momentous as it is recalcitrant to correction. Among the factors in the contemporary world which militate against the formulation of an educational ideal related to the humanistic traditions of the past, this seems to me to be the most decisive.

The Freud/Jung Letters

[A review of *The Correspondence Between Sigmund Freud and C. G. Jung,* edited by William McGuire, translated by Ralph Manheim and R. F. C. Hull, *The New York Times Book Review,* April 21, 1974]

THE relationship between Sigmund Freud and C. G. Jung had its bright beginning in 1906 and came to its embittered end in 1913. Its disastrous course was charted by the many letters the two men wrote each other. Of these a few have been lost but there are 360 extant, of which 164 are from Freud, 196 from Jung. In 1970 the Freud and Jung families made the enlightened decision that this correspondence was to be edited as a unit, and it is now published, simultaneously in German and in English. In no way does it disappoint the large expectation it has naturally aroused. Both as it bears upon the personal lives of the men between whom the letters passed and upon the intellectual history of our epoch, it is a document of inestimable importance.

In 1906 Freud was 50 years old, by no means an anonymous figure in psychiatry but far from content with the acceptance that had so far been accorded his ideas. Jung was 31, already well established in his profession, second in command at the widely-known psychiatric hospital at Zürich, the Burghölzli, whose chief was the redoubtable Eugen Bleuler. The relationship began with Jung's sending Freud a copy of a volume of studies he had supervised in which the importance of psychoanalysis was handsomely acknowledged. Freud received the gift with delight; actually, indeed, having heard how gratifyingly his name had figured in the book, he had already bought a copy. With his brief but fervent note of thanks the correspondence begins.

For a time the two men exerted a powerful enchantment over each other. Ernest Jones has told us of the special appeal that Jung had for Freud because he was, with the exception of Jones himself, the first non-Jewish disciple. Freud saw him as his heir-apparent, the champion and continuator of the new science; it was he who would bring to the understanding of the psychoses the psychoanalytic concepts that Freud had derived from his work with the neuroses.

But Jung's place in Freud's regard was not determined only by practical considerations. Freud, as we know, was exceptionally sensitive to the thought of growing old, and he delighted in this new coadjutor who had youth and to spare, being not only young in fact but young by his very name, and young (it seems clear) by virtue of his being Germanic and not Jewish. Jung, for his part, received from Freud the heady sense of having been chosen for a high destiny. A family legend had it that his grandfather, of the same name as himself, was an illegitimate son of Goethe, and it might be said that Freud licensed Jung's ambition to rival in fame this supposititious ancestor.

It isn't likely that the admirers of either man will be gratified by the part he plays in the correspondence. Freud and Jung were not good for one another; their connection made them susceptible to false attitudes and ambiguous tones. In the early stages of the association it is Freud who might most distress his partisans—they cannot but be uneasy as they watch him seeking to bind the new young colleague to his cause and to himself. Every wile of love and praise is used to assure that there will be no defection, the possibility of which is often referred to openly by both correspondents; for example, Jung has heard from Freud the story of the unhappy friendship with Wilhelm Fliess and he is at pains to write to Freud that he "may rest assured, not only now, but for the future, that nothing Fliess-like is going to happen."

Freud is never anything but specific about the advantages of the relationship he envisages. Jung, he says, is the Joshua to his Moses, fated to enter the Promised Land which he himself will not live to see. Again and again he speaks of Jung as his "heir," once as "my successor and crown prince," and even as "spirit of my spirit." He cannot be explicit enough in referring to the gratitude this precious new son deserves, to the uniqueness of the place he holds in his father's confidence. So that there will be no uncertainty of the specialness of his regard, he speaks condescendingly of colleagues with whom he is on close terms, Sandor Ferenczi especially and also Karl Abraham and Jones.

But if the admirers of Freud are troubled by discerning so much purpose in his relation to Jung, they are not likely to be reassured by those many passages in the letters which suggest that the courtship was not only professional and calculated but also personal and very deeply felt, much more so, indeed, than Freud permitted himself to know. No man is to be faulted for the love he gives or the love he seeks, yet moved as we may be by Freud's need for Jung's loyal affection, I think we have the right to ask of the father of psychoanalysis a little more consciousness of the nature and extent of the claims he makes on Jung than Freud here shows.

Through the greater part of the correspondence Jung's behavior is unexceptionable. He isn't—perhaps could scarcely be—wholly comfortable in the role that has been assigned to him and he often speaks of his difficulties. Although at one moment he says that he wants to enjoy Freud's friendship "not as one between equals but as that of father and son," he also can say that it is hard to have to work alongside the "father creator" and that he lives "from the crumbs that fall from the rich man's table." Still, in a trying situation he handles himself in a composed and serious way.

But when the relationship goes into its last stage, something quite extreme takes place in this mannerly person. His poise leaves him; he is overcome by uncontrollable rage and to the man whom he often said he venerated, even "unconditionally," he now speaks in jeers. This behavior is the uglier because it alternates with efforts to maintain "correctness." Never, I think, has spite been so palpable on the page as in the underbred sarcasms of Jung's last letters. They are met by Freud with a hard, dry disdain. It should perhaps be added that although Jung was by no means inaccessible to anti-Jewish thoughts and feelings—this is made clear by Jones and of course by Jung's deplorably compromised relation to the Nazi ideology—there is no adumbration of anti-Semitism in the quarrel with Freud.

So far as the crack in the golden bowl of the friendship was intellectual, it appeared early, actually in Jung's first letter. No one will be surprised to hear that it was a difference of view about the place that sex should have in psychoanalytic thought. Beyond a certain point in the sexual etiology of the neurosis Jung could not go. Often his objection was frankly opportunistic—more people, he believed, would be attracted to psychoanalysis if they were not scared away by sex, and again and again Freud had to insist to him that, as he once put it, there was no way to "sweeten the sour apple." Sometimes the objection was made on the ground of theory —did it not needlessly limit the psyche to make sex definitive of its nature and function? The resistance which Jung offered to Freud's sexual doctrine was strengthened by his increasing commitment to the occult, which Freud, despite his efforts to accommodate it (for Ferenczi's sake as much as for Jung's), could not stomach.

The intellectual and professional differences between the two men, profound as these eventually became, would perhaps not of themselves have brought about a break so drastic as did take place had not their alienating tendency been reinforced by personal conflicts. It is scarcely possible to suppose that Freud was wholly without ambivalence in his response to Jung's rapid success—his famous fainting spell when he, Jung and Ferenczi were lunching in

Bremen the day before they sailed for America to attend the Clark University celebration of 1909 is often explained by Jung's having been invited to take part in the occasion on equal terms with him.

If Freud did indeed regard Jung with ambivalence, his effort to resolve this doubleness of feeling might account for his having been excessive in his conciliation of the cherished son. This, we can't but see, was counter-productive. Jung could not maintain his equanimity under all that wooing. On one occasion he explained his discomfort by referring to an episode of his boyhood in which he was the victim of a sexual assault by an older man whom he had "worshipped."

Whatever developing recalcitrance Freud may have perceived in his filial colleague, his letters were but little disposed to confront it. We of course must remark that in 1911 he was writing *Totem and Taboo*, which deals with the murder of the primal father by the sons, and that he told Jung that he "will feel almost obligated *not* to discuss" his findings with him. Still, such anxiety as he may have felt about the relationship does not envisage a crisis in it. But then the full extent of the estrangement is made plain when into the dialogue of the two men a third voice intrudes itself. It is a woman's voice, that of Jung's wife, Emma. She speaks to Freud privately; her husband, she says, is not to know of their colloquy.

The four letters which Emma Jung wrote Freud in October and November of 1911 are unforgettable in their effort to bring the light of psychoanalytic reason to the troubled mind of Sigmund Freud. The occasion of the first letter was the visit Freud had recently paid the Jungs at their home in Küsnacht, during which, Emma says, he had treated Carl with marked reserve. After telling Freud of how much courage she needs to write to him, Emma goes on to speak of the strain that has developed between him and Carl, its cause being, she believes, his disapproval of the line Carl had taken in his important paper, "Transformations and Symbols of the Ego." Her tone to Freud is warmly affectionate and what she addresses herself to is his state of feeling. About this she says an astonishing thing: ". . . I cannot bear to see you so resigned. . . ." She asks whether his resignation relates only to what he had told her about his "real children" or to his "spiritual sons" as well.

To this Freud replied with a "nice kind letter"—it has not survived, nor have any of his letters to Emma—and Emma writes again and ventures further. Why, she wants to know, should Freud have said that his "marriage had long ago been 'amortized,' [that] now there was nothing more to do except—die"? When they had last talked together, she had taxed him with not paying enough attention to his children's relation with him, necessarily more difficult because he was so distinguished a man, and he had replied that he hadn't time to analyze his children's dreams because he must earn money so that they could go on dreaming: did he think this a right attitude to take?

For her part, she says, she prefers to "think that one *should not* dream at all, one should live." She rebukes him for being "resigned," for not confronting and enjoying his "well-earned fame and success," for thinking of himself as older than in fact he is. She concludes by urging him to give up his paternal relation to her husband, to think of Carl "not with a father's feeling: 'He will grow and I must dwindle,' but rather as one human being thinks of another, who like you has his own law to fulfill."

The advice was good, and, in the event, what was there for Freud to do save act on it? By the time Emma was writing her letters of 1911 Jung had come to feel that the fulfillment of his own law must proceed at an accelerated pace. In the autumn of 1912, on his return from America, where he had gone to lecture in New York, Chicago, and Washington, he wrote Freud a letter charged with grievance and provocation. From this the situation might well have seemed hopeless, but a few days later the two men met at the conference on organizational matters that Freud had convened in Munich and there seemed reason to suppose that the basis for at least an accommodation had been established. Freud and Jung went for a long walk together; Freud was able to explain to Jung's satisfaction an incident which Jung had understood to be an intentional slight. They returned to a vivacious lunch with their colleagues at which Freud had his second fainting spell in Jung's presence.

A few days later Jung wrote to Freud, coolly but with amenity, even with the avowal of the wish to continue in personal if no longer in intellectual closeness. Freud replied in kind; he commented on the fainting episode, about which Jung had enquired, and concluded by saying, "A bit of neurosis that I ought really look into." The minimizing phrase seems to have put Jung into a state of hysterical rage. He insolently replies that "this 'bit' should, in my opinion, be taken very seriously indeed because it leads 'usque ad instar voluntariae mortis, ('to the semblance of voluntary death'). I have suffered from this bit in my dealings with you . . ." and more to the same effect and in the same tone.

A few weeks later, after a further acerb exchange, he writes that he sees through Freud's "little trick," which is that Freud goes "around sniffing out" symptoms, "thus reducing everyone to the level of sons and daughters" while himself remaining "on top as the father, sitting pretty. . . . You see, my dear Professor, so long as you hand out this stuff I don't give a damn for my symptomatic actions; they shrink to nothing in comparison with the formidable beam in my brother Freud's eye."

With this burst of *ressentiment,* which transforms the judging father into the condemned brother, Jung stands on the verge of freedom. There are a few more letters exchanged, partly because business remained to be transacted, partly because the two men cannot quite give each other up even though there is only bitterness between them. Nothing now holds Jung back from going on to fulfill his own law. That he did so cannot be doubted, and there are many who are gratified by what his autonomy has yielded. There are also many, of whom the present reviewer is one, who see his effort of self-fulfillment as an elaborate act of intellectual super-erogation, both as it issues in his cultural and general psychological concepts and in his clinical theory.

When Freud's son Ernst and Jung's son Franz met in the former's home in St. John's Wood, London, to exchange their fathers' letters and to agree that they should be published together, it was naturally understood that the letters were to be edited with entire impartiality. This task was put into the charge of William McGuire, the supervising editor of Jung's Collected Works, and he has carried it out in a way that is admirable in every respect. For anyone concerned with the history of the psychoanalytic movement through the years over which the correspondence extends, his editorial apparatus, at once elegant and compendious, is of the greatest value. Freud's letters have been translated by Ralph Manheim with his justly-admired skill; the equally successful translation of Jung's letters was made by R. F. C. Hull, the translator of the Collected Works.

Whittaker Chambers' Journey

[Introduction to the republication of *The Middle of the Journey*, Secker & Warburg, London, 1975; first published, under the title used here, in the *Times Saturday Review*, London, April 5, 1975]

THE re-issue of *The Middle of the Journey* so many years after it was first published makes an occasion when I might appropriately say a word about the relation which the novel bears to actuality, especially to the problematical kind of actuality we call history. The relation is really quite a simple one but it is sometimes misunderstood.

From my first conception of it, my story was committed to history—it was to draw out some of the moral and intellectual implications of the powerful attraction to Communism felt by a considerable part of the American intellectual class during the Thirties and Forties. But although its historical nature and purpose are attested to by the explicit reference it makes to certain of the most momentous events of our epoch, the book I wrote in 1946–47 and published in 1947 did not depict anyone who was a historical figure. When I have said this, however, I must go on to say that among the characters of my story there is one who had been more consciously derived from actuality than any of the others—into the creation of Gifford Maxim there had gone not only such imagination as I could muster on his behalf but also a considerable amount of recollected observation of a person with whom I had long been acquainted; a salient fact about him was that at one period of his life he had pledged himself to the cause of Communism and had then bitterly repudiated his allegiance. He might therefore be thought of as having moved for a time in the ambience of history even though he could scarcely be called a historical figure; for that he clearly was not of sufficient consequence. This person was Whittaker Chambers.

But only a few months after my novel was published, Chambers' status in history underwent a sudden and drastic change. The Hiss case broke upon the nation and the world and Chambers became beyond any doubt a historical figure.

The momentous case had eventuated from an action taken by Chambers almost a decade earlier. In 1939 he had sought out an official of the government—Adolf Berle, then Assistant Secretary of State—with whom he lodged detailed information about a Communist espionage apparatus to which he himself had belonged as a courier and from which he had defected some years earlier. What led him to make the disclosure at this time was his belief that the Soviet Union would make common cause with Nazi Germany and come to stand in a belligerent relation to the United States. As a long-belated, circuitously reached outcome of this communication, Alger Hiss was intensively investigated and questioned, a procedure which by many was thought bizarre in view of the exceptional esteem in which the suspected man was held—he had been an official in President Roosevelt's administrations since 1933 and a member of the State Department since 1936; he had served as adviser to the President at Yalta, and as temporary Secretary General of the United Nations; in 1946 he had been elected president of the Carnegie Endowment for International Peace. The long tale of investigation and confrontation came to an end when a Federal grand jury in New York, after having twice summoned Hiss to appear before it, indicted him for perjury. The legal process which followed was prolonged, bitter, and of profound moral, political, and cultural importance. Chambers, who had been the effectual instigator of the case, was the chief witness against the man whom he had once thought of as a valued friend. He was as much on trial as Alger Hiss—people commonly spoke of the Hiss–Chambers case—and his ordeal was perhaps even more severe.

At the time I wrote *The Middle of the Journey,* Chambers was a successful member of the staff of *Time* and a contributor of signed articles to *Life* and therefore could not be thought of as having a wholly private existence, but he was not significantly present to the consciousness of a great many people. Only to such readers of my novel as had been Chambers' college-mates or his former comrades in the Communist Party or were now his professional colleagues would the personal traits and the political career I had assigned to Gifford Maxim connect him with the actual person from whom these were derived.

In America *The Middle of the Journey* was not warmly received upon its publication or widely read—the English response was more cordial—and some time passed before any connection was publicly made between the obscure novel and the famous trial. No sooner was the connection made than it was exaggerated. To me as the author of the novel there was attributed a knowledge of events behind the case which of course I did not have. All I actually knew that bore upon what the trial disclosed was Whittaker Chambers' personality and the fact that he had joined, and then defected from, a secret branch of the Communist Party. This was scarcely arcane information. Although Chambers and I had been acquainted for a good many years, anyone who had spent a few hours with him might have as vivid a sense as I had of his comportment and temperament, for these were out of the common run, most memorable, and he was given to making histrionic demonstration of them. As for his political career, its phase of underground activity, as I shall have occasion to say at greater length, was one of the openest of secrets while it lasted, and, when it came to an end, Chambers believed that the safety of his life depended upon the truth being widely known.

That there was a connection to be drawn between Whittaker

Chambers and my Gifford Maxim became more patent as the trial progressed, and this seemed to make it the more credible that my Arthur Croom derived from Alger Hiss; some readers even professed to see a resemblance between Nancy Croom and Mrs. Hiss. If there is indeed any likeness to be discerned between the fictive and the actual couples, it is wholly fortuitous. At no time have I been acquainted with either Alger Hiss or Priscilla Hiss, and at the time I wrote the novel, we did not, to my knowledge, have acquaintances in common. The name of Hiss was unknown to me until some months after my book had appeared.

It was not without compunction that I had put Whittaker Chambers to the uses of my story. His relation to the Communist Party bore most pertinently upon the situation I wanted to deal with and I felt no constraint upon my availing myself of it, since Chambers, as I have indicated, did not keep it secret but, on the contrary, wished it to be known. But the man himself, with all his idiosyncrasies of personality, was inseparable from his political experience as I conceived it, and in portraying the man himself to the extent I did I was conscious of the wish that nothing I said or represented in my book could be thought by Chambers to impugn or belittle the bitter crisis of conscience I knew him to have undergone. His break with the Communist Party under the circumstances of his particular relation to it had been an act of courage and had entailed much suffering, which, I was inclined to suppose, was not yet at its end.

Such concern as I felt for Chambers' comfort of mind had its roots in principle and not in friendship. Chambers had never been a friend of mine though we had been in college at the same time, which meant that in 1947 we had been acquainted for twenty-three years. I hesitate to say that I disliked him and avoided his company —there was indeed something about him that repelled me, but there was also something that engaged my interest and even my respect. Yet friends we surely were not.

Whether or not Chambers ever read my book I cannot say. At

the time of its publication he doubtless learned from reviews, probably also from one of the friends we had in common, that the book referred to him and his experience. And then when the trial of Alger Hiss began, there was the notion, quite widely circulated and certain to reach him, that *The Middle of the Journey* had evidential bearing on the case. In one of the autobiographical essays in his posthumous volume *Cold Friday,* Chambers names me as having been among the friends of his college years, which, as I have said, I was not, and goes on to speak of my having written a novel in which he is represented. He concludes his account of my relation to him by recalling that when "a Hiss investigator" tried to induce me to speak against him in court, I had refused and said, "Whittaker Chambers is a man of honor." I did indeed use just those words on the occasion to which Chambers refers and can still recall the outburst of contemptuous rage they evoked from the lawyer who had come to call on me to solicit my testimony. I should like to think that my having said that Chambers and I were not friends will lend the force of objectivity to my statement, the substance of which I would still affirm. Whittaker Chambers had been engaged in espionage against his own country; when a change of heart and principle led to his defecting from his apparatus, he had eventually not only confessed his own treason but named the comrades who shared it, including one whom for a time he had cherished as a friend. I hold that when this has been said of him, it is still possible to say that he was a man of honor.

Strange as it might seem in view of his eventual prominence in the narrative, Chambers had no part in my first conception and earliest drafts of *The Middle of the Journey*. He came into the story fairly late in its development and wholly unbidden. Until he made his appearance I was not aware that there was any need for him, but when he suddenly turned up and proposed himself to my narrative, I could not fail to see how much to its point he was.

His entrance into the story changed its genre. It had been my intention to write what we learned from Henry James to call a *nouvelle,* which I take to be a fictional narrative longer than a long short-story and shorter than a short novel. Works in this genre are likely to be marked by a considerable degree of thematic explicitness—one can usually paraphrase the informing idea of a *nouvelle* without being unforgivably reductive; it needn't be a total betrayal of a *nouvelle* to say what it is "about." Mine was to be about death—about what had happened to the way death is conceived by the enlightened consciousness of the modern age.

The story was to take place in the mid-Thirties and the time in which it is set is crucial to it. Arthur and Nancy Croom are the devoted friends of John Laskell; during his recent grave illness it was they who oversaw his care and they have now arranged for him to recruit his strength in the near vicinity of their country home. Upon his arrival their welcome is of the warmest, yet Laskell can't but be aware that the Crooms become somewhat remote and reserved whenever he speaks of his illness, during which, as they must know, there had been a moment when his condition had been critical. To Laskell the realization of mortality has brought a kind of self-knowledge, which, even though he does not fully comprehend it, he takes to be of some considerable significance, but whenever he makes a diffident attempt to speak of this to his friends, they appear almost to be offended. He seems to perceive that the Crooms' antagonism to his recent experience and to the interest he takes in it is somehow connected with the rather anxious esteem in which they hold certain of their country neighbors. In these people, who, in the language of the progressive liberalism of the time were coming to be called "little people," the Crooms insist on perceiving a quality of simplicity and authenticity which licenses their newly conceived and cherished hope that the future will bring into being a society in which reason and virtue will prevail. In short, the Crooms might be said to pass a *political* judgment upon Laskell for the excessive attention he pays to the fact that he had approached death and hadn't died. If Laskell's preoccupation were looked at closely and objectively, they seem to be saying, might it not be understood as actually an affirmation of death, which is, in practical outcome, a negation of the future and of the hope it holds out for a society of reason and virtue. Was there not a sense in which death might be called reactionary?

This was the *donnée* which I undertook to develop. As I have said, the genre that presented itself as most appropriate to my purpose was the *nouvelle,* which seemed precisely suited to the scope of my given idea, to what I at first saw as the range of its implications. After Chambers made his way into the story, bringing with him so much more than its original theme strictly needed, I had to understand that it could no longer be contained within the graceful limits of the *nouvelle:* it had to be a novel or nothing.

Chambers was the first person I ever knew whose commitment to radical politics was meant to be definitive of his whole moral being, the controlling element of his existence. He made the commitment while he was still in college and it was what accounted for the quite exceptional respect in which he was held by his associates at that time. He entered Columbia in 1920, a freshman rather older than his classmates, for he had spent a year between high school and college as an itinerant worker. He was a solemn youth who professed political views of a retrograde kind and was still firm in a banal religious faith. But by 1923 his principles had so far changed that he wrote a blasphemous play about the Crucifixion, which, when it was published in a student magazine, made a scandal that led to his withdrawal from college. He was subsequently allowed to return, but in the intervening time he had lost all interest in academic life—during a summer tour of Europe he had witnessed the social and economic disarray of the continent and discovered both the practical potential and the moral heroism of revolutionary activity. Early in 1925 he joined the Communist Party.

Such relation as I had with Chambers began at this time, in 1924–25, which was my senior year. It is possible that he and I never exchanged a single word at college. Certainly we never conversed. He knew who I was—that is, he connected me with my name—and it may be that the report I was once given of his having liked a poem of mine had actually originated as a message he sent to me. I used to see him in the company of one group of my friends, young men of intimidating brilliance, of whom some remained loyal to him through everything, though others came to hold him in bitterest contempt. I observed him as if from a distance and with considerable irony, yet accorded him the deference which my friends thought his due.

The moral force that Chambers asserted began with his physical appearance. This seemed calculated to negate youth and all its graces, to deny that they could be of any worth in our world of pain and injustice. He was short of stature and very broad, with heavy arms and massive thighs; his sport was wrestling. In his middle age there was a sizable outcrop of belly and I think this was already in evidence. His eyes were narrow and they preferred to consult the floor rather than an interlocutor's face. His mouth was small and, like his eyes, tended downward, one might think in sullenness, though this was not so. When the mouth opened, it never failed to shock by reason of the dental ruin it disclosed, a devastation of empty sockets and blackened stumps. In later years, when he became respectable, Chambers underwent restorative dentistry, but during his radical time, his aggressive toothlessness had been so salient in the image of the man that I did not use it in portraying Gifford Maxim, feeling that to do so would have been to go too far in explicitness of personal reference. This novelistic self-denial wasn't inconsiderable, for that desolated mouth was the perfect insigne of Chambers' moral authority. It annihilated the hygienic American present—only a serf could have such a mouth, or some student in a visored cap who sat in his Moscow garret and thought of nothing save the moment when he would toss the fatal canister into the barouche of the Grand Duke.

Chambers could on occasion speak eloquently and cogently, but he was not much given to speaking—his histrionism, which seemed unremitting, was chiefly that of imperturbability and long silences. Usually his utterances were gnomic, often cryptic. Gentleness was not out of the range of his expression, which might even include a compassionate sweetness of a beguiling kind. But the chief impression he made was of a forbidding drabness.

In addition to his moral authority, Chambers had a very considerable college prestige as a writer. This was deserved. My undergraduate admiration for his talent was recently confirmed when I went back to the poetry and prose he published in a student magazine in 1924–25. At that time he wrote with an elegant austerity. Later, beginning with his work for the *New Masses,* something went soft and "high" in his tone and I was never again able to read him, either in his radical or in his religiose conservative phase, without a touch of queasiness.

Such account of him as I have given will perhaps have suggested that Whittaker Chambers, with his distinctive and strongly marked traits of mien and conduct, virtually demanded to be co-opted as a fictive character. Yet there is nothing that I have so far told about him that explains why, when once he had stepped into the developing conception of my narrative, he turned out to be so particularly useful—so necessary, even essential—to its purpose.

I have said that he entered my story unbidden and so it seemed to me at the time, although when I bring to mind the moment at which he appeared, I think he must have been responding to an invitation that I had unconsciously offered. He presented himself to me as I was working out that part of the story in which John Laskell, though recovered from his illness, confronts with a quite intense anxiety the relatively short railway journey he must make to visit the Crooms. There was no reason in reality for Laskell to feel as he did, nor could he even have said what he was apprehensive of—his anxiety was of the "unmotivated" kind, what people call neurotic, by which they mean that it need not be given credence either by him who suffers it or by them who judge the suffering.

It was while I was considering how Laskell's state of feeling should be dealt with, what part it might play in the story, that Chambers turned up, peremptorily asserting his relevance to the question. That relevance derived from his having for a good many years now gone about the world in fear. There were those who would have thought—who did think—that his fear was fanciful to the point of absurdity, even of madness, but I believed it to have been reasonable enough, and its reason, as I couldn't fail to see, was splendidly to the point of my story.

What Chambers feared, of course, was that the Communist Party would do away with him. In 1932—so he tells us in *Witness*—after a short tour of duty as the editor of the *New Masses,* he had been drafted by the Party into its secret apparatus. By 1936 he had become disenchanted with the whole theory and ethos of Communism and was casting about for ways of separating himself from it. To break with the Communist Party of America—the overt Party, which published the *Daily Worker* and the *New Masses* and organized committees and circulated petitions—entailed nothing much worse than a period of vilification, but to defect from the underground organization was to put one's life at risk.

To me and to a considerable number of my friends in New York it was not a secret that Chambers had, as the phrase went, gone underground. We were a group who, for a short time in 1932 and even into 1933, had been in a tenuous relation with the Communist Party through some of its so-called fringe activities. Our relation to the Party deteriorated rapidly after Hitler came to power in early 1933 and soon it was nothing but antagonistic. With this group Chambers retained some contact despite its known hostility to what is now called Stalinism. Two of its members in particular remained his trusted friends despite his involvement in activities which were alien, even hostile, to their own principles.

Although I knew that Chambers had gone underground, I formed no clear idea of what he subterraneously did. I understood, of course, that he was in a chain of command that led to Russia, by-passing the American Party. The foreign connection required that I admit into consciousness the possibility, even the probability, that he was concerned with something called military intelligence, but I did not equate this with espionage—it was as if such a thing hadn't yet been invented.

Of the several reasons that might be advanced to explain why my curiosity and that of my circle wasn't more explicit and serious in the matter of Chambers' underground assignment, perhaps the most immediate was the way Chambers comported himself on the widely separated occasions when, by accident or design, he came into our ken. His presence was not less portentous than it had ever been and it still had something of its old authority, but if you responded to that, you had at the same time to take into account the comic absurdity which went along with it, the aura of parodic melodrama with which he invested himself, as if, with his darting, covert glances and extravagant precautions, his sudden mani-festations out of nowhere in the middle of the night, he were acting the part of a secret agent and wanted to be sure that everyone knew just what he was supposed to be.

But his near approach to becoming a burlesque of the under-ground revolutionary didn't prevent us from crediting the word, when it came, that Chambers was in danger of his life. We did not doubt that, if Chambers belonged to a "special" Communist unit, his defection would be drastically dealt with, by abduction or assassination. And when it was told to us that he might the more easily be disposed of because he had been out of continuous public view for a considerable time, we at once saw the force of the suggestion. We were instructed in the situation by that member of our circle with whom Chambers had been continuously in touch while making his decision to break with the apparatus. This friend made plain to us the necessity of establishing Chambers in a firm personal identity, an unquestionable social existence which could be attested to. This was ultimately to be established through a regular routine of life, which included an office which he would go to daily; what was immediately needed was his being seen by a number of people who would testify to his having been alive on a certain date.

To this latter purpose it was arranged that the friend would bring Chambers to a party that many of us planned to attend. It was a Hallowe'en party; the hostess, who had been reared in Mexico, had decorated her house both with the jolly American symbols of All Hallowmas and with Mexican ornaments, which speak of the returning dead in a more literal and grisly way. Years later, when Chambers wished to safeguard the microfilms of the secret documents that had been copied by Hiss, he concealed them in a hollowed-out pumpkin in a field. I have never understood why, when this was reported at the trial, it was thought to be odd behavior which cast doubt upon Chambers' mental stability, for the hiding-place was clearly an excellent one. But if a recondite psychological explanation is really needed, it is perhaps supplied by that acquaintance of Chambers—she had been present at the Hallowe'en party—who easily connected the choice of hiding-place with the jack-o'-lanterns of the party at which Chambers undertook to establish his existence in order to continue it.

Chambers was brought to the party when it was well advanced. If he had any expectations of being welcomed back from underground to the upper world, he was soon disillusioned. Some of the guests, acknowledging that he was in danger, took the view that fates similar to the one he feared for himself had no doubt been visited upon some of his former comrades through his connivance, which was not to be lightly forgiven. Others, though disenchanted with Communist policy, were not yet willing to believe that the Communist ethic countenanced secrecy and violence; they judged the information they were given about Chambers' danger to be a libelous fantasy and wanted no contact with the man who propagated it. After a few rebuffs, Chambers ceased to offer his hand in greeting and he did not stay at the party beyond the time that was needed to establish that he had been present at it.

In such thought as I may have given to Chambers over the next years, that Hallowe'en party figured as the culmination and end of his career as a tragic comedian of radical politics. In this, of course, I was mistaken, but his terrible entry upon the historical stage in the Hiss case was not forced upon him until 1948, and through the intervening decade one might suppose that he had permanently forsaken the sordid sublimities of revolutionary politics and settled into the secure anti-climax of bourgeois respectability. In 1939 he had begun his successful association with *Time*. During the years which followed, I met him by chance on a few occasions; he had a hunted, fugitive look—how not?—but he was patently surviving, and as the years went by he achieved a degree of at least economic security and even a professional reputation of sorts with the apocalyptic pieties of his news-stories for *Time* and the sodden profundities of his cultural essays for *Life*. Except as these may have made me aware of him, he was scarcely in my purview—until suddenly he thrust himself, in the way I have described, into the story I was trying to tell. I understood him to have come—he, with all his absurdity—for the purpose of representing the principle of reality.

At this distance in time the mentality of the Communist-oriented intelligentsia of the Thirties and Forties must strain the comprehension even of those who, having observed it at first hand, now look back upon it, let alone of those who learn about it from such historical accounts of it as have been written.[1] That mentality

---

[1] The relation of the class of bourgeois intellectuals to the Communist movement will, I am certain, increasingly engage the attention of social and cultural historians, who can scarcely fail to see it as one of the most curious and significant phenomena of our epoch. In the existing historiography of the subject, the classical document is *The God That Failed*, edited by Richard Crossman (New York: Harper, 1949; London: Hamish Hamilton, 1950), which consists of the autobiographical narratives of their relation to Communism of six eminent cultural figures, Arthur Koestler, Ignazio Silone, Richard Wright ("The Initiates"), and André Gide, Louis Fischer, Stephen Spender ("Worshippers From Afar"). The American situation is described in a series of volumes called *Communism in American Life*, edited by Clinton Rossiter (various publishers and dates), of which the most interesting are the two volumes by Theodore Draper, *The Roots of American Communism* (New York: Viking, 1957; London: Macmillan, 1957) and *American Communism and*

was presided over by an impassioned longing to believe. The ultimate object of this desire couldn't fail to be disarming—what the
fellow-travelling intellectuals were impelled to give their credence
to was the ready feasibility of contriving a society in which reason
and virtue would prevail. A proximate object of the will to
believe was less abstract—a large segment of the progressive intellectual class was determined to credit the idea that in one country, Soviet Russia, a decisive step had been taken toward the establishment of just such a society. Among those people of whom this
resolute belief was characteristic, any predication about the state
of affairs in Russia commanded assent so long as it was of a
"positive" nature, so long, that is, as it countenanced the expectation that the Communist Party, having actually instituted the
reign of reason and virtue in one nation, would go forward to do
likewise throughout the world.

Once the commitment to this belief had been made, no evidence
might, or could, bring it into doubt. Whoever ventured to offer
such evidence stood self-condemned as deficient in good will. And
should it ever happen that reality did succeed in breaching the
believer's defenses against it, if ever it became unavoidable to
acknowledge that the Communist Party, as it functioned in Russia,
did things, or produced conditions, which by ordinary judgment
were to be deplored and which could not be accounted for by
either the state of experimentation or the state of siege in which the
Soviet Union notoriously stood, then it was plain that ordinary
human judgment was not adequate to the deplored situation, whose
moral justification must be revealed by some other agency, commonly "the dialectic."

But there came a moment when reality did indeed breach the

Soviet Russia (New York: Viking, 1960; London: Macmillan, 1960), and Daniel
Aaron's *Writers on the Left* (New York: Harcourt, Brace & World, 1961). The
most recent and in some respects the most compendious record of the relation of
intellectuals to Communism and the one that takes fullest account of its sadly comic
aspects is David Caute's *The Fellow Travellers* (London and New York: Macmillan,
1972).

defenses that had been erected against it, and not even the dialectic itself could contain the terrible assault it made upon faith. In 1939 the Soviet Union made its pact with Nazi Germany. There had previously been circumstances—among them the Comintern's refusal to form a united front with the Social Democrats in Germany, thus allowing Hitler to come to power; the Moscow purge trials; the mounting evidence that vast prison camps did exist in the Soviet Union—which had qualified the moral prestige of Stalinist Communism in one degree or another, yet never decisively. But now to that prestige a mortal blow seemed to have been given. After the Nazi–Soviet pact one might suppose that the Russia of Stalin could never again be the ground on which the hope of the future was based, that never again could it command the loyalty of men of good will.

Yet of course the grievous hurt was assuaged before two years had passed. In 1941 Hitler betrayed his pact with Stalin, the German armies marched against Russia and by this action restored Stalinist Communism to its sacred authority. Radical intellectuals, and those who did not claim that epithet but modestly spoke of themselves as liberal or progressive or even only democratic, would now once again be able to find their moral bearings and fare forward.

Not that things were just as they had been before. It could not be glad confident morning again, not quite. A considerable number of intellectuals who had once been proud to identify themselves by their sympathy with Communism now regarded it with cool reserve. Some even expressed antagonism to it, perhaps less to its theory than to the particularities of its conduct. And those who avowed their intention of rebutting this position did not venture to call themselves by a name any more positive and likely to stir the blood than that of anti-anti-Communists.

Yet that meeching phrase tells us how much authority Stalinist Communism still had for the intellectual class. Anti-anti-Communism was not quite so neutral a position as at first it might seem to have been: it said that although, for the moment at least, one need not be actually *for* Communism, one was morally compromised, turned toward evil and away from good, if one was against it. In the face of everything that might seem to qualify its authority, Communism had become part of the fabric of the political life of many intellectuals.

In the context, *political* is probably the mandatory adjective though it might be wondered whether the Communist-oriented intellectuals of the late Forties did have what is properly to be called a political life. It must sometimes seem that their only political purpose was to express their disgust with politics and make an end of it once and for all, that their whole concern was to do away with those defining elements of politics which are repugnant to reason and virtue, such as mere opinion, contingency, conflicts of interest and clashes of will and the compromises they lead to. Thus it was that the way would be cleared to usher in a social order in which rational authority would prevail. Such an order was what the existence of the Soviet Union promised, and although the promise must now be a tacit one, it was still in force.

So far as *The Middle of the Journey* had a polemical end in view, it was that of bringing to light the clandestine negation of the political life which Stalinist Communism had fostered among the intellectuals of the West. This negation was one aspect of an ever more imperious and bitter refusal to consent to the conditioned nature of human existence. In such confrontation of this tendency as my novel proposed to make, Chambers came to its aid with what he knew, from his experience, of the reality which lay behind the luminous words of the great promise.

It was considerably to the advantage of my book that Chambers brought to it, along with reality, a sizable amount of nonsense, of factitiousness of feeling and perception. He had a sensibility which was all too accessible to large solemnities and to the more facile paradoxes of spirituality, and a mind which, though certainly not without force, was but little trained to discrimination and all too easily seduced into equating portentous utterance with truth. If my novel did have a polemical end in view, it still was a novel and not a pamphlet, and as a novel I had certain intentions for it which were served by the decisive presence in it of a character to whom could be applied the phrase I have used of Chambers, a tragic comedian. I had no doubt that my story was a serious one, but I nevertheless wanted it to move on light feet; I was confident that its considerations were momentous, but I wanted them to be represented by an interplay between gravity and levity. The frequency with which Chambers verged on the preposterous, the extent to which that segment of reality which he really did possess was implicated in his half-inauthentic profundities made him admirably suited to my purpose. If I try to recall what emotions controlled my making of Gifford Maxim out of the traits and qualities of Whittaker Chambers, I would speak first of respect and pity, both a little wry, then of intellectual and literary exasperation and amusement.

It was not as a tragic comedian that Chambers ended his days. The development of the Hiss case made it ever less possible to see him in any kind of comic light. The obloquy in which he lived forbade it. He had, of course, known obloquy for a long time, ever since his defection from Communism and the repudiation of the revolutionary position. Even gentle people might treat him with a censorious reserve which could be taken for physical revulsion. Such conduct he had met in part by isolating himself, in part by those histrionic devices which came so easily to him, making him sometimes formidable and sometimes absurd. But the obloquy that fell upon him with the Hiss case went far beyond what he had hitherto borne and there was no way in which he could meet it, he could only bear it, which he did until he died. The educated, progressive middle class, especially in its upper reaches, rallied to the cause and person of Alger Hiss, confident of his perfect innocence, deeply stirred by the pathos of what they never doubted was the injustice being visited upon him. By this same class

Whittaker Chambers was regarded with loathing—the word is not too strong—as one who had resolved, for some perverse reason, to destroy a former friend.[2]

The outcome of the trial did nothing to alienate the sympathy of the progressive middle class from Hiss or to exculpate Chambers. Indeed, the hostility to Chambers grew the more intense when the verdict of Hiss's guilt became a chief ground upon which the unprincipled junior Senator from Wisconsin, Joseph McCarthy, based his notorious anti-radical campaign.

So relentlessly was Chambers hated by people of high moral purpose that the news-letter of his college class, a kind of publication which characteristically is undeviating in its commitment to pious amenity, announced his death in 1961 in an article which surveyed in detail what it represented as his unmitigated villainy.

If anything was needed to assure that Chambers would be held in bitter and contemptuous memory by many people, it was that his destiny should have been linked with that of Richard Nixon. Especially because I write at the moment of Nixon's downfall and disgrace, I must say a word about this connection. The two men came together through the investigation of Hiss which was undertaken by the Committee of the House of Representatives on Un-American Activities; Nixon, a member of the Committee, played a decisive part in bringing Hiss to trial. The dislike with which a large segment of the American public came to regard Nixon is often said to have begun as a response to his role in the Hiss case, and probably in the first instance it was he who suffered in esteem from the connection with Chambers. Eventually, however, that situation reversed itself—as the dislike of Nixon grew concomitantly with his prominence, it served to substantiate the

[2] A psychoanalyst, Dr. Meyer Zeligs, has undertaken to give scientific substantiation to this belief in *Friendship and Fratricide* (New York: The Viking Press, 1967; London: André Deutsch, 1967), a voluminous study of the unconscious psychological processes of Chambers and Hiss and of the relations between the two men. In my opinion, no other work does as much as this one to bring into question the viability of the infant discipline of psycho-history.

odium in which Chambers stood. With the Watergate revelations, the old connection came again to the fore, its opprobrium much harsher than it had ever been, and as discredit overtook the President, partisans of Hiss's innocence were encouraged to revive their old contention that Hiss had been the victim of Chambers and Nixon in conspiracy with each other.

The tendentious association of the two men does Chambers a grievous injustice. I would make this assertion with rather more confidence in its power to convince if it were not the case that there grew up between Chambers and Nixon a degree of personal relationship and that Chambers had at one period expressed his willingness to hope that Nixon had the potentiality of becoming a great conservative leader. The hope was never a forceful one and it did not long remain in such force as it had—a year before his death Chambers said that he and Nixon "have really nothing to say to each other." The letters in which he speaks of Nixon—they are among those he wrote to William Buckley[3]—are scarcely inspiriting, not only because of the known nature and fate of the man he speculates about but also because it was impossible for Chambers to touch upon politics without falling into a bumble of religiose portentousness. But I think that no one who reads these letters will fail to perceive that the sad and exhausted man who wrote them had nothing in common morally, or, really, politically, with the man he was writing about. In Whittaker Chambers there was much to be faulted, but nothing I know of him has ever led me to doubt his magnanimous intention.

[3] See *Odyssey of a Friend. Whittaker Chambers: Letters to William F. Buckley, Jr. 1954–1961*, edited with notes by William F. Buckley, Jr. (New York, privately printed, 1969).

Why We Read Jane Austen

[A paper prepared for the Jane Austen Conference, University of Alberta, Canada, October 1975.
Incomplete at Lionel Trilling's death, November
5, 1975. Published as it was left, *Times Literary
Supplement*, March 5, 1976.]

MY subject is of a speculative kind and as it develops it
will lead us away from Jane Austen and toward the
consideration of certain aspects and functions of literature and art generally. It did not have its origin in reflections upon
our author's canon of work in itself but was proposed by a phenomenon of our contemporary high culture, the large and ever-
growing admiration which Jane Austen's work is being given. This
phenomenon may be thought the more significant because, contrary to what would have been the case at an earlier time, young
people have a salient part in it, and what I shall begin by talking
about is the intensity of feeling which students at my university
directed to Jane Austen when I gave a course in her novels two
years ago.

An account of the incident I refer to must touch upon some
dull scholastic details. As I envisaged my course, it was not to be
given in lectures but as a "class." That is to say, each of its two
meetings a week would start with my remarking on some significant aspect of the novel that was being considered and to this the
members of the class would address themselves, developing or
disagreeing with what I and then their fellow-students had said.

This method of instruction is likely to be held in greater regard than it deserves. In any class there will be students who cannot be induced to say anything at all, and there will be those who cannot be kept from trying to say everything, and of course even a measured articulateness does not ensure the cogency of what is said. But if through luck or cunning one can get the method working at all well, it has a quite special pedagogic value.

For this way of teaching, the optimum number of students would seem to be twenty and a practicable maximum probably cannot be higher than thirty. To my amazement and distress the number of students who attended the first meeting of the course was something like 150. Although there was no clear principle by which I could choose among such a number, I was determined to stay with the method of instruction I had originally proposed to myself. I addressed my little multitude and said that the course as I had planned it could not accommodate nearly as many students as were now gathered, and that beginning at once and going on for as long as was necessary, I would interview students in my office and post a list of those who might register. There were the conventional student sounds of dismay but no polemical challenge was offered to my decision and by the time I reached my office a long line had formed outside it.

All through that afternoon, through the whole of the next day and the day after that I conducted interviews, and with each one the absurdity of the procedure became more apparent. As I have said, there was no reasonable criterion by which I might judge the applicants. I had to see that the comments I jotted down about each student were subjective and in some sense discriminatory; they expressed my estimate of the applicant's intellectual aptitude, range of knowledge, and—inevitably—personal interestingness. Yet despite my growing discomfort, I continued as I had begun, feeling that I had made my decision for good reason.

The reason deserves some notice. It had to do with my ambiguous feelings about the position Jane Austen had come to occupy in our

literary culture and about the nature of the esteem and the degree
of attention she was being given by scholars and critics. If I looked
back over the period of my life during which I was at all aware of
Jane Austen, I had of course to recognize that a decisive change had
taken place in the way she was being thought about. One could not
adequately describe this change by saying that she stood now in
higher esteem than formerly. A glance through Chapman's critical
bibliography makes plain to what heights the esteem had long ago
ascended, how grand were the terms in which admiration had
been expressed, including comparison with Shakespeare. Indeed,
when it came to the question of how much praise she deserved, a
personage no less authoritative than Henry James could say that
she was given too much of it, or at least that it was of the wrong
sort and given by people of the wrong sort. And as if at the instance
of Henry James's little burst of temper over this state of affairs, the
regard in which Jane Austen was held began to change its nature
in a radical way—she ceased to be a darling and a pet, she ceased to
be what James deplored her being, "dear Jane." She became ever
less the property of people who, through being nice people, were
excluded from the redemptive strenuosities of the intellectual life.
One was the less disposed to share the views of this order of her
admirers because it had been shown that Jane Austen herself actually hated such people. And now having been delivered from
their deplorable adulation, she was safe and presumably happy in
the charge of scholars and critics of the most enlightened and energetic kind.

Instructed and lively intellects do not make pets and darlings
and dears out of the writers they admire but they do make them
into what can be called *figures*—that is to say, creative spirits whose
work requires an especially conscientious study because in it are
to be discerned significances, even mysteries, even powers, which
carry it beyond what in a loose and general sense we call literature,
beyond even what we think of as very good literature, and bring it

to as close an approximation of a sacred wisdom as can be achieved in our culture. Flaubert is of course a figure *par excellence;* Stendhal somewhat less of one; Balzac, though certainly much admired, remains a writer. Dickens became a figure quite some time back; there has been a large increase in the admiration we now give Trollope, but it is unlikely that he will ever become a figure. Kafka was a figure from the first; Gide was a figure twenty-five years ago but seems now to have lost much of his figurative ground.

The making of Jane Austen into a figure has of recent years been accelerated, probably in part by the contemporary demand for female figures, though certainly not for that reason alone. I find it difficult to say why I am not on comfortable terms with the figurative process generally and as it touches Jane Austen in particular, but a chief reason for my not wanting to give the course as lectures was that lectures would almost certainly have to take account of the enormous elaboration of articulate sensibility which has developed around Jane Austen and would put me under the obligation of trying to add to it. Perhaps because I somewhere held the primitive belief that there really was such a thing as life itself, which I did not want interfered with by literature or by the ingenuities of academic criticism, I did not wish either to encompass or to augment the abundant, the superabundant, the ever more urgent intellectual activity that was being directed toward a body of work whose value I would be the first to assert.

How, then, did I want my students to think of Jane Austen? Was she perhaps to be thought of as nothing more than a good read? I do not accept that my purpose can be thus described, though now that we have before us that British locution, which Americans have lately taken to using, the question might be asked why the phrase should have come to express so much force of irony and condescension, why a good read should necessarily imply a descent into mere creature-comfort, into downright coziness. As my case stood, I would have granted that we must get beyond the unexamined pleasure with which we read in childhood and be prepared to say why and how it is that pleasure comes to us from stories; we keep it in mind here that some of my students were in graduate school and going on to the teaching of literature as their profession. But it seemed to me that the enterprise of consciousness could best be forwarded, could best be kept direct and downright, by the colloquial give-and-take of class discussion rather than by lectures.

As the interviews got under way, however, I found myself becoming doubtful that the directness and downrightness I hoped for could actually be achieved, for such qualities of literary discourse did not consort well with the prevailing emotional tone of the interviews. Many of these did of course proceed in, if I may put it so, a normal enough way. An undergraduate had read *Pride and Prejudice,* had liked it and wanted more of the same; a graduate student concentrating in the Romantic period might naturally wish to give close attention to the six novels. But most of the students had no special scholarly reason for reading Jane Austen and yet displayed a degree of anxiety about their admission to the course which seemed to say that their motive was something other than that of ordinary literary interest. There was something they wanted, not from me, as was soon apparent, but from Jane Austen, something that was making for an intensity in their application for the course such as I had no preparation for in all my teaching career. So far as I could make out, they did not think it absurd that they should be required to formulate reasons why they should be allowed to take the course—why should not the sincerity of their vocation be tested? Several of them, after their interviews, wrote me pleading notes. Several sought out colleagues of mine with whom they were in good repute and asked them to intercede with me. Two messages came from friends who taught in other colleges in the city telling me that certain graduate students who had worked with them as undergraduates deserved my most thoughtful consideration.

When at last I posted my roster, with all due misgiving and such compunction as led me to revise upward to forty my notion of what is a feasible number for classroom discussion, there were appeals made to me to reconsider my decisions. There were even expressions of bitterness.

The course as it was given must have gone well enough, for I recall that I enjoyed giving it. The bizarre show of almost hysterical moral urgency which marked its beginning disappeared as soon as we got down to business. Although there might have been some pedagogic value in my doing so, I did not revert to that uncanny episode to try to explain it. But the occurrence deserves some effort of explanation.

One line of understanding which inevitably proposes itself is that the students were so especially eager to take the course because they had formed the impression that Jane Austen's novels presented a mode of life which brought into question the life they themselves lived and because it offered itself to their fantasy as an alternative to their own mode of life. If this was indeed the case, nothing could have been more characteristic of our high culture—we have built into the structure of our thought about society the concept of *Gemeinschaft* in its standing criticism of *Gesellschaft* and we can readily suppose that the young men and women who so much wanted to study Jane Austen believed that by doing so they could in some way transcend our sad contemporary existence, that, from the world of our present weariness and desiccation, they might reach back to a world which, as it appears to the mind's eye, is so much more abundantly provided with trees than with people, a world in whose green shade life for a moment might be a green thought.

The use of social-political terms to explain the literary predilection I was dealing with is lent a degree of substantiation by the circumstance that five years before there had been given to another English literary figure a devotion which, though of a different kind, was as intense as that which was now being given to Jane Austen and which clearly received its impetus from feelings about social existence. American undergraduates seem to be ever more alienated from the general body of English literature, but they had for some time made an exception of William Blake, pledging him their unquestioning allegiance, and in 1968, when the large majority of the students at my university were either committed to or acquiescent in its disruption, they found him uniquely relevant to their spiritual aspirations. It might seem that, no less than Blake, Jane Austen offered a position from which to scrutinize modern life with adverse intention. The style phases of our culture are notoriously short; it was not to be thought anomalous that at one moment disgust with modern life should be expressed through devotion to a figure proposing impulse, excess, and the annihilation of authority, and then a scant five years later through devotion to the presiding genius of measure, decorum, and irony.

It is not hard to say what are the attributes of the world of Jane Austen's novels which might make it congenial to the modern person who feels himself ill-accommodated by his own time. I have referred in passing to an aspect of the visual character of that world, its abundance of trees as compared with the number of people who come into our or each other's ken; and in general it is a thing taken for granted by readers that the novels represent a world which is distinctly, even though implicitly, gratifying to the eye and to the whole sensory and cognitive system. We are seldom required by Jane Austen to envision a displeasing scene, such as Fanny Price's parental home, and almost all places, even those that are not particularly described, seem to have some degree of pleasantness imputed to them. Notable among the elements of visuality which lead to the effect of amenity is that of *scale,* the relation in size between human beings and the components of their environment. No one needs to be reminded that the dialectic over what sort of scale is to be preferred is ancient and ceaseless—sometimes the hygiene of the soul is thought to be best served by spaces and objects whose magnitude overawes and quiets the will, or, alternatively, challenges it to heroic assertion; sometimes the judgment goes that the most salubrious situation is one in which moderate though generous size conveys the idea of happy accommodation. At the present time the sensibility of educated persons is likely to set particular store by this latter sort of scale as it is represented in Jane Austen's novels.

But it is plain that the charming visual quality of Jane Austen's "world," even when we grant it all the moral significance it can in fact have, will not of itself account for the present appeal that the novels make. If it could do so, we might expect that William Morris's *News from Nowhere* would rival the Austen novels in interest, for no one ever gave so much moral weight as Morris did to the *look* of human existence, especially to the question of scale, making it one of the traits of his redeemed Londoners of the future that they should hold in contempt the dimensions of St. Paul's and the coarseness of the mind of Christopher Wren in having fixed upon them. But of course to the modern taste Morris's utopian romance is little more than a pleasing curiosity. It is a tribute to Morris's honesty that we can so easily perceive why this is so, for Morris is explicit in saying that the one discontent that at least a few of the inhabitants of Nowhere might be expected to feel is that being a person is not interesting in the way that novelists had shown it to be in the old unregenerate time.

It might be said that Morris, for his own reasons, adumbrates the programmatic negation of character which increasingly marks the novel of our day, the contemporary novelist finding it ever more beside the point to deal with destinies as if they were actually personal, or at least to do so in any other way than that of pastiche and parody. Surely one obvious reason why the students turned so eagerly to Jane Austen is that they felt the need to see persons represented as novels once typically represented them; that, without formulating their need, they were in effect making a stand against the novel in its contemporary mode. We should never take it for granted that young people inevitably respond affirmatively to what is innovative and anti-traditional in the high artistic culture of their time; there is the distinct possibility that the students with whom I was dealing saw the contemporary novel as being of a piece with those elements of the modern dispensation which they judged to be maleficent, such as industrialism, urbanization, the multiversity. This maleficence would have to do with the reduction of their self-hood, and presumably it could be neutralized by acquaintance with the characters of Jane Austen's novels, an association that was indeed licensed by the aesthetic of the works. That is, these fictive persons would be experienced as if they had actual existence, as if their "values" were available to assessment, as if their destinies bore upon one's own, and as if their styles of behavior and feeling must inevitably have a consequence in one's own behavior and feeling.

If this was really what the students felt in reading Jane Austen, they were of course fulfilling the aim of traditional humanistic education. In reading about the conduct of other people as presented by a writer highly endowed with moral imagination and in consenting to see this conduct as relevant to their own, they had undertaken an activity which humanism holds to be precious, in that it redeems the individual from moral torpor; its communal effect is often said to be decisive in human existence.

Humanism does not in the least question the good effect of reading about the conduct of other people of one's own time, but it does put a special value upon ranging backward in time to find in a past culture the paradigms by which our own moral lives are put to test. In its predilection for the moral instructiveness of past cultures, humanism is resolute in the belief that there is very little in this transaction that is problematic; it is confident that the paradigms will be properly derived and that the judgments made on the basis they offer will be valid. Humanism takes for granted that any culture of the past out of which has come a work of art that commands our interest must be the product, and also, of course, the shaping condition, of minds which are essentially the same as our own.

Perhaps this is so, but after the Jane Austen course had gone on for a time, the enormous qualifying power of that word "essentially" became manifest to me. Essentially like our own that past culture and those minds, or selves, which created it and were created by it doubtless were, but between them and us there stretched a great range of existential differences.

The word "code" has a traditional place in discourse about society, but in our day it has acquired a new force which isn't quite continuous with what used to be intended by such phrases as "the social code" or "the code of honor." The question I tried to raise with my class was the extent to which any of us who delighted in Jane Austen's novels and found them so charged with moral significance could comprehend the elaborately encoded values of the society they depicted and read accurately the signals being sent out.

A certain amount of difficulty was produced by the question of what kind of society was being represented by the novels. There was a general readiness among the students to say that the society was "aristocratic," but one young man remarked that it was an aristocracy without any nobles—he actually used that by now oddly vulgar word. This observation had the effect of somewhat relaxing the inhibition which American students are likely to feel about taking note of social gradations and we managed to achieve a reasonably complicated view of the system of status and deference on which the novels are based. I had the sense, however, that the students were never quite easy with it and didn't finally believe in its actuality.

Then, following my observation that Jane Austen does not find the relation between servants and their masters or mistresses as interesting as many English novelists do and therefore gives but little help to the modern reader in understanding the part servants played in the life of her time, I had to particularize for the students such matters as what it was that servants were needed for and how many were required for one or another kind of domestic establishment. It turned out that most of the students, though of the middle class, had no real conception of what a servant was or did and could not imagine what the existence of a servant class might imply for a culture—to take a simple example, what effect, for good or ill, their relationships with servants might have upon the children of the house.

We gave some attention to the nature of familial and personal relationships. In the fall of 1973, when my course was being given, the debate in *The Times Literary Supplement* over how brothers and sisters might naturally have felt toward each other early in the nineteenth century had not yet begun, but we remarked the relations between sister and sister in Jane Austen's novels and agreed that this relation was represented as having the possibility of greater closeness than is now likely. And at a moment when notions of youthful solidarity and community were strong, we came to the conclusion that the ideal of friendship had become considerably less vivid than it once was.

We remarked on the circumstance that no one in the novels sought personal definition through achievement. For instance, to none of her heroines and to none of her male characters does Jane Austen attribute her own impulse to literary composition. In 1973 the "work ethic" was still under a cloud, yet I could not fail to see that for all their readiness to be wry about "performance" and "roles," the students expected the interest of life to be maintained by some enterprise requiring effort. But although they could perceive that the idea of vocation lent dignity to Mr. Gardner or Charles Bertram or Captain Wentworth, it did not occur to them to find alien to their conception a society in which most persons naturally thought that life consisted not of doing but only of being.

And then there was the question of the way and the degree in which a person might be morally conscious. The students were not in the least inclined to cynicism but they were gently amused when Eleanor Dashwood, in response to Marianne's question, says that what had sustained her in a bad time was the consciousness that she was doing her duty. They thought it downright quaint of Anne Elliot to say to Captain Wentworth that she had been right in submitting to Lady Russell because a "strong sense of duty is no bad part of a woman's portion," and we did what we could to take account of the cultural implications of that highly charged word "portion."

Inevitably we went into manners in its several meanings, including, of course, the one that Hobbes assigns to it when he says that manners are small morals. I sought to elicit an explanation of the legendary propriety of the novels in relation to what might be concluded about the sexual mores of the age and about those curious moments in the author's published letters which E. M. Forster speaks of as the "deplorable lapses of taste over carnality."

All this might well suggest that the direction of the discussion was toward subverting the basic assumption of humanistic literary pedagogy: so far from wishing to bring about the realization of how similar to ourselves are the persons of a past society, it was actually the dissimilarity between them and us that I pressed upon. At the time, I was conscious of no reason why I inclined to cast doubt upon the procedure by which humanism puts literature at the service of our moral lives, but my more or less random undertaking has since been given a measure of rationalization by certain formulations which have been put forward by a distinguished anthropologist.

I refer to the lecture, delivered in the spring of 1974, in which Professor Clifford Geertz examines the epistemology of cultures, asking what knowledge we can have of cultures unlike our own and what are the means by which we gain this knowledge.[1] The chief intention of the lecture is to say that, contrary to common belief, the faculty of empathy plays but a minimal part in the knowledge an anthropologist gains of unfamiliar cultures and to describe

---

1 "From the Native's Point of View: On the Nature of Anthropological Understanding," *Bulletin of the American Academy of Arts and Sciences*, Vol. XXVIII, No. 1.

the means by which reliable understanding actually is achieved. Drawing upon his own experience, Mr. Geertz puts the matter thus:

In all three of the societies I have studied intensively, Javanese, Balinese, and Moroccan, I have been concerned, among other things, with attempting to determine how the people who live there define themselves as persons, what enters into the idea they have (but . . . only half realize they have) of what a self, Javanese, Balinese, or Moroccan style, is.

He goes on:

In each case I have tried to arrive at this most intimate of notions not by imagining myself as someone else—a rice peasant or a tribal sheikh, and then seeing what I thought—but by searching out and analyzing the symbolic forms—words, images, institutions, behaviors—in terms of which, in each place, people actually represent themselves to themselves and to one another.

Mr. Geertz then specifies the method by which these symbolic forms are to be induced to yield up their meaning: he tells us that one follows "what Dilthey called the hermeneutic circle," in which a conceived whole is referred to its particularities and then the particularities are referred to the conceived whole, and so on in ceaseless alternation.

Mr. Geertz cites two examples of the hermeneutic circle, or, as it sometimes appears, the hermeneutic spiral. One of these is the process by which we comprehend a baseball game. "In order to follow a baseball game, one must understand what a bat, a hit, an inning, a left fielder, a squeeze play, a hanging curve, or a tightened infield are, and what the game in which these 'things' are elements is all about." The second example of the hermeneutic circle or spiral is one that I shall have occasion to return to. It is the attempt of "an *explication de texte* critic like Leo Spitzer" to interpret Keats's "Ode on a Grecian Urn." The attempt, Mr. Geertz says, will involve the critic in "repetitiously asking himself the alternating questions, 'What is the whole poem about?' and 'What exactly has Keats seen (or chosen to show us) depicted on the urn he is describing?'; at the end of an advancing spiral of general observations and specific remarks he emerges with a reading of the poem as an assertion of the aesthetic mode of perception over the historical."

With reference to the two examples· of the hermeneutic process which Mr. Geertz considers appropriate to ethnology, he says, "In the same way, when a meanings-and-symbols ethnographer like myself attempts to find out what some pack of natives[2] conceives a person to be, he moves back and forth between asking himself, 'What is the general form of this life?' and 'What exactly are the vehicles in which that form is embodied?,' emerging at the end of a similar sort of spiral with the notion that they see the self as a composite, or a persona, or a point in a pattern."

No student of literature can read Mr. Geertz's lecture without having it borne in upon him that anthropologists conceive unfamiliar cultures to be much more difficult to comprehend than do humanist scholars or the ordinary readers they instruct. Mr. Geertz spends years trying to discover the concepts on which the members of one or another unfamiliar culture base their sense of being persons or selves, and eventually, by following the hermeneutic circle or spiral, he is able to tell us what these concepts are. By and large, the humanist way of dealing with alien cultures feels itself to be under no such necessity. I recently read for the first time the well-known Icelandic story called "Audun and the Bear," which tells about a rather poorly-off man from the Westfirths who takes ship for Greenland and there buys a bear, said to be "an absolute treasure," which he wants to present as a gift to King Svein of Denmark; King Harald of Norway, Svein's enemy, would like to have this treasure of a bear for himself but behaves very well about it and there follows a series of incidents in which Audun and the two kings adumbrate a transcendent ethos of magnanimity and munificence. I had no difficulty in "understanding" this story. I did ex-

---

[2] The phrase is used by Mr. Geertz with ironic force: it expresses his uneasiness over the condescension which is implicit in the situation of someone "studying" a group of strangers in whose land he sojourns.

actly what Mr. Geertz says he does not do when he wants to arrive at the understanding of what a self is in an alien culture: I made use of empathy, I imagined myself someone else, a not very well-off man from the Westfirths, and this seemed to suit my purpose admirably, leading me to know all that I felt I needed to know about bears and their excellence, and kings, and gift-giving.

But actually, of course, if Mr. Geertz is right, I don't know anything at all about Audun and his bear and his two kings, or at best I know something that merely approximates the cultural fact—and it was in this pleasant but wholly imprecise way of empathy that my students knew the culture represented in Jane Austen's novels. Humanism brushes aside the imprecision, and doubtless would brush aside gross error if it were proved; humanism takes the line that we are to be confident of our intuitive understanding of behavior in Iceland a thousand years ago; we understand it because it is part of "Western" culture and as such pretty directly continuous with our own culture of the present time. Just so we know all about Abraham or Achilles because of what we call the "Judaeo-Hellenic tradition," which constitutes a considerable part of the tradition we conceive ourselves to be in. Of course neither the Jews nor the Greeks thought like humanists—they believed that nothing could be, or should be, more incomprehensible than alien cultures, the ways that *goyim* or *barbaroi* chose to go about being persons or selves.

In thinking about the cultures of the past which are presumably continuous with our own, humanists of our time do of course acknowledge one striking and quite invincible alienation—they know that we of the present time may not do certain things that were done in the cultures of the past even though they are things upon which we bestow the very highest praise. For example, although we are of course enlightened and exalted and generally made better by the art of, say, Giotto or Michelangelo, we know that we must not make use of the idioms of their art or of the art of their epochs in our own creative enterprises. When we bring into conjunction with each other the certitude that great spiritual good is to be derived from the art of the past and the no less firmly held belief that an artistic style cannot be validly used in any age other than that in which it was invented, we confront what is surely one of the significant mysteries of man's life in culture.

It is at this point, when I may have succeeded in bringing at least a little complication to humanism's rather simple view of the relation in which our moral lives stand to other cultures, that I should like to recur to the second of the two examples offered by Mr. Geertz as he explains the hermeneutic circle. This is the one in which he speaks of Keats's "Ode on a Grecian Urn" as it is interpreted by a critic of Leo Spitzer's persuasion. Whether or not Mr. Geertz consciously framed the example to this end, we must see, I think, that Keats's poem bears decisively upon the question of how we respond to observed cultures.

I myself should not say of "Ode on a Grecian Urn," as Mr. Geertz does say, following Mr. Spitzer, that it asserts "the aesthetic mode of perception over the historical." Actually, indeed, I think that the poem may be said to assimilate the two modes to each other in that it conceives the essence of the aesthetic object as having *pastness* as one of its attributes. The aesthetic essence of what is depicted on the urn is that it will never proceed into the future; the culture of the little hillside town is no longer in process. This is true also of the dramatic action represented on the urn—although the lover pursues his beloved, it is of decisive consequence in the poem that neither he nor she is in motion; the distance between them will never change. They exist in an eternal present which momently becomes the past. In the comparison which the poem institutes between them and actual persons, they are represented as lacking in certain of the attributes of life, as being in some degree or in some sense *dead,* and it is in their being so that we find their significance.

This significance consists in the paradox that their motion is to be seen as fixity; its evanescence has, through representation, become permanence. In *Disorder and Early Sorrow* Thomas Mann speaks of the impulse of the historian—which of course is what the urn is explicitly said to be—to bring the processes of life to a stop so as to be able to conceive and, as it were, *possess,* a coherent and comprehensible event. "The past is immortalized; that is to say, it is dead," says the protagonist of the story, Professor Cornelius, ". . . and death is the root of godliness and of all abiding significance." And Mann suggests that this death, which brings everlastingness and abiding significance, may be a decisive element in personal love. The father in Mann's great story, who actually is a historian, wants his beloved little daughter to be always as she now is, as he now knows her and loves her; he fears the changes that the processes of life will bring. That is why, in a moment of distressing perception, he is able to say that in his love for his little daughter "there is something not perfectly right and good." He wishes to believe that he and she can exist in the fixity of conception, of art, like Keats's lovers, that forever will he love and she be a child and his darling; his desire is, in effect, that she forgo her development, or, to put the matter in Yeats's terms, her life in nature. It is not alone the art and thought of Yeats's Byzantium that has in it the element of fixity, of movelessness, or what I am calling death —all thought and art, all conceptual possession of the processes of life, even that form which we call love, has inherent in its celebration and sanctification of life some element of this negation of life. We seek to lay hold of the fluidity of time and to make perdurable the cherished moments of existence. Committed to will as we of the West are, we yet on certain occasions seek to qualify and even to negate its authority and to assert the life-affirming power of idea, or, to use the word that has been proposed by the latest translator of Schopenhauer's great work, to say that life is best affirmed by *representation,* by will realized and negated. Nowadays it is not often observed as a paradox of the human spirit in the West that, for all its devotion to will in action, it finds pleasure and the image of perfection in what is realized and brought to its end—in the perception that art, even when it is at pains to create the appearance of intense and vigorous action, has the effect of transmuting that which is alive into that which has the movelessness and permanence of things past, assimilating it in some part to death.

And surely what can be said of love and thought and art can also be said of culture, more, doubtless, of some cultures than of others, but in a measure of all cultures. Of the three cultures Mr. Geertz touches on his lecture, at least two of them, the Javanese and the Balinese, may readily be thought of as bringing life under the dominion of some form of conceptual or aesthetic "death." Javanese culture may indeed verge upon the bizarre in the overtness of its intention to control, up to the point of actually negating, what we think of as the characteristic processes of life.

Among the Javanese, Mr. Geertz tells us, the problem of the person or self is pursued with "the sort of intensity which would be very rare with us." The person is conceived by means of two dualities; the terms of one of them may be given as "inside"/"outside," of the other as "refined"/"vulgar." The goal of the Javanese person-system is to order inward feelings and outward actions in such a way that the result may be described as "refined" (or "polished," "exquisite," "ethereal," "subtle," "civilized": the native word is *alus*) rather than as "vulgar" (or "impolite," "insensitive," "rough," "uncivilized," "coarse": the native word is *ḳaser*). Mr. Geertz tells us how this effort is to be achieved:

Through meditation the civilized man thins out his emotional life to a kind of constant hum; through etiquette, he both shields that life from external disruptions and regularizes his outer behavior in such a way that it appears to others as a predictable, undisturbing, elegant, and rather vacant set of choreographed motions and settled forms of speech.

It might, Mr. Geertz says, lie beyond our powers to take seriously the possibility of such a conception of selfhood, being kept from doing so "by our own notions of the intrinsic honesty of deep feeling and the moral importance of personal sincerity." Perhaps, he says, it can have credibility for us only when we have seen, as he has, a young man whose wife—a woman he has raised from childhood and who had been the center of his life—has suddenly and inexplicably died, greeting everyone with a set smile and formal apologies for his wife's absence and trying by mystical techniques to flatten out, as he himself put it, the hills and valleys of his emotion into an even level plain. ("That is what you have to do," he said to me, "be smooth inside and out.")

The Javanese sense of personhood is indeed at a far remove from our own, yet surely it is considerably more accessible to us than Mr. Geertz says it is. Doubtless if any of us were to see a friend respond to the death of his wife as the Javanese young man did, we would conclude that he was in a state of severe mental pathology. But when we regard the Javanese behavior apart from the context of our own lives, we do not, I think, experience an insuperable difficulty in giving credence to the concepts on which it is based, and, what is more, for many of us it will be not merely comprehensible but actually may have quite considerable charm.

If I try to account for the possibility of our forming this judgment, I almost certainly must begin by observing that the Javanese culture has as one of its definitive functions to induce its members to become as much as possible like works of art: the human individual is to have the shapedness, the coherence, the changelessness of an object, if not actually of high art, then at least of *vertu*. This, it needs scarcely be said, is at the furthest possible remove from the dominant avowed intentions of Western culture in regard to personhood, yet we ought to consider that not all the intentions of Western culture in regard to personhood are avowed, and that some of them, even though they are not actually dominant, are quite strong. However committed to expressive action and significant utterance the Western paradigm of personhood may be, the Western person, as I have suggested, is not wholly without the capability of finding value in what is fixed, moveless, and silent.

For example, it will not, I believe, carry us beyond the bounds of rationality if we consider whether there is not a similarity to be discerned between the charm which we can discover in the Javanese ideal of personhood as embodied in the young widower and the gratification which we experience as we watch a tragic drama approach its end. We know that soon now, for Hamlet or Macbeth or Lear, the process of destiny must come to a stop: a point is reached at which each hero ceases to be a manifestation of will and comes to exist for us as idea or representation, as an object completed and, as it were, perfected. We may speculate that somewhere involved in the tragic gratification is the security which we derive from seeing what is intrinsically and ineluctably painful when it is an element of the experience of will being transmuted into an object of representation, carried by appropriate death beyond the reach of contingency. Tragic drama generates and confirms a supposition which we cherish: that life may be transmuted into art and thus put into our possession and control.

The culture of Bali may not engage us for even so long as that of Java has done, though certainly it commands no less interest by its overt purpose of bringing life within the presumably reassuring categories of art. Mr. Geertz tells us "that there is in Bali a persistent and systematic attempt to stylize all aspects of personal expression to the point where anything idiosyncratic, anything characteristic of the individual mainly because he is who he is physically, psychologically, or biographically, is muted in favor of his assigned place in the continued, and so it is thought, never changing pageant that is Balinese life. It is dramatis personae, not actors, that in the proper sense really exist. Physically men come and go—mere incidents in a happenstance history of no importance even to themselves. But the masks they wear, the stage they occupy, the parts they play"—Mr. Geertz later particularizes such parts as "king," "grandmother," "third-born," "Brahman," all of them unimpassioned, or, as we say, undramatic parts—"and, most important, the spectacle they mount remain and comprise not the façade but the substance of things, not least the self. . . . There is no make-believe; of course players perish, but the play doesn't and it is the latter, the performed rather than the performer, that really matters."

It has become part of the jargon of our Western selfhood and society to speak of the "roles" which we "play," but this locution manifestly has only a metaphorical intention as compared with the literal force that the idea of a dramaturgic existence has for the Balinese. Sometimes, Mr. Geertz tells us, it happens that a Balinese person becomes aware that there is a core of personality (as we would call it) which can break through and dissolve "the standardized public identity" and that for this to happen would be thought a disaster, though the normal expectation is that it will not happen but that all will go well, which is to say that the integrity of the dramaturgic mode will be maintained.

That people—that an organized culture—should deal with life in this way cannot fail, at some point in our encounter with the possibility, to be received incredulously. Life, we do indeed believe, is real, life is earnest, and for it to achieve a praiseworthy aesthetic condition through a negation of its lifelikeness is not its goal. Yet at the same time we cannot deny that in some fashion, for some reason, our hearts go out to this dramatis-personification of personhood, just as our hearts go out to the Javanese transformation of persons into objects of art or of *vertu*.

We of the West perhaps cannot ever do quite what the Balinese and the Javanese do in the way of turning life into art. We believe, indeed, that we ought not to do it. Yet there are moments of fantasy, of fantasy that may barely be conscious of what it is, in which we are drawn to deal with our personhood somewhat in this manner, when we find in the negation of the literal and immediate actuality of Western personhood such gratification as comes with the promise of integration or perfection of being. The communal life of the little town on Keats's Grecian urn is part of what is apostrophized in the poem as an "attitude" ("O Attic shape! Fair attitude!"), which is the technical term for an archaic device of dramaturgic presentation, that in which all the actors simultaneously "freeze," holding themselves motionless in whatever posture the moment of attitude has caught them. It is thus that the participants in the festival have their existence, and, yet more memorably, the two lovers, she fixed in the attitude of flight, he in that of pursuit. All these persons are imbued with life, yet they do not live as we live, we of the West. They are, in the matter of speaking I have taken license to use, touched with death, in that they are stopped in all vital process, made motionless and changeless, yet by very reason of the deprived condition of their existence, are thought to celebrate and perpetuate life.

This we understand, and at moments, as I have said, it makes a strong appeal to us. But then again, when we consciously regard such cultures as those of Java and Bali, we can be aware that, along with the complex gratification which we take in their approximation to art, there exists a certain condescension. Surely, we find ourselves asking, this cannot be the way cultures, or individuals, ought to confront their destinies, their lives as given? Surely it is not by being urged toward becoming a kind of simulacrum of art that life can be given its right meed of dignity? We of the West are never finally comfortable with the thought of life's susceptibility to being made into an aesthetic experience, not even when the idea is dealt with as one of the received speculations of our intellectual culture— sooner or later, for example, we find ourselves becoming uneasy with Schiller's having advanced, on the basis of Kant's aesthetic theory, the idea that life will be the better for transforming itself into art, and we are uneasy again with Huizinga's having advanced the proposition, on the basis of Schiller's views, that life actually does transform itself into art: we feel that both authors deny the earnestness and literalness—the necessity—of which, as we of the West ultimately feel, the essence of life consists.

It is, I think, open to us to believe that our alternations of view on this matter of life seeking to approximate art are not a mere display of cultural indecisiveness but, rather, that they constitute a dialectic, with all the dignity that inheres in that word. . . .

APPENDIX

Some Notes for an
Autobiographical Lecture

[In the spring of 1971 the English department of Purdue University held a series of graduate seminars on contemporary literary theory at which practicing critics were asked to discuss their own work. These are the notes for the talk given by Lionel Trilling at the seminar concerned with his writing.]

I N a long career of teaching, this is the first time that I have been the subject of my own instruction.

I am sure that you will readily understand why this singular pedagogic undertaking is not exactly simple and easy, and why, as one way of responding to its peculiar difficulties, I might be impelled to take refuge in diffidence or irony, or both.

But you members of this seminar have done me the considerable honor of reading what I have written in the genre of literary criticism and have put yourselves to the task of thinking about it in a serious way and I must therefore see that I am under obligation to consider the subject with a seriousness that is not less entire than yours. I must put aside any impulse I may have to defend myself against its inherent embarrassments by escaping into either diffidence or irony. I must deal with it as directly and objectively as I would with any other topic of literature. And since I believe that objectivity in literary study and instruction begins with what might be called a programmatic prejudice in favor of the work or author being studied, I shall make every effort to regard myself with sympathy and even with admiration.

Yet the statement with which I should like to begin my discussion of my own work might seem to be charged with exactly that diffidence and irony which I have made a point of repudiating. I hope, however, that you will believe that I mean it to be understood in the very simplest and most literal sense.

It is this: that I am always surprised when I hear myself referred to as a critic. After some thirty years of having been called by that name, the role and the function it designates seem odd to me.

I do not say alien, I only say odd. With the passing years I have learned to accept the name—to live with it, as we say—and even to be gratified by it. But it always startles me, takes me a little aback, if only momentarily, and raises an internal grin.

If I ask myself why this is so, the answer would seem to be that in some sense I did not ever undertake to be a critic—being a critic was not, in Wordsworth's phrase, part of the plan that pleased my boyish thought, or my adolescent thought, or even my thought as a young man. The plan that did please my thought was certainly literary, but what it envisaged was the career of a novelist. To this intention, criticism, when eventually I began to practice it, was always secondary, an afterthought: in short, not a vocation but an avocation.

This isn't the occasion on which I might appropriately attempt to say why I did not pursue, or not beyond a certain point, the career of a writer of prose fiction, and perhaps such an occasion will not ever present itself. But that early, and in some sense abiding, intention of mine requires to be mentioned because to me it seems definitive of the nature of my work in criticism.

I shall not attempt to be more specific about this than to say that my conception of what is interesting and problematical in life, of what reality consists in and what makes for illusion, of what must be held to and what let go, was derived primarily from novelists and not from antecedent critics or from such philosophers as speculate systematically about the nature and function of literature. Derived from novelists and not from poets—that is, from practitioners of the genre which was traditionally the least devoted to the ideals of *form* and to the consciousness of formal considerations; the genre which, despite an occasional revolt against its characteristic shaggy-bagginess, was of all genres the most indifferent to manifest shapeliness and decorum, and the most devoted to substance, which it presumes to say is actuality itself; the genre which is least disposed to say that it is self-sufficient and unconditioned.

In remarking that my work in criticism took its direction from the novel, I have it in mind to point to its tendency to occupy itself not with aesthetic questions, except secondarily, but rather with moral questions, with the questions raised by the experience of quotidian life and by the experience of culture and history. Indeed, so far as the genre of the novel can be thought of as having, in some large part of its sense of itself, a degree of bias against accepted literary forms and attitudes, to the extent that some part of its impulse might be called *anti-literary,* I would discover in this position the source, or the encouragement, of a tendency which I am aware of in my critical writing, which is to be a little skeptical of literature, impatient with it, or at least with the claims of literature to be an autonomous, self-justifying activity.

To this tendency—which now and then presents itself to my view as a failure of sensibility—I shall presently return.

When I said that my early conception of a life in literature did not include criticism, it seemed to me for a moment that this was a silly thing to have said, since, in the nature of the case, a boy or youth cannot be expected to imagine the critical enterprise or to respond to it if he should be made aware of it. Actually this is not true at the present time—although the predilection for criticism is certainly not now what it was twenty years ago, when all my conscious and gifted undergraduates made it the dream of their lives to be critics, it is nowadays not uncommon for quite young students to be animated by a desire to comprehend literature in a profound way and to express their achieved understanding of it. But there was no likelihood at all that this undertaking would engage the imagination of a young literary person when I was at secondary school. It did, however, begin to be possible in my college time—possible, I mean, not as the development of an individual consciousness but as an option offered by the culture.

What I have in mind is the great burst of national self-consciousness in the 1920's—in the years following the First World War.

The intense and pervasive questioning of the prevailing way of doing things—that is to say, of the majority's way of doing things, and of the business community's way of doing things.

Questions of social justice. But perhaps even more compelling were the questions asked about a condition which is now very salient in our consciousness and which has been given a name—the QUALITY OF LIFE, including perhaps especially the quality of intellectual life and the quality of emotional life.

This particular concern was not, of course, a new thing in the world: the Victorian tradition—Ruskin, Matthew Arnold, William Morris, Oscar Wilde: followed by Shaw and Wells and Lawrence.

Not a new thing in America: Emerson, Thoreau.

But in America in the Twenties, it recruited great numbers and became, as it were, institutionalized. If I mention the names of Van Wyck Brooks and Lewis Mumford and Randolph Bourne, I shall have indicated the ideational tendency I speak of. And if I mention *The Nation* and

The New Republic and *The Freeman* and the influence
they had, I shall have indicated the growing sense of identity and solidarity of the rapidly developing *intellectual
class.*

Shall not attempt to define the nature and function of the intellectual class beyond saying that essential to it is the idea of
society and the idea of *culture,* both of which are believed
to be susceptible to a conscious intention to change and
correct them.

* * * *

Perhaps there was no college in the country at which a student
might be as accessible to this new movement as Columbia
College.

It wasn't only that the intellectual movement was based in New
York—the University itself was part of the movement,
many of its members were leading figures in it.

JOHN DEWEY

Beard/Hayes/Tugwell

The great word in the College was INTELLIGENCE.

As I utter that word in reminiscence, it occurs to me that of late
years it has fallen out of use—it seems to me a long time
since I have heard a man praised for his *intelligence:* that is,
for the activity of his mind, for its centrality, its flexibility,
its awareness of difficulty and complexity, and its readiness to confront and deal with difficulty and complexity.
Something has happened in our sense of the relation of the
individual mind to the experience of the world that has
led us to devalue the word.

But with us at Columbia College in the Twenties it was the great
word. It did not necessarily imply exceptional powers of
abstract thought, chiefly an ability to bring thought cogently to bear upon all subjects to which thought might be
appropriate.

An eminent teacher of ours, John Erskine, provided a kind of slogan by the title he gave to an essay of his which, chiefly through its title, gained a kind of fame: THE MORAL OBLIGATION TO BE INTELLIGENT.

I did not count myself among those who were intelligent. I would have been the first to say that I was observant, even perceptive, of certain things, that I was intuitive; and I rather prided myself on a quality that went by the name of subtlety. But intelligence I scarcely aspired to: it did not seem to me that this was a quality that a novelist needed to have, only a quick eye for behavior and motive and a feeling heart.

But eventually I was seduced into bucking to be intelligent by the assumption which was prepotent in Columbia College— that intelligence was connected with literature, that it was advanced by literature.

Here I should make the point that literature at Columbia College was taught on principles that were very different from those that prevailed in the Graduate School of the University. And they were, I think, different principles than those that were in force even in undergraduate instruction at Harvard and at Yale.

Literature was not taught as a disciplined study, as essentially a subject of scholarship, with a quasi-German, quasi-scientific apparatus and an ideal of exactitude of knowledge. It did not have in mind a learned man, a scholar, but a well-read man, a widely-read man, precisely an intelligent man, for there was an intelligence of the emotions and of taste.

It was, I am persuaded, in many respects a right way to go about the teaching of literature. It didn't, you may be certain, assure that literature was well taught. Often it was not. But sometimes it was. If you read Dante with Raymond Weaver, or Shakespeare with Mark Van Doren, although you learned nothing about the problems of scholarship these authors raised, and possibly not quite enough about the substance of their works, you had the sense of having come very close to them, of having annihilated a sizable piece of intervening time to do so. This was the kind of thing you could do if you were intelligent, and doing it made you more intelligent.

A characteristic and striking expression of what might be called the Columbia College *mystique* of education was the course called General Honors which John Erskine instituted, although only after overcoming great opposition from many powerful colleagues. It was a two-year course for selected juniors and seniors, meeting on Wednesday evenings for two hours or more in groups of fifteen, under two teachers drawn from various departments, philosophers, historians, classicists, economists, specialists in their own fields but teaching a course which, by the variety of its subject-matter, was in no field at all. Its curriculum was the classics of the Western World, the Great Books, beginning with Homer and coming down through the 19th century—in those days there were as yet no recognized 20th-century classics: *Ulysses* was a new book—including not only works of literature but also philosophy and history, which were likely to be dealt with as if they were works of literature. We were assigned nothing else but the great books themselves, confronting them as best we could without the mediation of ancillary works: it was this primitive simplicity, or purity, of the course which had aroused members of the faculty who were devoted to the ideal of exact scholarship to say that the course must inevitably be superficial. To this John Erskine had made answer that for every book which deserves frequent reading and long study there must be a *first* reading; and that the first—the contemporary—audience of every book had read it without the help of scholarship.

The reason he gave for why certain books should be read—why they *must* be read—I shall touch on in a moment.

I must not seem to idealize the course. It was nothing like as good as it might have been. It was not exigent enough: we were not pressed hard enough by our teachers. Yet it embodied a powerful idea and for many of us it was a salutary and decisive experience.

It will not be a digression if I say that it was from this course that the movement of General Education in the humanities took its rise and established itself not only in Columbia College but in numerous colleges throughout the nation. It was a movement that flourished for some two decades, through the Forties and Fifties, as, if not the pre-eminent and characteristic tendency of American undergraduate education, at least as one tendency that was especially salient. It is now, I need scarcely remark, in eclipse. Even in Columbia College it is in process of being attenuated and I believe that it will soon be wholly rejected. [Implications of this]

What was Erskine's idea which for a time gained so wide an acceptance and whose present devaluation makes, as I think, a landmark in our cultural history?

Erskine had been the pupil at Columbia of George Edward Woodberry, who at Harvard had been the pupil of Charles Eliot Norton, who had been the friend of Carlyle, Ruskin, and Matthew Arnold. This lineage makes clear the provenance of the idea that was at the root of the General Honors course—the idea that great works of art and thought have a decisive part in shaping the life of a polity.

But of course the provenance of the idea extends further back than that. Erskine was a scholar of Elizabethan literature and it was under him that I first read Sir Philip Sidney's *Defence of Poesie*. Recently, when I re-read this notable document of English humanism, I was struck by how closely it bore upon the rationale of the Columbia course. Sidney directed his argument to aristocrats; Erskine and the members of the lineage I have attributed to him had in mind a democratic society; but their assumptions and intentions were the same. They believed that men who were in any degree responsible for the welfare of the polity and for the quality of life that characterized it must be large-minded men, committed to great ends, devoted to virtue, assured of the dignity of the human estate and dedicated to enhancing and preserving it; and that great works of the imagination could foster and even institute this large-mindedness, this *magnanimity*.

A less grandiose way of putting the matter is to say that the Columbia *mystique* was directed to showing young men how they might escape from the limitations of their middle-class or their lower-middle-class upbringings by putting before them great models of thought, feeling, and imagination, and great issues which suggested the close interrelation of the private and personal life with the public life, with life in society.

The besetting danger of the humanistic tradition as it is applied to education is that it will deteriorate into becoming what Santayana called the *genteel tradition*. The conception of the "good life," of the "examined life," of life illuminated by *reason* and shaped by *art*, can be inert and passionless, or encapsulated. [Charles Eliot Norton] But we at Columbia in my student time were preserved from that fate by the nature of the time as we in New York experienced it. We could not fail to be aware of a genuine issue: What were the polity and the culture to be like? Who was to make their terms?

It was at this time that the university began to play a decisive part in the cultural life of America. It was now, almost suddenly, that the academic disciplines seemed to many men to offer attractive professional careers and that literary men

—poets and novelists—came to believe that the university offered a suitable base of operations. The English teaching profession became attractive not only because it was the profession that allowed one to escape from the established professions, to support oneself without taking part in the middle-class competitive life, but also because a large number of young literary men were drawn to conceiving their life in letters as properly consisting not only of creative activity but also of intellectual activity, of dealing with ideas, with theories—and could there be a more appropriate place for this enterprise than the university?

In any complex and highly developed culture, art generates ideas and theories about art. But surely no artistic epoch has ever been so ideational and theoretical as the great epoch, now at an end, which we call modern. Everything about art was problematical—its essential nature, its purposes, its privileges, its duties, the conditions under which it might best be made.

That last problematical concern was of decisive importance to the developing intellectual class in America. What bound its members together was the perception that art had a hard time of it in America. There was no proper audience, the national purpose was not directed to the establishment of the kind of life in which art was a matter of great moment. The social arrangements were all wrong for the making of art. The culture stood in need of radical revision.

And in Europe, where envious American eyes could see that a fully achieved and truly great art had recently come into being, the great question of the culture was no less exigent. Indeed, it was, if anything, more so—how could one read Yeats or Joyce or Lawrence or Eliot or Proust or Mann or Kafka without understanding that the culture of humanism was at a point of crisis? That the society which had sustained this culture was in dire straits?

Problems, problems. It was a problem how one was to write and
how one was to read and how one was to judge what one
read. The books that undertook to solve these problems
had great standing.

> T. S. Eliot   *The Sacred Wood*
> I. A. Richards   *The Principles of Literary Criticism*
> [and for teachers of literature, even more
> exciting *Practical Criticism*]
> Edmund Wilson   *Axel's Castle*
> F. R. Leavis   *Revaluations*

The sense of cultural crises that literature conveyed—that sense of
crisis that made for so intense a *critical* activity—was paral-
leled and enforced by the work of two commanding, pre-
eminent minds, Marx and Freud.

It is much to the point that both had been schooled, and rigorously
schooled, in the tradition of humanism, in the severe discipline of the German *Gymnasium* instruction in the classical languages and literatures. Their loyalty to that tradition never wavered. Their intellects were shaped by the
humanist ideal. Perhaps this would have seemed a strange
thing to emphasize about them when their work first made
its impact upon the world, but I think that at this point in
history it cannot be surprising.

If we speak of the two men, Marx and Freud, together, although of
course we are aware of what separated them ideationally
and in some respects makes them antithetical to each
other, we cannot fail to see that in one respect they are pro-
foundly in accord—in their programmatic rejection of the
settled, institutionalized conception of reality and how it
works, in their discovery of principles of causation which
lead to the conclusion that the settled, institutionalized reality is a falsehood, or, as we might say, a mask. They were
not unique in this—what has been called the "unmasking

principle" is characteristic of much of the intellectual life of Europe since the 18th century and the French Revolution. But as exponents of the unmasking principle they were surely pre-eminent. They taught the intellectual classes that nothing was as it seemed, that the great work of intellect was to strike through the mask.

Their influence on the intellectual life went, I need scarcely say, beyond this. They worked a revolution in the world-picture that was available to anyone who undertook to think at all —they enforced a relationship to the past which was more comprehensive, more intimate, and more *active* than any that had existed before; and they similarly intensified the relation of the individual to society, and to culture, and to the whole of mankind.

Perhaps no system of secular thought ever so invaded the private life and brought it into open connection with the public life. Both systems, the Marxian and the Freudian, raised unremitting questions about motive and intention; they implicated one in the largest possible issues and events.

Upon my work in criticism, upon my intellectual life in general, the systems of Marx and Freud had, I have never doubted, a decisive influence.

Only for a very short time, and then quite presumptuously, did I think of myself as a Marxist. To Freud as a systematic thinker I became more committed and I remain so. But what I would wish to acknowledge by way of influence is not so much a doctrinal authority but rather that effect which I have just spoken of—their power of enforcing upon such minds as respond to them the sense of the actuality and intimacy of history, of society, of culture; this and the felt necessity they induce of discovering the causative principles of these entities.

It was this that controlled my first more-or-less mature critical undertaking, my study of Matthew Arnold.

I am appalled when I remember the state of ignorance and naïveté
I was in when I ventured upon this enterprise. I had no
wish to be a scholar, but having chosen the English-teach-
ing profession as a means of subsistence, I discovered that
I could not stay in it unless I became a Doctor of Philosophy. This meant writing a dissertation and at Columbia
in those days this was rather a whopping job. But I
thought that I might circumvent the difficulties by writing
a book about a man whom I conceived of as a minor but
still highly accredited poet. All I knew about Matthew
Arnold I had derived from an affection for some of his
poems whose melancholy spoke to me in an especially
personal way. I thought it would be interesting to discover
and explain in historical-cultural terms why he was so sad.
Of *Essays in Criticism*, of *Culture and Anarchy*, of the educational
writings, of the religious writings, I was only dimly aware.
They were not part of the sense of Arnold with which I
began—they came to me as a revelation and as a reason
for consternation. (If a graduate student . . .)
How the book got done I no longer understand. It did not occur to
me until I was pretty well into it that I had chosen for my
subject a man who touched almost every problematical
aspect of a great and complex cultural epoch. And being
once in the subject, I had not the sense to get out. The
great mass of special studies of Arnold that have since
appeared have made me conscious of all I did not know
and should have known. . . .
[Here I might say that something of the intellectual temper of the
time—of the late Twenties and early Thirties—is suggested by my determination that the work should find its
audience not among scholars but among the general public,
that it was to be a work of criticism, not of scholarship—
in those days this distinction could be made, and made
polemically: at my "defense" one of my examiners said

severely that what I had presented was no doubt a good *book* but was by no means a good *dissertation*.]

The Arnold that engaged my first interest was, as I have said, the melancholy poet, the passive sufferer from the stresses and tendencies of his culture. When the book was finished my concern was with the man who had pitted himself against the culture, who had tried to understand the culture for the purpose of shaping it—with the critic, with (perhaps it can be said) the first literary intellectual in the English-speaking world.

When the book was finished, I resolved to put Arnold out of my mind—I had no wish, I remember saying, to be what would be known in academic circles as "an Arnold man."

Yet no sooner was the book out of the way than I found myself confronting a situation that I had inevitably to understand in Arnold's own terms.

Arnold, I need scarcely remind you, called himself a liberal, yet his major effort in criticism was to bring into question the substance of liberal thought—the liberal assumptions, the liberal line of reasoning, the liberal conception of the *quality* life should have.

I found myself in a similar situation. [Arnold's call for ideas] In the later Thirties and through the Forties the cultural tendency to which I referred earlier had accelerated itself and established itself. The growing intellectuality—or, rather, *intellectualism*—of the middle class.

The ideational life. The rational life. Every aspect of existence was touched by ideas, or the simulacra of ideas. Not only politics, but child-rearing, the sexual life, the life of the psyche, the innermost part of existence was subject to ideation.

I say not only politics, but certainly most especially politics. A new phenomenon of which we grow increasingly aware: the *politics of culture*. That is to say, a politics in which the concern is not with immediate personal interest but with the interest of others—with the moral assumptions of the polity, with the quality of life that the polity generates and sustains.

To be quite specific here: the enormous influence of a species of Marxism: of *Stalinism*. The Russian Revolution. What has happened to that Revolution, as early as 1922 and certainly by the 1930's. See Mrs. Mandelstam's book for the nature of this development. But of this in the Thirties and Forties among the intellectual classes of America (and of the West generally) there was no consciousness. The liberal intellectual middle-class acceptance of Stalinist doctrine in all aspects of life—in art and thought.

The Nation/The New Republic/The New York Times . . .

The task, as I saw it, was that of *unmasking*. Not merely of saying what lay behind the false representations, but of discovering and disclosing what was really being served in the personal existence by the attachment to Stalinist-colored liberal ideas. The undertaking was the more complex because the people I had in mind thought of themselves as devoted precisely to the work of *unmasking*—of disclosing the falsehood of the established order. To unmask the unmaskers—to show that the very ideals they were committed to were betrayed to very death by their way of dealing with ideas: as if they were totems, in the way of piety.

Not alone in this: *Partisan Review:* committed to the radical position, but . . . Hated.

Behind my sense of the situation was, I think, a kind of perception that I might call novelistic—that there was in the prevailing quality of the intellectual-political life a kind of self-deception: an impulse toward moral aggrandizement through the taking of extreme and apocalyptic positions which, while they *seemed* political, actually expressed a desire to transcend the political condition—which, as I saw things, and still do, meant an eventual acquiescence in tyranny.

Or it meant the converse of that: it meant the desire to exercise power. I account as one of the most significant moments of my intellectual life an encounter I had in my late twenties with a Russian emigré, an aging man of impressive mien, a Menshevik who had spent years in the Czar's prisons and in Siberia, who had fled his native land after the defeat of the revolutionary programs of his party by the Bolsheviks. In the course of conversation he said that what motivated intellectuals was the desire for *power*. He did not mean merely that they wished to make their ideals prevail, believing them to be good for mankind—he meant that behind the ideals there lay the desire for power in itself. He meant that the intellectual, however disinterested he claimed to be, was not *innocent*.

Defense of this. Hawthorne.

Never seemed to me a final condemnation of the function of the intellectual. But power blinds us to the object: to the work of art, to the complexity. . . .